API Development with Laravel

A Quick Start Guide

Adegoke Akintoye

Apress®

API Development with Laravel: A Quick Start Guide

Adegoke Akintoye
Ota, Nigeria

ISBN-13 (pbk): 979-8-8688-1575-1   ISBN-13 (electronic): 979-8-8688-1576-8
https://doi.org/10.1007/979-8-8688-1576-8

Managing Director, Apress Media LLC: Welmoed Spahr
Acquisitions Editor: Divya Modi
Editorial Assistant: Gryffin Winkler
Copy Editor: Kezia Endsley

Cover designed by eStudioCalamar

Cover image designed by Pete Linforth from Pixabay

Distributed to the book trade worldwide by Springer Science+Business Media New York, 1 New York Plaza, New York, NY 10004. Phone 1-800-SPRINGER, fax (201) 348-4505, e-mail orders-ny@springer-sbm.com, or visit www.springeronline.com. Apress Media, LLC is a Delaware LLC and the sole member (owner) is Springer Science + Business Media Finance Inc (SSBM Finance Inc). SSBM Finance Inc is a **Delaware** corporation.

For information on translations, please e-mail booktranslations@springernature.com; for reprint, paperback, or audio rights, please e-mail bookpermissions@springernature.com.

Apress titles may be purchased in bulk for academic, corporate, or promotional use. eBook versions and licenses are also available for most titles. For more information, reference our Print and eBook Bulk Sales web page at http://www.apress.com/bulk-sales.

Any source code or other supplementary material referenced by the author in this book is available to readers on GitHub. For more detailed information, please visit https://www.apress.com/gp/services/source-code.

If disposing of this product, please recycle the paper

This book is dedicated to the loving memory of my late father, Jackson Folabi Akintoye (a.k.a. Ever White). Thank you for your love, care, and guidance. And thank God for making you my father—I'm grateful. You are one in a billion. I love you and I always will. I also dedicate this book to the loving memory of my late grandmother, Mama Mobisola Ikusika (nee Akinbanni). To both of you, I say thank you.

Table of Contents

About the Author

 **Adegoke Akintoye** is a writer, techpreneur, and technology enthusiast with a diverse background in technology and programming. Holding a B.Tech in physics with electronics from the Federal University of Technology, Akure (FUTA), Nigeria, Adegoke has a strong foundation in both science and technology. With a passion for sharing knowledge, Adegoke has authored over 16 books, primarily focused on programming topics. His dedication to educating others through his writing showcases his commitment to helping individuals navigate the world of technology. Adegoke's interests extend beyond writing, delving into software development, embedded systems, and electronic system design and fabrication. His expertise in these areas highlights his versatile skill set and innovative mindset. As a techpreneur, Adegoke combines his entrepreneurial spirit with his technical acumen to drive innovation and create impactful solutions. Outside of his professional pursuits, Adegoke finds joy in family life, as he is happily married with children. Residing in Ota, Ogun State, Nigeria, Adegoke balances his career with his personal life, finding inspiration in God's word and His creation. Adegoke Akintoye's multifaceted background, passion for technology, entrepreneurial drive, and dedication to sharing knowledge make him an asset to the programming and tech communities.

About the Technical Reviewer

 **Sourabh Mishra** is a seasoned entrepreneur, developer, technical author, speaker, corporate trainer, and animator with a deep-rooted passion for technology. A recognized Microsoft MVP and a proud .NET Warrior, Sourabh has been working in the tech industry since the age of 15, turning his childhood fascination with computers into a thriving career.

With hands-on expertise across a wide range of technologies—including C/C++, C#, ASP.NET, VB.NET, MVC, Web API, WCF, Entity Framework, SQL Server, Azure, Angular, jQuery, and Highcharts—Sourabh brings both breadth and depth to every technical topic he explores. He is especially known for his enthusiasm for Microsoft technologies and his commitment to staying at the forefront of innovation.

Sourabh is the founder of IECE Digital and Sourabh Mishra Notes, platforms dedicated to making complex technical concepts easy to understand for learners and professionals alike. Through his writing, training sessions, and active involvement in online developer communities, he continues to empower others by sharing practical knowledge and real-world insights.

Acknowledgments

First and foremost, I give thanks to God, my greatest help and constant source of strength. Without His grace, none of this would be possible.

To my beloved wife, Adeola Akintoye, and our precious children, Deborah Akintoye, Elijah Akintoye, and Elisha Akintoye—thank you for your unwavering love, patience, and understanding. Your support has been my anchor throughout this journey.

To my mother, Florence Morenike Akintoye, whose love and guidance have shaped me into who I am—thank you for being there. I love you, ma'am.

To my siblings—I am deeply grateful for your love, encouragement, and the many ways you've supported me along the way. Thanks.

To my friends—thank you for standing by me and offering your help and encouragement when it mattered most.

To the incredible team at Apress—your professionalism, dedication, and kindness made this process a joy. It has truly been a pleasure working with you.

With heartfelt gratitude, I acknowledge each of you for the role you've played in bringing this book to life.

Introduction

APIs are the invisible engines powering modern software. From mobile apps and e-commerce platforms to payment systems and connected devices, they make everything talk. Whether you're just getting into API development or want to learn Laravel, *API Development with Laravel: A Quick Start Guide* will get you learning Laravel and building real-world APIs—fast.

This is a practical, straight-to-the-point guide written for developers who prefer hands-on learning. You'll build a RESTful Payment Processing API complete with a dashboard using Laravel 12, while learning key concepts like routing, validation, authentication, and deployment as you go.

By the end of this book, you'll be able to:

- Develop RESTful APIs with Laravel 12

- Set up and configure your Laravel development environment

- Authenticate and authorize API users

- Test your APIs using EchoAPI

- Automatically generate clean, professional API documentation with Scramble

- Implement webhooks, version control your API, and deploy it using CapRover

- Build a user-facing dashboard for managing API access

You'll also gain confidence in using modern tools and best practices to make your APIs secure, scalable, and easy to maintain.

This book is written for beginner-to-intermediate developers who have a basic understanding of PHP and web technologies. If you're comfortable navigating files and using a web browser, you're willing to use the command-line interface for basic operations, and you're ready to explore API development with Laravel, you're in the right place.

With nearly a decade of experience building and integrating APIs, I've created the guide I wish I had when I started—focused, practical, and project-driven.

Let's dive in, build something meaningful, and learn by doing.

Note   The source code for this book is available on GitHub via `https://github.com/Apress/API-Development-with-Laravel`.

PART I

Fundamentals of API

CHAPTER 1

Introduction to API

This chapter introduces Application Programming Interface (API). It explains what it is, how it work, and it various forms. It also looks in-depth at REST as an API development architecture. The chapter explores the core principles of the REST architecture in an easy-to-digest way. You will learn about resources, endpoints, HTTP methods, and HTTP response codes. Finally, you learn how they all work together to make things happen in RESTful API development.

APIs and Why Are They Important

An API is a powerful and popular tool in modern software development. APIs enable different software systems to communicate and exchange data seamlessly, acting as intermediaries between various applications.

In simple terms, an API is a set of rules and definitions that dictate how one piece of software can interact with another. APIs define the kind of requests that can be made, how to make those requests, and the format of the responses. Think of an API as a waiter in a restaurant. The customer (the user) tells the waiter what they want (makes a request), and the waiter relays this request to the kitchen (the system). Once the food is ready, the waiter delivers it back to the customer (the response).

APIs are important because they:

1. **Promote efficiency:** Developers don't need to build systems from scratch. APIs allow integration with existing systems, saving time and resources.

2. **Enable connectivity:** They allow different software systems to work together, even if they are built on entirely different technologies or platforms.

© Adegoke Akintoye 2025
A. Akintoye, *API Development with Laravel*, https://doi.org/10.1007/979-8-8688-1576-8_1

3. **Drive innovation:** APIs provide developers with tools to build creative solutions, leveraging the functionalities of existing platforms or services.

4. **Encourage modularity:** By compartmentalizing functionality, APIs enable software to be more flexible, scalable, and easier to maintain.

How Do APIs Work?

This section takes a high-level view of how a typical API works.

1. **Request:** The client sends a request to the API endpoint. This request includes details such as the action to be performed, the parameters, and the authorization tokens.

2. **Processing:** The API server processes the request, interacting with the underlying system or database if necessary.

3. **Response:** The server sends a structured response, often in JSON or XML format, back to the client.

For example, let's say you are using a weather app. When you open it, the app sends a request to a weather API with your location. The API fetches the relevant weather data and sends it back, which is then displayed in the app.

Types of APIs

APIs come in various forms, each designed for specific purposes:

*   **Open APIs:** Publicly available and often used for third-party integrations, such as social media APIs, payment processing APIs, and so on.

*   **Internal APIs:** Restricted to internal use within an organization to streamline processes and systems.

*   **Partner APIs:** Shared with specific partners to enable collaboration, such as payment processing or logistics.

Types of API Architectures

This section looks at various API architectures. To build an API, you can use one of these architectures.

1. **REST (Representational State Transfer):**

   - Uses standard HTTP methods (GET, POST, PUT, and DELETE).

   - Stateless and highly scalable.

   - Popular due to its simplicity and ease of use.

2. **SOAP (Simple Object Access Protocol):**

   - Uses XML for communication.

   - More rigid but highly secure.

   - Often used in enterprise-level applications.

   - Has dwindled in popularity.

3. **GraphQL:**

   - Flexible and allows clients to request only the data they need.

   - Ideal for complex queries and applications.

   - Not as popular relative to REST.

This book uses the REST architecture. REST has been the most widely adopted API design approach for years. It is still the default choice for many developers. Also, tools and libraries for REST exist in nearly every programming language. Later in this chapter, you'll look deeper into the REST architecture and its use in API development.

API Monetization: Turning Code into Cash

Apart from being able to make money developing APIs for clients or helping clients connect their applications to a third-party API (for payment processing, social media feeds, etc.), an API built around an application can be monetized. In today's interconnected digital world, APIs are more than just tools for developers; they are opportunities to generate revenue. With businesses and developers increasingly relying on APIs for functionality, data, and integration, monetizing an API can be a lucrative venture. Here's how you can turn your API into a revenue-generating asset.

1. **Offer API access using a subscription model:** One of the most common ways to make money with an API is through subscription-based pricing. Businesses often charge users a monthly or yearly fee to access their API. This model works particularly well for APIs that provide high-value services like financial data, customer analytics, or communication tools. For example, services like Twilio (for messaging) and Stripe (for payments) offer tiered pricing based on use.

2. **Charge per use or transaction:** Usage-based pricing allows you to charge customers based on how much they use your API. This is ideal for APIs where users need flexibility, such as data-retrieval services or APIs that facilitate transactions. Companies like AWS offer APIs that follow this pay-as-you-go model, making it scalable for both small businesses and enterprise clients.

3. **Adopt a freemium model:** The freemium model offers basic API access for free while charging for premium features. This approach is excellent for attracting a wide user base and gradually converting free users into paying customers. For example, Mapbox provides free access to basic location data, but charges for advanced analytics and custom map designs.

4. **Create a developer ecosystem:** Building an ecosystem around your API can open doors to partnerships and revenue-sharing opportunities. By encouraging developers to build applications using your API, you can grow your user base and share profits with third-party app creators. This strategy works well for platforms like Shopify, which allows developers to build and sell apps using its API.

5. **Sell data access:** If your API provides access to unique or valuable data, you can monetize it by selling access to that data. APIs that offer market insights, financial trends, or consumer behavior analytics are highly sought after in industries like finance, marketing, and real estate.

6. **Use APIs to drive indirect revenue:** Not all APIs generate money directly. Some APIs are designed to enhance your core product or service, thereby increasing overall customer satisfaction and loyalty. For instance, an e-commerce platform could use an API to streamline shipping processes, improve user experience, and boost sales.

7. **Partner with enterprises:** If your API has niche applications or serves a specialized market, partnering with larger enterprises can be a smart move. You can charge these companies for dedicated access, customized features, or enhanced support.

These are just some of the ways that APIs can be monetized.

Note   A *third-party API*, specifically, is an interface provided by an external provider to enable developers to access their data, services, or functionalities. Examples include the Google Maps API for location-based services, the Twitter API for social media integration, the Stripe API for payment processing, and the OpenWeather API for weather data/forecast (see Figure 1-1).

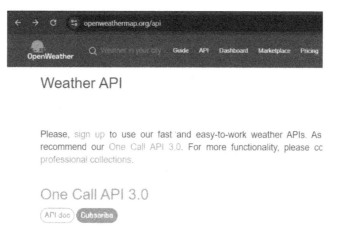

Figure 1-1. *The OpenWeather API page (https://openweathermap.org/api)*

Tip   An API marketplace serves as a centralized platform where developers can explore, evaluate, and even purchase APIs. These platforms often provide detailed documentation, pricing structures, and user reviews to help developers make informed decisions. Popular API Marketplaces include RapidAPI, API Layer (see Figure 1-2), and Postman API Network.

Figure 1-2. *The API Layer web page (https://apilayer.com/)*

Tip   By leveraging third-party APIs, developers can reduce the time and resources needed to build certain features from scratch. For instance, integrating an authentication system via an API like Auth0 is far quicker than designing and deploying a custom solution.

Likewise, a developer can gain access to advanced and specialized features, such as machine learning models, weather forecasts, analytics tools, and so on, without needing to be an expert in those areas, by simply using a third-party API.

RESTful API

A RESTful API system is a framework that allows different applications to communicate over the web, enabling data sharing and interaction through structured HTTP requests (see Figure 1-3). The design of RESTful APIs is guided by REST (Representational State Transfer) principles, which prioritize simplicity, scalability, and resource orientation. This approach has become the backbone of modern web and mobile applications, as it allows client applications to request, create, update, and delete resources on a server through clearly defined endpoints.

REST is simply a set of design guidelines rather than a strict standard. RESTful APIs follow REST principles, aiming to make web services scalable and flexible. These APIs expose resources (such as user data, blog posts, products, and so on) via URLs, allowing clients to perform actions on these resources using HTTP methods like GET, POST, PUT, and DELETE.

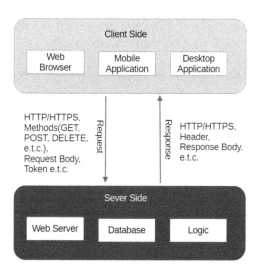

Figure 1-3. *A basic RESTful API system*

REST, an architectural style, was defined by Roy Fielding in his doctoral dissertation, and it has since become the foundation for web-based interactions due to its simplicity, scalability, and flexibility. Fielding's guidelines specify how systems should be organized to efficiently communicate, focusing on six key constraints: client-server separation, statelessness, cacheability, a uniform interface, layered system, and code on demand. The next section delves into these principles and explains how they apply to RESTful APIs.

Core Principles of REST (Roy Fielding's Guidelines)

Roy Fielding outlined six principles that define REST. They describe what a RESTful API system should look like. However, as stated earlier, these are a set of design guidelines rather than a strict standard and in real-world applications you may see systems that do not follow all the guidelines. The more of these guidelines an API system implements, the more RESTful the system will be.

The following are the guidelines defined by Fielding:

1. **Client-server separation:** The client-server model is the foundation of the REST architecture, where the client (usually a browser, mobile app, or another service) and the server (where the data and logic reside) remain independent of each other. This separation ensures that the client and server can evolve independently. The client interacts with the server solely through HTTP requests and responses, while the server processes these requests and sends back the required resources.

   For example, when a user views their profile on a web app, the frontend sends a GET request to the server. The server returns a JSON representation of the user profile, and the frontend presents it to the user without needing to understand the server's inner workings.

2. **Statelessness:** In a RESTful API, each request from a client to the server must contain all the information needed for the server to fulfill it. RESTful systems are stateless, meaning that no session or context data is stored on the server between requests. Statelessness simplifies interactions, making the system more scalable since each request is self-contained. For instance, if a user requests their profile page, every necessary detail—like the user's ID and request method—should be included in that request. This approach allows the server to treat each request independently, which means scaling up by adding servers becomes straightforward.

3. **Cacheability:** In REST, resources should be defined as cacheable whenever possible to improve performance. By allowing responses to be stored in a cache, RESTful APIs reduce the need for repeated server processing, enhancing speed and efficiency.

RESTful APIs specify which resources are cacheable, often using HTTP headers like Cache-Control or Expires to indicate how long responses can be cached.

For example, if an API retrieves a list of popular articles, caching this resource allows the client to use the cached version instead of making repeated requests to the server.

4. **Uniform interface:** The uniform interface principle is one of REST's most essential constraints, aiming to make APIs consistent and predictable. This principle encourages a standardized way of interacting with resources, which allows clients and developers to understand the API without needing extensive documentation for each endpoint.

    Fielding's uniform interface includes the following components:

    - **Identification of resources:** Each resource should have a unique identifier (e.g., URL path).

    - **Resource manipulation through representations:** Clients should use standard representations (e.g., JSON, XML) to interact with resources.

    - **Self-descriptive messages:** Each message should include enough information for the recipient to understand and process it.

    - **Hypermedia as the engine of application state (HATEOAS):** Responses should provide relevant links, enabling clients to navigate the API's resources dynamically.

      For example, in a RESTful API for a library system, each book resource might have URLs like /books for the list of books or /books/1 for a specific book. The response for /books/1 might also include links to related resources like /authors/1 for the book's author, adhering to the HATEOAS principle.

5. **Layered system:** A RESTful system is designed to support a layered architecture, where components like servers, databases, proxies, and caches are organized in layers. Each layer has its distinct role, and interactions occur only between adjacent layers,

meaning a client does not know if it's communicating directly with the server or a proxy. This layered approach improves scalability, allowing each layer to be independently upgraded or replaced. For instance, a client request might go through a caching layer and load balancers before reaching the server. As a result, the server can focus on its primary role, relying on other layers to handle additional functions like caching and load balancing.

6. **Code on Demand (Optional):** The final REST constraint, code on demand, is optional and allows the server to send executable code to the client. This feature lets clients enhance their functionality dynamically, for instance, by receiving JavaScript code that the client can execute directly. However, this constraint is less commonly used, as it can complicate the client's design and raise security considerations.

   For example, a web application might request JavaScript code to validate form inputs dynamically. The server sends the necessary code, and the client executes it without needing built-in logic for validation.

The next section looks at the endpoint, resource, HTTP methods, and HTTP response codes concepts in relation to RESTful API in more detail.

Resources

In the context of a RESTful API, a resource is a fundamental concept, representing any piece of data or object that can be accessed, modified, or manipulated through the API.

Resources can represent real-world objects, like books, users, and cars, as well as more abstract items, like settings, permissions, and reports—depending on what you are modelling. Each resource is identified by a unique URL, or a Uniform Resource Identifier (URI), which allows clients to access or interact with it.

For example:

- In an API made for a library, a book can be considered a resource.

- In an e-commerce API, products, customers, and orders are individual resources.

- In a social media API, resources might include posts, comments, and users.

Note   A URI (Uniform Resource Identifier) is a broad concept that refers to a string of characters used to identify a resource on the Internet. The key here is identification. A URI can locate the resource, describe it, or both. Essentially, it serves as an umbrella term for ways to refer to resources, regardless of how they're accessed or described. An example of a URI that is not a URL is the ISBN number of a book—a book is identified by this number, but it doesn't tell you where to find it.

A URL (Uniform Resource Locator) is a subset of a URI that not only identifies a resource but also provides a means to locate it. In other words, a URL specifies where a resource is located and how it can be accessed, typically using a protocol such as HTTP, HTTPS, FTP, and so on.

When specifying a URL, for example `https://mydomain.com/user/1`, we sometimes specify it as `/user/1`, omitting the base URL `https://mydomain.com`. In Laravel, the base URL must still be provided by the developer in the configuration (`.env`) file (you'll see how this is done later). Laravel knows how to fetch it and create a full URL for you. This is also an advantage, since the base URL only needs to be changed in one location (inside the `.env` configuration file).

Resource Representation

A resource is usually described or represented with data corresponding to its attributes. Since the attributes of a given resource can be infinite, we only deal with ones that are relevant to the application at hand. For example, a given application might only need the name of a person, while in another application, we may also require the address and nationality. When a client requests a resource, the server provides a representation of it, containing all the relevant data fields. This data representation includes properties of the resource (e.g., for a book, the title, author, and year published) and sometimes additional links to related resources.

For example, a GET request to /books/1 might return a JSON representation like this:

```json
{
  "id": 1,
  "title": "1984",
  "author": "George Orwell",
  "publishedYear": 1949
}
```

Uniform Resource Identifier (URI)

In RESTful APIs, each resource is accessible via a URI, making it easy to locate, retrieve, update, or delete. The URI is a standardized URL format, such as /books/1, where /books represents the collection of book resources, and /1 refers to a specific book with an ID of 1.

This structure provides a clear and predictable way to access resources. For instance:

- /users represents all users, while /users/123 represents a specific user with ID 123.

- /products lists all products, while /products/789 shows details for a specific product with ID 789.

A good URI structure helps create a straightforward, user-friendly API design that clients can easily understand and use. URIs are a key part of the uniform interface principle in REST, as they allow clients to interact with each resource in a predictable way.

Resource Relationships

Resources are often interconnected, and in RESTful APIs, these relationships are represented by linking related resources. This approach is known as Hypermedia as the Engine of Application State (HATEOAS), one of the core principles of REST, which suggests that clients should be able to navigate an API through the links provided in the resource representation.

For example:

- A book resource might include links to related resources, such as /authors/1 (the author of the book) and /genres/fiction (the genre of the book).

- A customer resource in an e-commerce API might have links to /orders (listing the customer's orders) and /cart (showing items in their shopping cart).

Collections versus Individual Resources

In RESTful APIs, resources are often organized into collections. A *collection* is a group of related resources that can be accessed through a shared endpoint. For example:

- /books is a collection of book resources.

- /users is a collection of user resources.

When interacting with a collection, you typically perform actions like retrieving all resources (GET /books) or creating a new resource within the collection (POST /books). When interacting with an individual resource, you specify the resource's unique identifier (e.g., /books/1) and can perform actions such as reading (GET), updating (PUT/PATCH), or deleting (DELETE) that specific resource. Table 1-1 compares collection endpoints and individual resource endpoints.

Table 1-1. *Examples of Collection Endpoints Versus Individual Resource Endpoints, Mapping HTTP Methods to Actions on Collections and Single Resources*

Action	Collection URI	Resource URI
Get all	GET /books	
Get one		GET /books/1
Create	POST /books	
Update		PUT /books/1
Delete		DELETE /books/1

Endpoints

Essentially, an *endpoint* is a specific URL or URI on a server that a client can send a request to, and it defines how a resource or service can be accessed or interacted with. An endpoint refers to a specific path or address on a server where a particular resource or functionality is available. Figure 1-4 illustrates a basic endpoint structure.

Each endpoint corresponds to an operation or set of operations that a client can perform, such as fetching data, creating new resources, updating existing resources, or deleting resources. For example:

- GET /api/users: Retrieves a list of users.

- POST /api/users: Creates a new user.

- GET /api/users/1: Retrieves details of a specific user with ID 1.

- PUT /api/users/1: Updates information about the user with ID 1.

- DELETE /api/users/1: Deletes the user with ID 1.

Endpoints are commonly defined using HTTP methods such as GET, POST, PUT, PATCH, and DELETE, each representing a specific action.

Components of an Endpoint

An endpoint is typically composed of the following components:

1. **Base URL:** The base URL is the consistent part of the API address. It identifies the server where the API resides.

   Example: https://api.example.com

2. **Path:** The path specifies the resource being accessed or manipulated. It is appended to the base URL.

   Example: /users

3. **HTTP method:** The HTTP method determines the type of operation the client wants to perform on the resource.

    GET: Retrieves data.

    POST: Creates a new resource.

    PUT/PATCH: Updates the resource.

    DELETE: Removes a resource.

4. **Query parameters (optional):** Query parameters are key-value pairs added to the endpoint to filter or modify the request. They follow the ? (question mark) in the URL.

    Example: /users?role=admin

5. **Headers (optional):** Headers provide additional context for the request, such as authentication tokens or content types.

6. **Request body (for certain HTTP methods):** For methods like POST and PUT, a request body is often sent to include the data being created or updated.

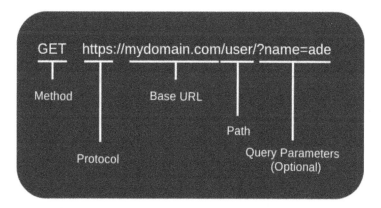

Figure 1-4. *A basic REST API endpoint*

HTTP Methods (Verbs)

HTTP methods are used in RESTful APIs to define the type of action or operation a client wants to perform on a given resource. RESTful APIs leverage these methods to establish clear communication between the client (e.g., a browser or app) and the server.

The most commonly used HTTP methods in RESTful APIs are:

- GET: Retrieves a resource or collection of resources.

- POST: Creates a new resource.

- PUT: Updates an existing resource.

- PATCH: Partially updates a resource.

- DELETE: Removes a resource.

Each method corresponds to a specific action, and when combined with the API's endpoint, they define how resources are accessed or manipulated. For example:

- GET /api/users: Retrieves all users.

- POST /api/users: Creates a new user.

- PUT /api/users/1: Updates a user with ID 1.

- DELETE /api/users/1: Removes a user with ID 1.

Note   Requests to endpoints based on methods like GET, PUT, and DELETE should be *idempotent*. This means that performing the operation multiple times on a resource should have the same effect as performing it once.

By using these methods appropriately, developers can create APIs that are intuitive, efficient, and adhere to RESTful principles. A well-designed API with clearly defined HTTP methods ensures a seamless experience for both developers and clients.

HTTP Response Codes in RESTful APIs

HTTP response codes are essential in RESTful APIs as they provide clients with information about the outcome of their requests. These codes are part of the HTTP protocol and indicate whether a request was successfully processed, if there was an error, or if additional actions are required. Understanding HTTP response codes is crucial for designing and consuming RESTful APIs effectively.

Structure of HTTP Response Codes

An HTTP response code is a three-digit number included in the server's response to a client's request. These codes are grouped into five classes based on the first digit:

1. **1xx (informational):** Request received, and processing is continuing.

2. **2xx (success):** The request was successfully received, understood, and processed.

3. **3xx (redirection):** Further action is required to complete the request.

4. **4xx (client errors):** The request contains errors, such as bad syntax or unauthorized access.

5. **5xx (server errors):** The server encountered an error while processing the request.

Table 1-2 summarizes these response codes.

Table 1-2. *Summary of Common HTTP Response Codes*

Code	Category	Description
200	Success	Request processed successfully
201	Success	Resource created
204	Success	No content to return
400	Client Error	Bad request (syntax error)
401	Client Error	Unauthorized access
403	Client Error	Access forbidden
404	Client Error	Resource not found
422	Client Error	Validation error
500	Server Error	Generic server error

HTTP response codes provide clients with essential feedback about the success, failure, or required actions related to their requests. By understanding and implementing these codes correctly, developers can ensure that their APIs are intuitive, reliable, and user-friendly.

Summary

This chapter introduced Application Programming Interfaces (APIs)—what they are, how they work, and their types. You also looked in-depth into REST as an API development architecture. The chapter explored the core principles of the REST architecture in an easy-to-digest way and explained resources, endpoints, HTTP methods, and HTTP response codes.

The next chapter introduces Laravel and explains why it's a good choice for API development. It also explores its various concepts in relation to RESTful API development. You also see how to set up a good and easy development environment for the project in this book.

## CHAPTER 2

Installing Laravel, Development, and Test Tools Installation

The last chapter explained at concepts such as REST and HTTP, and also discussed Roy Fielding's principles of the RESTful architecture. But how do you translate these abstract concepts into practical implementation? This is where Laravel, a popular PHP framework, comes into play. This chapter explores why Laravel is a great candidate for API development and how it can help you build RESTful APIs that align with Fielding's REST guidelines. You will also look at how to install Laravel, set up a local development environment using Uniform Server and VS Code, and create a test environment using EchoAPI.

What Is Laravel?

Laravel is an open-source PHP framework designed to simplify web development. Known for its elegant syntax, robust tools, and active community, Laravel makes it easier for developers to build secure, scalable, and maintainable applications.

For API development, Laravel shines because it provides a comprehensive toolkit that allows you to design APIs quickly without sacrificing quality. It also helps you adhere to best practices. Whether you're building a small CRUD API or something more elaborate, Laravel has your back.

© Adegoke Akintoye 2025
A. Akintoye, *API Development with Laravel*, https://doi.org/10.1007/979-8-8688-1576-8_2

Why Laravel Is Ideal for API Development

Let's start by discussing why Laravel is so well-suited for creating APIs in relation to Roy Fielding's RESTful guidelines.

1. **RESTful routing and controller structure:** Laravel's routing system is one of its standout features. The framework offers a clear and intuitive way to define RESTful routes that align perfectly with Fielding's principles. Using Laravel, you can map HTTP methods (GET, POST, PUT, and DELETE) to specific actions in your controllers, ensuring a consistent and predictable API design.

2. **Resources as the foundation of REST:** According to Roy Fielding, RESTful systems revolve around resources. In Laravel, these resources are represented by models and controllers, which are tightly integrated through its Eloquent ORM. For example, if you're working with a POST resource, Laravel allows you to interact with the database using an expressive syntax that treats each POST as an object.

3. **Statelessness and Laravel middleware:** One of the core tenets of REST is statelessness—each request from a client must contain all the information necessary for the server to fulfill it. Laravel enforces this principle naturally through its middleware system (see Figure 2-1).

   For instance, Laravel Sanctum allows you to implement token-based authentication, ensuring that each API request is self-contained and secure. Sanctum ensures that only authenticated requests can access protected resources, maintaining both security and statelessness.

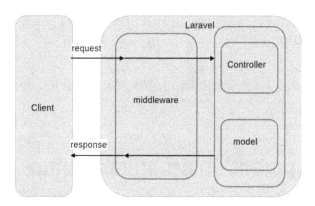

Figure 2-1. *Signal/response flow through middleware in Laravel*

4. **Layered system and middleware support:** Fielding's guidelines emphasize the use of a layered system where components are separated into logical layers. Laravel adheres to this guideline through its support for middleware, queues, and service containers.

   For example, you can create middleware to handle rate limiting, ensuring that your API adheres to best practices for scalability.

5. **HATEOAS and Laravel application:** Fielding's RESTful guidelines also emphasize HATEOAS (Hypermedia as the Engine of Application State), where clients receive not only data but also links to navigate the API. Laravel can generate hypermedia responses through API resources.

6. **Consistency and maintainability:** Laravel's expressive syntax and built-in tools like migrations, seeding, and testing ensure that your API remains consistent and easy to maintain over time. Its testing tools, in particular, allow you to write robust tests for your API endpoints to ensure that they work as expected.

Laravel simplifies the process of adhering to Fielding's RESTful principles while offering a rich set of tools to enhance your API's functionality. Its ability to seamlessly integrate RESTful routing, enforce statelessness, and provide hypermedia support makes it a natural choice for modern API development.

As you explore Laravel's capabilities in later parts of this book, you'll discover how to leverage its features to build APIs that are not only functional but are in line with industry standards.

The next section looks at how to put together a local development environment for your Laravel API project.

Local Development Environment Setup

This book uses Uniform Server `www.uniformserver.com` as the development environment because of its standout features, as outlined here (However, if you are not using Windows, you can use XAMPP, which is available for Mac and Linux users. For instructions on how to install XAMPP, visit `www.apachefriends.org`.):

- **No installation required:** It offers a hassle-free setup process. Developers simply need to download, extract, and run the server—no installation required. This reduces potential conflicts with existing software and avoids cluttering the system with additional registry entries or services. You can quickly set up a development environment without administrative privileges. This is perfect for testing environments or temporary projects.

- **Lightweight and resource-friendly:** It is designed to have a minimal footprint on system resources. Compared to other options, it uses less storage and memory. It doesn't run background services unless explicitly started, ensuring your system's performance remains optimal.

  The lightweight nature of Uniform Server makes it particularly suitable for older or less powerful machines, where heavier tools like Docker, Vagrant, or even XAMPP might struggle.

  For Laravel developers, this means a smooth and responsive local environment without unnecessary overhead.

- **Cost-free solution:** Uniform Server is completely free to use.

- **Full control and customization:** Uniform Server allows developers to customize the environment to their exact needs. Unlike XAMPP or Laragon, which come with predefined configurations, Uniform Server offers:

1. **Modifiable PHP settings:** Developers can directly edit php. ini to enable or disable extensions like curl, mbstring, or pdo_mysql required by Laravel.

2. **Flexible Apache settings:** Developers can configure virtual hosts or modify httpd.conf to suit project-specific requirements.

3. **Multiple PHP versions:** Developers can easily switch between PHP versions to match the Laravel project's compatibility.

   This level of control is invaluable for developers working on diverse projects with unique requirements.

Setting Up Uniform Server

Follow these steps to install Uniform Server:

1. Download the latest version of Uniform Server Zero from the official website: www.uniformserver.com. See Figures 2-2, 2-3, and 2-4.

Figure 2-2. *On the Uniform Server home page, click the Download Now button, and you'll be taken to the download page on SourceForge*

Figure 2-3. *On the SourceForge download page, click the Download Latest Version button to download the file to your computer. It may take a few seconds before the download starts*

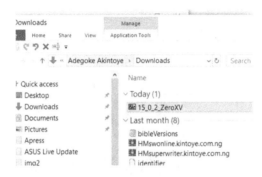

Figure 2-4. *The file was downloaded to my Downloads folder and named 15_0_2_ZeroXV.exe. Depending on the version you're downloading, the number part of the name may be different*

2. Double-clicking the file downloaded in Step 1 will display a dialog box asking you to select the directory to extract to (see Figures 2-5 and 2-6). Choose your preferred directory. In this book, I use the C:\ folder. It will extract itself inside the selected directory within a folder called UniServerZ (e.g., C:\UniServerZ based on the directory you choose). In the rest of this book, I assume Uniform Server is extracted into C:\UniServerZ directory.

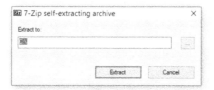

Figure 2-5. *Choose the directory to extract Uniform Server into*

Figure 2-6. *Clicking the Extract Button in Figure 2-5 will start the extraction process. Wait until it's done*

3. **Launch the Control Panel:**

- Once the extraction process has ended, navigate to the extracted folder in Step 2. Locate and double-click the UniController. exe file to launch the control panel. See Figures 2-7 and 2-8.

- From the Control Panel, you can start the Apache and MySQL servers. See Figure 2-8.

(C:) › UniServerZ	∨ ↺	Search UniServerZ	🔎
Name	Date modified	Type	
core	25/11/2023 21:13	File f...	
db_backup_restore	05/11/2013 10:48	File f...	
docs	25/11/2023 21:13	File f...	
home	25/11/2023 21:13	File f...	
htpasswd	25/11/2023 21:12	File f...	
logs	07/05/2019 14:46	File f...	
ssl	25/11/2023 21:11	File f...	
tmp	05/11/2013 10:48	File f...	
utils	25/11/2023 21:13	File f...	
www	25/11/2023 21:11	File f...	
15_0_2_ZeroXV_read_me	25/11/2023 19:40	TXT F	
UniController	21/07/2023 21:41	Appli	

Figure 2-7. *Uniform Server extracted folder with the controller highlighted*

Figure 2-8. *Uniform Server Controller, where you can control the server operation*

Figure 2-9. *A Dialog box asking you to set MySQL password if you are opening the UniServer Controller for the first time. Click Cancel - I'll show you another way to set the password later in this chapter*

Figure 2-10. *Yet another Dialog box. Just Click OK to continue*

4. **Configure PHP for Laravel application:**

    Laravel requires certain PHP extensions. To ensure the requirements are met, do the following:

    • First, on the Uniform Server Control panel, ensure that Apache and MySQL are both switched off, with the indicators turning red. See Figure 2-11.

Figure 2-11. *Ensure that on the Control Panel, the Apache and MySQL servers are both off indicated by the red color*

    • On the Control Panel, choose PHP ➤ Edit Basic and Modules ➤ PHP Modules Enable/Disable (see Figure 2-12). A page will then be displayed for you to enable/disable the PHP modules. See Figure 2-13.

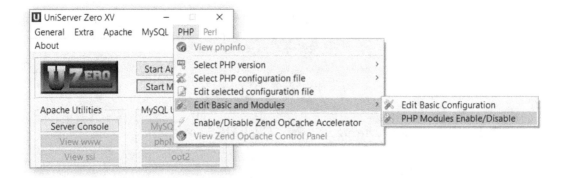

Figure 2-12. *Accessing the PHP Extension Enable/Disable page for the php.ini file update*

Figure 2-13. *The page for php.ini values update*

- On the page displayed in Step 2, ensure the following modules are checked and then close the page.

  - mbstring

  - openssl

  - pdo_mysql

  - fileinfo

- You can now restart Apache and MySQL.

Installing Composer

Composer is software that manages (adds, removes, or updates) other piece of software that Laravel operation depends on. These other software programs that Laravel depends on are referred to as Laravel's *dependencies*. You, therefore, need to install Composer in order to install Laravel. Follow these steps to install Composer:

1. **Download the Composer installer:**

   Visit Composer's website at getcomposer.org (see Figure 2-14) and download the installer by clicking the Download button.

Figure 2-14. *Composer's website. Click the Download button to download Composer*

2. **Run the installer:**

   - Locate the downloaded file (Composer-Setup.exe). Mine was downloaded into my Downloads folder. See Figure 2-15. Double-click the file to initiate installation. Figures 2-16 to 2-24 show how to proceed with the installation.

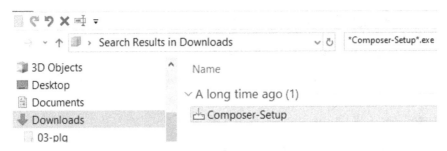

Figure 2-15. *Locating the Composer executable file called Composer-Setup.exe*

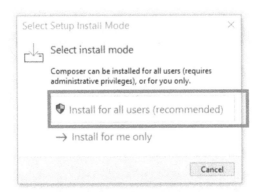

Figure 2-16. *Click Install for All Users (Recommended)*

Figure 2-17. *Click Next*

- During setup, specify the path to PHP used by Uniform Server.
  Based on the folder you extracted Uniform Server into, in this
  example, this should be:

```
C:\UniServerZ\core\php83\php.exe
```

Figure 2-18. *Navigate to your PHP folder and select the PHP executable file*

Figure 2-19. *Click Next*

Figure 2-20. *Composer is finally ready to install, so click Install*

Figure 2-21. *Composer is installing, so allow it to finish*

Figure 2-22. *When the installation is finished, click Next*

Figure 2-23. *Click Finish again to conclude the installation*

3. **Verify installation:**

- Open a command prompt and run the command shown in Listing 2-1.

Listing 2-1. Checking the version of Composer installed

```
composer --version
```

This should display the installed Composer version as well as the version of the PHP installed. See Figure 2-24a.

```
C:\Users\Adegoke Akintoye>composer --version
Composer version 2.8.4 2024-12-11 11:57:47
PHP version 8.3.0 (C:\UniServerZ\core\php83\php.exe)
```

Figure 2-24a. *Composer and the PHP version displayed as a proof that Composer was properly installed*

Installing Git

Git is a tool that helps track changes to files over time, making it easy to collaborate with others and manage different versions of a project. It's like a time machine for your files, allowing you to revert to previous states or make multiple versions simultaneously.

Later in this book, to deploy the app so that it's easily scalable, you'll use an open-source tool called *CapRover*. This tool requires that your project be a Git repository.

To install Git in Windows, run the command in Listing 2-2 from the command-line terminal while connected to the Internet.

Listing 2-2. Command for Installing Git in Windows

```
winget install --id Git.Git -e --source winget
```

Alternatively, you can also download Git installer for Windows by visiting https://git-scm.com/downloads/win;see Figure 2-24b. If your computer is a 64-bit system, you should download the 64-bit version of Git; otherwise, if you are using a 32-bit system, download the 32-bit version. Once it's downloaded, double-click the downloaded file to extract and launch the installer. Accept the default options to complete the installation.

Figure 2-24b. *The Git download page*

To install Git for Mac, visit `https://git-scm.com/downloads/mac`; and for Linux, visit `https://git-scm.com/downloads/linux`.

Adding and Committing File Changes

To add and commit file changes in Git, run the command shown in Listing 2-3.

Listing 2-3. How to add and commit changes made to your code in Git

```
git add . && git commit -m "Your commit message"
```

Laravel Installation

To install Laravel, follow these steps:

1. Open a command prompt and navigate to the www folder of Uniform Server by typing the command in Listing 2-4.

Listing 2-4. Moving into your server public folder from the Command line

```
cd C:\UniServerZ\www
```

Figure 2-25 shows the command prompt in the new folder (C:\ UniServerZ\www) when the command was executed.

```
C:\Users\Adegoke Akintoye>cd C:\UniServerZ\www

C:\UniServerZ\www>_
```

Figure 2-25. *The command prompt is now in the* www *folder of Uniform Server*

2. Use Composer to create a new Laravel project. To create a
    Laravel project, enter and run the command in Listing 2-5 in
    the command-line. Replace my_laravel_api with your desired
    project name.

Listing 2-5. Installing Laravel

```
composer create-project --prefer-dist laravel/laravel my_laravel_api
```

In the rest of this book, I assume the project name is my_laravel_
api, which is also the name of the project folder. Figure 2-26
shows a view of the Laravel installation progress in the command
terminal.

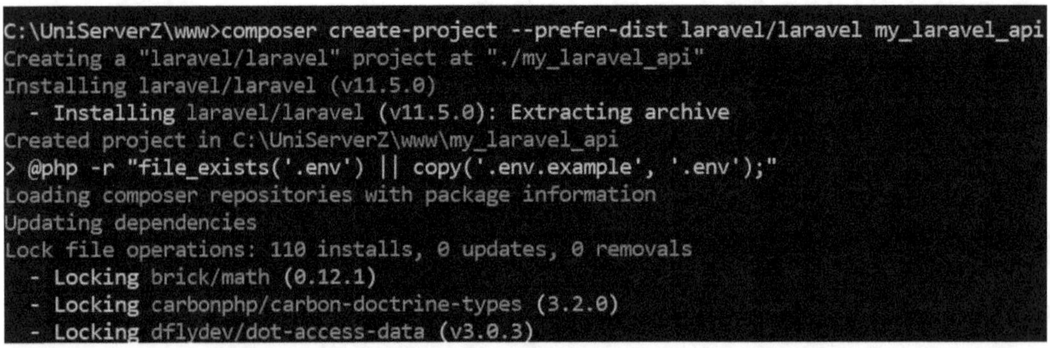

```
C:\UniServerZ\www>composer create-project --prefer-dist laravel/laravel my_laravel_api
Creating a "laravel/laravel" project at "./my_laravel_api"
Installing laravel/laravel (v11.5.0)
  - Installing laravel/laravel (v11.5.0): Extracting archive
Created project in C:\UniServerZ\www\my_laravel_api
> @php -r "file_exists('.env') || copy('.env.example', '.env');"
Loading composer repositories with package information
Updating dependencies
Lock file operations: 110 installs, 0 updates, 0 removals
  - Locking brick/math (0.12.1)
  - Locking carbonphp/carbon-doctrine-types (3.2.0)
  - Locking dflydev/dot-access-data (v3.0.3)
```

Figure 2-26. *Part of the output of executing the command for installing Laravel*

3. Wait for Composer to download and set up the Laravel framework.
    Once it's complete, run the command in Listing 2-6 to navigate
    into your Laravel project directory.

Listing 2-6. Changing into you Laravel project folder

```
cd my_laravel_api
```

Figure 2-27 shows what executing the command and its output looks like in the command terminal.

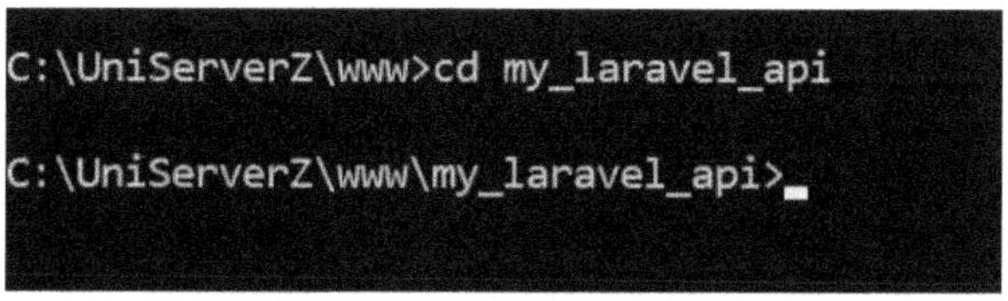
C:\UniServerZ\www>cd my_laravel_api
C:\UniServerZ\www\my_laravel_api>

Figure 2-27. *Moving the command prompt into the my_laravel_api project folder*

Laravel Installation Folder Structure

After installation, your Laravel installation should look like Figure 2-28.

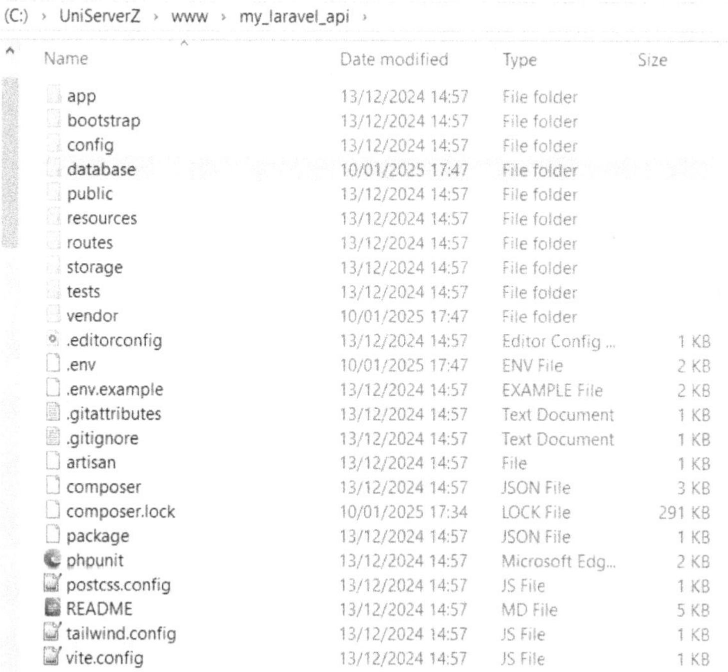
(C:) › UniServerZ › www › my_laravel_api ›
Name Date modified Type Size
app 13/12/2024 14:57 File folder
bootstrap 13/12/2024 14:57 File folder
config 13/12/2024 14:57 File folder
database 10/01/2025 17:47 File folder
public 13/12/2024 14:57 File folder
resources 13/12/2024 14:57 File folder
routes 13/12/2024 14:57 File folder
storage 13/12/2024 14:57 File folder
tests 13/12/2024 14:57 File folder
vendor 10/01/2025 17:47 File folder
.editorconfig 13/12/2024 14:57 Editor Config ... 1 KB
.env 10/01/2025 17:47 ENV File 2 KB
.env.example 13/12/2024 14:57 EXAMPLE File 2 KB
.gitattributes 13/12/2024 14:57 Text Document 1 KB
.gitignore 13/12/2024 14:57 Text Document 1 KB
artisan 13/12/2024 14:57 File 1 KB
composer 13/12/2024 14:57 JSON File 3 KB
composer.lock 10/01/2025 17:34 LOCK File 291 KB
package 13/12/2024 14:57 JSON File 1 KB
phpunit 13/12/2024 14:57 Microsoft Edg... 2 KB
postcss.config 13/12/2024 14:57 JS File 1 KB
README 13/12/2024 14:57 MD File 5 KB
tailwind.config 13/12/2024 14:57 JS File 1 KB
vite.config 13/12/2024 14:57 JS File 1 KB

Figure 2-28. *Laravel installation folder structure*

Files and Folders in the Laravel Directory Structure

In a Laravel installation directory, the files and folders serve specific purposes for developing and managing applications. The following list explains the key files and folders in the Laravel directory structure:

1. `app/`: Contains the core logic of your application, such as controllers, models, and middleware.

2. `bootstrap/`: Contains the `app.php` file, which initializes the Laravel framework. It also holds a `cache/` directory for optimizing performance (e.g., configuration and route caching).

3. `config/`: Contains configuration files for your application. Each file corresponds to a specific aspect, such as `app.php` (general app settings), `database.php` (database connections), and `mail.php` (email settings).

4. `database/`: Manages database-related files.

5. `factories/`: Houses factory classes for generating dummy data.

6. `migrations/`: Contains migration files for managing database schema.

7. `seeders/`: Holds seeder classes to populate the database with initial or test data.

8. `public/`: Purpose: The public-facing directory of your application. This directory contains a file named `index.php`, which serves as the entry point for all requests. It routes them to the framework. The folder also stores publicly accessible assets like CSS, JavaScript, and images.

9. `resources/`: Contains view templates, raw assets, and language files.

10. `routes/`: Defines application routes. It contains the following files:
    `web.php`: Routes for web interfaces
    `api.php`: Routes for APIs (stateless requests)
    `console.php`: Artisan command routes
    `channels.php`: Defines broadcast channels for real-time events

11. `storage/`: Stores files generated or used by the application.

12. `tests/`: Houses test classes for unit, feature, and integration testing.

13. `vendor/`: Contains all Composer-installed dependencies and libraries.

14. `artisan`: The CLI entry point for Laravel. Run commands to manage the application, such as migrations, caching, and testing.

15. `composer.json`: Lists the dependencies of the project and their versions. It also includes autoloading information.

16. `.env`: Environment configuration file that stores sensitive or environment-specific settings (e.g., database credentials and API keys).

17. `.env.example`: A template for the `.env` file, useful for sharing with other developers.

18. `.gitignore`: Specifies files and folders that Git should ignore in version control.

19. `package.json`: Specifies Node.js dependencies and scripts used in the project.

20. `vite.config.js`: Configuration file for Vite, used for compiling and bundling frontend assets.

21. `phpunit.xml`: Configuration file for PHPUnit testing.
     This structure is designed to separate concerns, making Laravel projects modular, maintainable, and scalable.

Adding Git to Your Laravel Application

To make your Laravel application a Git repository, you need to run a Git command from within the application folder. To do this in Windows, right-click the application folder and click the Git Bash Here option shown in Figure 2-29. This will open the command-line so that you can run the command from within the application folder.

Figure 2-29. *Right-click the application folder and click the Git Bash Here option to open the command-line interface*

From the opened command-line interface, run the command in Listing 2-7 to make your Laravel project a Git repository (see Figure 2-30).

Listing 2-7. Initializing Git for your Laravel folder

```
git init
```

Figure 2-30. *Initializing the application as a Git repository*

Create a Database

Next, you create a database for your Laravel app. You use phpMyAdmin. Follow these steps to set up the database:

Note   The name of the database and the password you set in this section will be required in later sections for use in your Laravel app. Be sure to write them down somewhere for later reference.

---

1. Ensure that the Uniform Server Control Panel is open and that the Apache and MySQL servers are turned on. Launch phpMyAdmin by clicking the button labelled phpMyAdmin. See Figure 2-31.

Figure 2-31. *To launch phpMyAdmin, open the Uniform Server controller and ensure that Apache and MySQL are on (indicated by the green color beside them), then click the phpMyAdmin button*

2. On the phpMyAdmin page, clicking the Databases menu button at the top or the New button to the left (see Figure 2-32). Doing so will open another page for you to create the database.

Figure 2-32. *The phpMyAdmin database page*

3. On the opened page from Step 2, enter your database name (I chose to name the database my_laravel_api) and select a collation option (I recommend utf8mb4_general_ci). See Figure 2-33. Then click the Create button to create the database. The newly created database will appear in the list of databases, as shown in Figure 2-34.

Figure 2-33. *Enter a name for the database and choose the collation type to create your database*

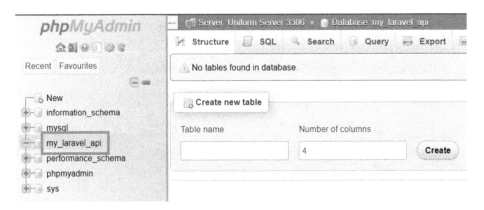

Figure 2-34. *You can see the new database to the left of the page*

4. Next you need to set a password for your database. First ensure that the Apache and MySQL servers are switched off. See Figure 2-35.

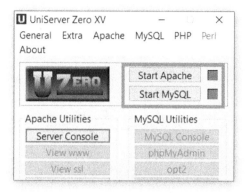

Figure 2-35. *Ensure that the Apache and MySQL servers are off before attempting to create a password*

5. Choose MySQL ➤ Change MySQL Password. See Figure 2-36.

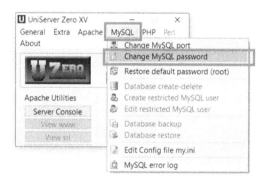

Figure 2-36. *Steps to open the dialog box and set your password*

6. Enter a password in the dialog box. I entered a value of 1234. See Figure 2-37. Enter your password for the database and click the OK button to accept and dismiss the dialog box. Another dialog will show up notifying you of the changed password. Here again, click the OK button (see Figure 2-38).

Figure 2-37. *Enter your password and click the OK button*

Figure 2-38. *Click the OK button again*

Configure Laravel Environment

1. Locate the .env file in your Laravel project directory and open it in Notepad or your code editor. See Figure 2-39. Update the database credentials in the .env file to match your Uniform Server's MySQL database name and password. See Figure 2-40.

) › UniServerZ › www › my_laravel_api ›		
Name	Date modified	Type
app	13/12/2024 14:57	File
bootstrap	13/12/2024 14:57	File
config	13/12/2024 14:57	File
database	10/01/2025 17:47	File
public	13/12/2024 14:57	File
resources	13/12/2024 14:57	File
routes	13/12/2024 14:57	File
storage	13/12/2024 14:57	File
tests	13/12/2024 14:57	File
vendor	10/01/2025 17:47	File
.editorconfig	13/12/2024 14:57	Edit
.env	10/01/2025 17:47	ENV
.env.example	13/12/2024 14:57	EXA
.gitattributes	13/12/2024 14:57	Text

Figure 2-39. *The .env file is located inside your Laravel installation folder—my_laravel_api in this case*

Figure 2-40. *After making the change, select File ➤ Save or press Ctrl+S to save the changes*

2. Open the /my_laravel_api/config/database.php file (see Figure 2-41a) and update the MySQL section with database credentials in the file to match your Uniform Server's MySQL database name and password setup. See Figure 2-41b.

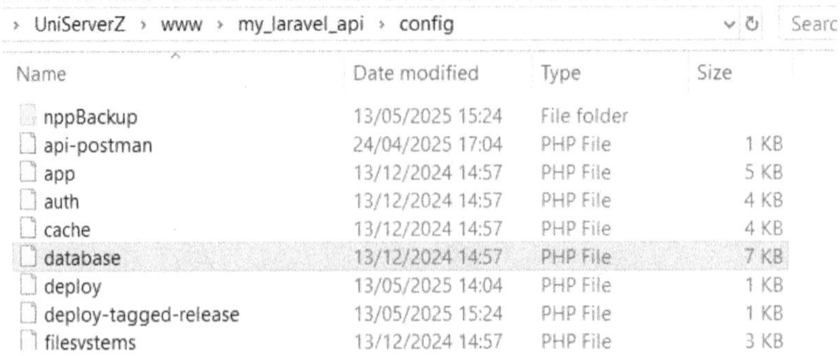

Figure 2-41a. *The /my_laravel_api/config/database.php file*

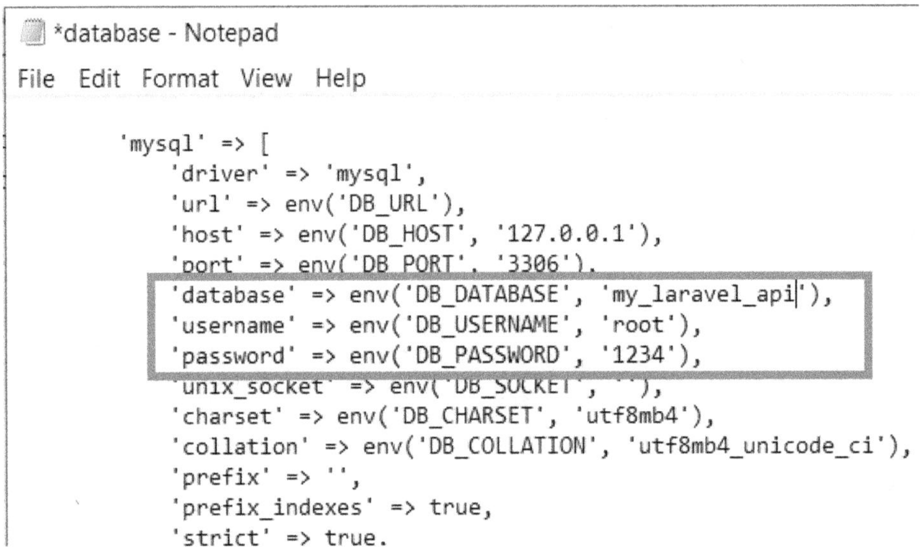

Figure 2-41b. *After making the change, select File ➤ Save or press Ctrl+S to save the changes*

Add Default Laravel's Database Tables

1. Open a command prompt and navigate to the Laravel project directory by running the command in Listing 2-8. If you installed Laravel in the `C:\UniServerZ\www\my_laravel_api` directory, your command will be the same. However, if you installed Laravel in a different directory, use that directory instead.

Listing 2-8. Changing into your Laravel project folder

```
cd C:\UniServerZ\www\my_laravel_api
```

See Figure 2-41c for a screenshot of the command executed in the command-line.

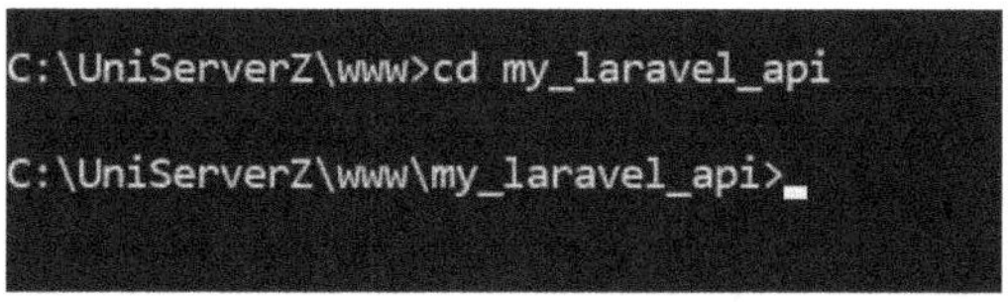

```
C:\UniServerZ\www>cd my_laravel_api

C:\UniServerZ\www\my_laravel_api>_
```

Figure 2-41c. *Move the command prompt into your Laravel project folder if you are not already there*

2. Once inside your Laravel project folder, enter the command in Listing 2-9 at the command prompt.

Listing 2-9. Running database migration

```
php artisan migrate
```

Figure 2-42 shows the screenshot of the command when it's executed.

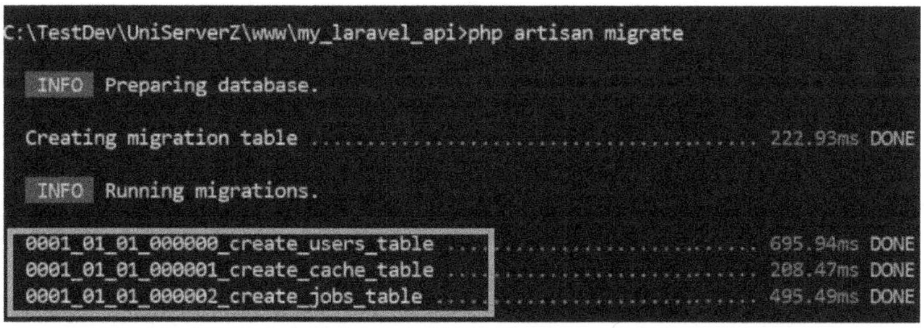

```
C:\TestDev\UniServerZ\www\my_laravel_api>php artisan migrate

  INFO  Preparing database.

  Creating migration table ....................................... 222.93ms DONE

  INFO  Running migrations.

  0001_01_01_000000_create_users_table ....    ................... 695.94ms DONE
  0001_01_01_000001_create_cache_table ....    ................... 208.47ms DONE
  0001_01_01_000002_create_jobs_table ....     ................... 495.49ms DONE
```

Figure 2 42. *Entering the Artisan command will create some tables—three in this case*

3. Once the command has finished executing, open phpMyAdmin and click the database you created earlier (my_laravel_api). The added tables will be displayed, as shown in Figure 2-43.

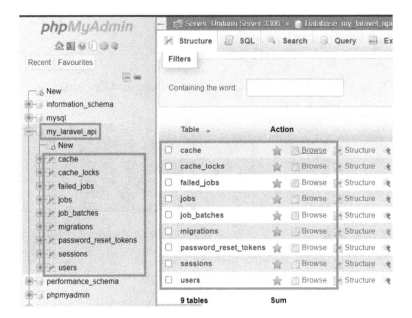

Figure 2-43. *After you run the Artisan migration command, you can see the generated tables in the database*

Setting the Laravel Public Folder as Your Root Folder

Currently, if you want to access your Laravel app's home URL, you have to type the URL as `http://localhost/my_laravel_app` instead of as `http://localhost`. In this section, you learn how to change your Uniform Server root folder from `www` to the `public` folder of the Laravel app to correct this. Follow these steps to make this change:

1. Open the Uniform Server Control panel, as shown in Figure 2-44. Choose Apache ➤ Change Apache Root Folders ➤ Select New Server Root-Folder (www).

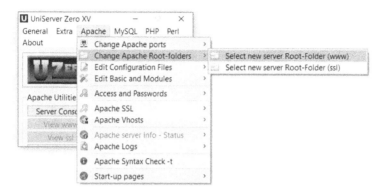

Figure 2-44. *Accessing the dialog box for changing the root folder of Uniform Server*

2. Following Step 1 will bring up a dialog to choose a new root folder. See Figure 2-45. Select your Laravel app's `public` folder. Then click Select Folder.

Figure 2-45. *Navigate to your Laravel application folder, click the public folder to highlight it, and then click the Select Folder button to select it*

3. Go to your Laravel public folder and open the `.htaccess` file in Notepad. You're going to replace its contents with the contents in Listing 2-10 (see Figure 2-46).

Figure 2-46. *Navigate to your Laravel application's public folder and open the .htaccess file in a text editor like Notepad, then replace its contents with that of Listing 2-10*

4. Change the .htaccess contents to the contents in Listing 2-10.

Listing 2-10. Updating the .htaccess file on your server

```
<IfModule mod_rewrite.c>
<IfModule mod_negotiation.c>
    Options +MultiViews +Indexes +FollowSymLinks +SymLinksIfOwnerMatch
</IfModule>

RewriteEngine On
DirectoryIndex index.php
# Handle Authorization Header
RewriteCond %{HTTP:Authorization} .
RewriteRule .* - [E=HTTP_AUTHORIZATION:%{HTTP:Authorization}]

# Redirect Trailing Slashes If Not A Folder...
RewriteCond %{REQUEST_FILENAME} !-d
RewriteCond %{REQUEST_URI} (.+)/$
RewriteRule ^ %1 [L,R=301]

# Send Requests To Front Controller...
RewriteCond %{REQUEST_FILENAME} !-d
RewriteCond %{REQUEST_FILENAME} !-f
RewriteRule ^ index.php [L]
</IfModule>
```

5. That's all. Restart Apache and MySQL (see Figure 2-47a) and
    visit the localhost in your browser. It will serve your Laravel app
    from the `public` folder, displaying the Laravel Welcome Page (see
    Figure 2-47b).

Figure 2-47a. *Restart the Apache and MySQL servers*

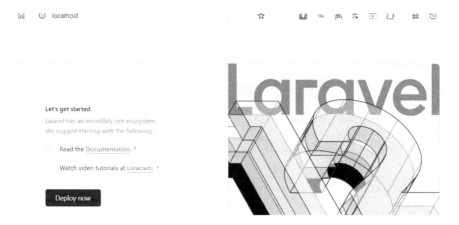

Figure 2-47b. *Laravel welcome page, indicating a successful installation
of Laravel*

Code Editor

You need a place to write and edit your code—a code editor—and there are many
options that are all viable and okay. However, in this book, I use VS Code. Among other
things, it has various extensions, one of which you'll use to test the API, EchoAPI, as well
as an built-in command-line tool. The fact that you can use these tools directly from
within VS Code while coding, without having to open external applications, makes it

convenient. Of course, if you use a different code editor, EchoAPI also has a cross-platform desktop application version that can be installed as a standalone application. Note that VS Code, being a cross-platform application, is available for macOS and Linux as well.

Installing Visual Studio Code on Windows

If you don't yet have it installed, follow these steps to install VS Code:

1. Download the installer:

    -   Visit the official Visual Studio Code website at `https://code.visualstudio.com`. Click the Download for Windows button to download the installer or click the Other Platforms link to download versions for other platforms. See Figure 2-48.

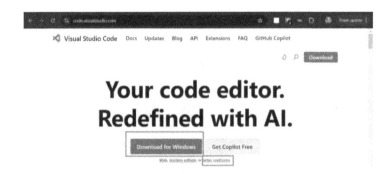

Figure 2-48. *VS Code website*

2. Run the Installer. Locate the downloaded file (usually in your `Downloads` folder) and double-click it to launch the installer. See Figure 2-49.

Figure 2-49. *Downloaded VS Code executable file*

3. Follow the Setup Wizard:

    •   Agree to the license terms and select the installation location. See
        Figure 2-50.

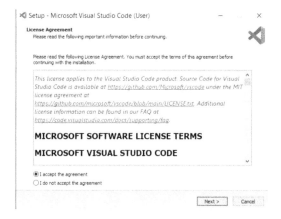

Figure 2-50. *Select I Accept the Agreement and click the Next button*

    •   Choose the installation folder. See Figure 2-51.

Figure 2-51. *Click Next*

- Select the Start Menu folder. See Figure 2-52.

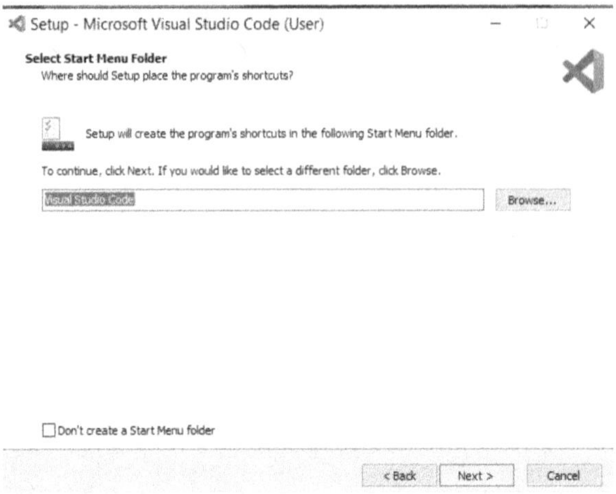

Figure 2-52. *Click Next*

- Choose additional options such as creating a desktop shortcut and adding VS Code to your system PATH (recommended). See Figure 2-53.

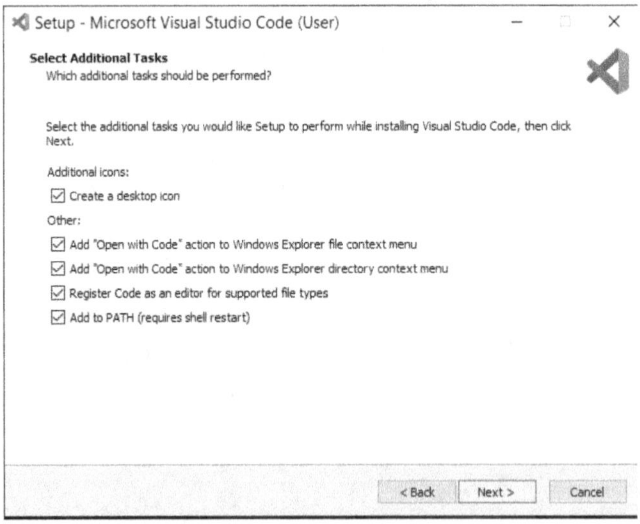

Figure 2-53. *Ensure all the options are ticked and click Next*

4. Complete the installation. Click Install and wait for the process to complete. See Figures 2-54 and 2-55.

Figure 2-54. *If you are okay with the options, click Next, if not click Back to make whatever changes you want*

Figure 2-55. *Allow VS Code to finish installing*

• Once it's finished, you can tick Launch VS Code and click Finish to launch VS Code. See Figure 2-56.

Figure 2-56. *Click the Finish button*

- Clicking the Finish button will launch VS Code, as shown in
  Figure 2-57.

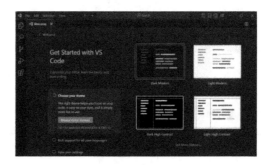

Figure 2-57. *Your newly installed VS Code interface*

Now you have VS Code ready. Next you learn how to open your Laravel project in VS Code as well as how to access its built-in command-line interface.

Opening Your Laravel Project in VS Code

In order to open your Laravel project in VS Code for editing, you need to take the following steps. Select File ➤ Open Folder. Navigate to the Laravel project folder (in this book, I use my_laravel_api as the name of the project/project folder). With the path to the project folder being C:/UniServerZ/www/my_laravel_api/, click Select Folder. See Figures 2-58 and 2-59. Figures 2-60 and 2-61 show the additional steps to take and the project folders/files now available for editing from within VS Code.

Figure 2-58. *To open the Laravel project in VS Code, select File ➤ Open Folder*

Figure 2-59. *Navigate to Uniform Server Root Folder (www) click to highlight it, then click the Select Folder button to select it*

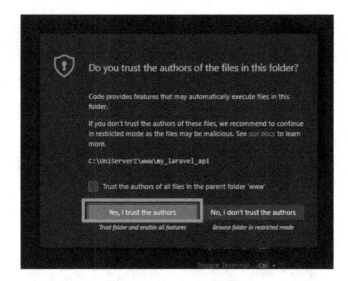

Figure 2-60. *Click the Yes, I Trust the Authors button to proceed*

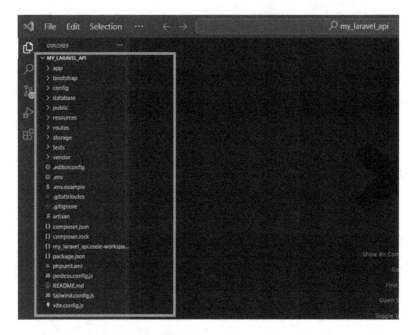

Figure 2-61. *The Laravel project folder now open in VS Code*

Now that you have your project open in VS Code, you can learn how to access and use the command-line interface from within VS Code.

Using VS Code's Built-In Command-Line (Terminal) Tool

To open and use the command-line (terminal) within Visual Studio Code, follow these steps:

1. Make sure Visual Studio Code is open.

2. Go to the top menu bar and choose View ➤ Terminal. See Figure 2-62.

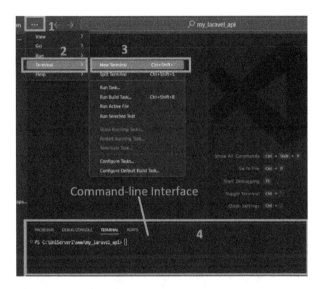

Figure 2-62. *Opening the command-line (Terminal) interface in VS Code*

That is it—you should see the command-line or terminal open. In this case it appeared at the bottom of VS Code; however, it's possible it may be placed to the side depending on your display configuration. By default, the VS Code command-line interface will always open into your project root folder, except you navigate away.

EchoAPI: Offline API Test Tool

To test your API, you'll be using software called EchoAPI. In this section, you learn how to install it. EchoAPI is a free-to-use tool, designed to make the process of developing and testing RESTful APIs very easy. One of its standout features is its ability to work offline. It can also be used to generate documentation.

Additional information about EchoAPI is available on its website at
`https://www.echoapi.com`

Installing EchoAPI as a VS Code Extension

Installing EchoAPI as a VS Code extension is straightforward and can be completed in
just a few steps:

1. **Open VS Code:** Ensure that you have VS Code installed and
   updated to the latest version.

2. **Access the extensions marketplace:** Click the Extensions icon
   in the Activity Bar on the side of the VS Code window or press
   Ctrl+Shift+X. In the search bar at the top, type **EchoAPI** and press
   Enter. Locate the EchoAPI extension in the search results and click
   it. See Figure 2-63.

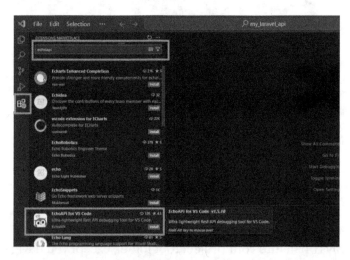

Figure 2-63. *Searching for and installing the EchoAPI VS Code extension*

3. **Install the extension:** Click the Install button of EchoAPI and wait
   for the installation to complete (see Figure 2-64).

Figure 2-64. *Click the Install button to install EchoAPI*

4. **Accessing EchoAPI:**

   - Once it's installed, EchoAPI will be accessible through the
     Extensions sidebar or via the Command Palette (Ctrl+Shift+P).
     See Figure 2-65.

Figure 2-65. *The EchoAPI VS Code extension interface to the left of VS Code*

   - However, if EchoAPI icon is not visible, right-click the extension
     icon and ensure that the EchoAPI option is ticked. The EchoAPI
     icon should now be visible on the sidebar. See Figure 2-66.

Figure 2-66. *Getting the EchoAPI icon to show up if it's not visible*

Summary

You've finally come to the end of this chapter! This chapter explored why Laravel is a great candidate for API development and how it can help you build RESTful APIs that align with Fielding's REST guidelines. You also installed Laravel and Git, set up a local development environment using Uniform Server and VS Code, and created a test environment using EchoAPI.

CHAPTER 3

Laravel for API Development

This chapter explains various concepts in Laravel for API development. This includes covering Artisan commands, routes, named routes, route parameters, route binding, models, migration, eloquent ORM, mass assignment, accessors, mutators, resource classes, request objects, pagination, controllers, validations, and more.

Artisan

Artisan is like a helper for Laravel developers. It can do a lot of things for you, like creating files, managing your database, and running tasks. Instead of doing everything manually, you can use Artisan commands to save time and effort.

When building RESTful APIs, Artisan makes it simple to create things like controllers, models, migrations, and so on. This lets you focus on building your application instead of doing repetitive setup work. Later, you'll look at some of the things you can use Artisan for.

Artisan commands are run from the command-line, and you must change your directory to your project folder from the command-line before running these commands. In Chapter 2, you learned how to open your project folder from within VS Code and how to access the VS Code command-line tool. Once you've done this, you can run Artisan commands as well as other commands in this book.

Additionally, to run Artisan commands, ensure that the MySQL server and web server, Apache in this case, are both turned on. If you are using Uniform Server, you can use it to do this. See Chapter 2 for details.

© Adegoke Akintoye 2025
A. Akintoye, *API Development with Laravel*, https://doi.org/10.1007/979-8-8688-1576-8_3

Routes

Routes allows developers to define the URLs of their application and link them to specific logic in the application using controllers or closures—you'll learn more about controllers and closures later, but for now just know that they are basically PHP classes and functions and they contain programming logic. Laravel uses routes to decide what to do when a user visits a specific URL.

In Laravel, files containing your routes—both the ones you define and the ones automatically generated for you by Laravel during installation—can be found in the route folder. This folder is inside your Laravel's installation folder. These route files can be edited to add or remove routes based on your needs. This directory typically contains files such as the following:

- `web.php`: For web routes requiring sessions, cookies, and CSRF protection, this file is usually auto-generated.

- `api.php`: For stateless API routes. These are not auto-generated by default.

- `console.php`: For defining custom Artisan commands. Usually auto-generated.

- `channels.php`: For broadcasting channels. Not auto-generated by default.

Although most of these files are auto-generated, you are free to add routes needed by your app to any of them.

A Simple Route

Listing 3-1 illustrates a basic example of how to define a route.

Listing 3-1. A basic Laravel route

```
use Illuminate\Support\Facades\Route;

Route::get('/', function () {
    return 'A Basic Route';
});
```

This route is explained here:

- **HTTP Verb**: The get() method specifies that this route responds to GET requests. There are other methods, depending on the type of request you are handling, such as post(), delete(), put(), and so on.

- **Path**: The / symbol indicates the root URL.

- **Callback function/action**: This is a closure—a function without a name. You place the code to be executed inside this function when this route is visited, say from a web browser. In this case, it returns the string 'A Basic Route' when the root URL is accessed.

Route Parameters

Laravel routes can accept dynamic parameters. These parameters are like placeholders or containers for values that can be passed to your application via a given URL. Parameters can either be required or optional. You define dynamic parameters by placing them in a pair of curly brackets ({ }).

Required Parameters

To make a parameter required, meaning that it must be included in the URL, simply place it in a pair of curly brackets, as shown in Listing 3-2.

Listing 3-2. A route using a required parameter

```
Route::get('/user/{id}', function ($id) {
    return "User ID: $id";
});
```

From this listing:

- {id} is a dynamic parameter.

- You can access the parameter's value in the callback function as $id.

67

Optional Parameters

By adding a question mark (?) to front of a parameter, it becomes optional. You can also provide a default value to be passed to the callback function if the parameter is not provided. See the code in Listing 3-3.

Listing 3-3. Example of how an optional parameter can be used

```
Route::get('/user/{name?}', function ($name = 'Guest') {
    return "Hello, $name!";
});
```

From the preceding code:

- The ? after the name parameter makes it optional.

- A default value (Guest) is used when no value is provided. You need to provide a default value because the callback function requires that the $name variable have a value. Therefore, if no value is passed via the URL to this function, the default value will be used.

Route Model Binding

One of the ways that Laravel makes it easy for developers to write code is through a concept called *route model binding*. Don't let the name confuse you, it's a simple concept. Imagine that you have a route defined as in Listing 3-4.

Listing 3-4. A Simple Route Without Model Binding

```
use App\Models\Post;
use Illuminate\Support\Facades\Route;

Route::get('/posts/{postid}', function ($postid) {
    $post = Post::find($postid);
    return response()->json($post);
});
```

The preceding code represents a route where postid is a route parameter. Whatever value you give to postid will be passed to the anonymous function or controller by Laravel so that you can then use the value. This code simply uses the value passed to retrieve a post whose id equals the value passed through the postid parameter. However, with route model binding, Laravel can automatically fetch the post for you; all you need to do is rewrite the code to let Laravel know that this is what you want. The same code, using route model binding, can be rewritten as shown in Listing 3-5.

Listing 3-5. The Same Code Rewritten with Route Model Binding

```
use App\Models\Post;
use Illuminate\Support\Facades\Route;

Route::get('/posts/{postid}', function (Post $post) {

    return response()->json($post);
});
```

By adding Post $post as a parameter to the anonymous function, you are simply telling Laravel that you want to retrieve a post whose id corresponds to postid (the route parameter). So Laravel will automatically fetch the post and pass it, rather than the postid itself, to you through your anonymous function or controller method. Of course, in order to use route model binding, you need to create model that is named appropriately. In this case, the model must be named Post. Later, you'll learn about models and how to create them.

Note that the resulting code is simpler, shorter, and easier to read. For example, you don't have to fetch the post, as it's done for you by Laravel automatically. This can result in considerable gain, especially when dealing with many route parameters.

This way of implementing route model binding is referred to as *implicit binding*.

Handling API Routes

As explained in Chapter 1, RESTful API development is about the manipulation of resources. This manipulation involves doing things like creating a new resource, reading the attributes of a resource, updating an existing resource, and deleting a resource. These actions are collectively referred to as CRUD operations.

Clients that want to manipulate a resource usually specify that intention to the server on which the resource is located—which also houses the Laravel API application—by sending the appropriate URL, HTTP verb (GET, POST, UPDATE, and so on), and header (specifying things like token, expected response, and so on.). The server can then carry out this operation. Therefore, to capture all the requests a client can make, you need at least four endpoints, which also translates to four routes. Actually, you will have six endpoints/routes as the READ and UPDATE operations are two types. You can read data about a specific user or get all users. For update, you can use either PATCH or PUT to change the data of a resource. Assuming you are dealing with a user resource containing data about your users, you would have the following endpoints:

1. **GET /users**: Retrieves all users.

2. **POST /users**: Creates a new user.

3. **GET /users/{id}**: Retrieves a specific user.

4. **PUT/PATCH /users/{id}**: Updates a specific user.

5. **DELETE /users/{id}**: Deletes a specific user.

The corresponding routes will then be as shown in Listing 3-6.

Listing 3-6. Typical corresponding routes for an API resource

```
1. Retrieve all users:
   Route::get('/users', function () {
       //Write code to get all user and return it to the client
   });
2. Create a new user:
   Route::post('/users', function (Request $request) {
       // Write code to create a new user
   });
3. Retrieve a specific user:
   Route::get('/users/{id}', function (User $user) {
       // Write code to retrieve a specific user and return it to
           the client.
       // note that here we are also using route model binding.

   });
4. Update all the data of a resource:
   Route::put('/users/{id}', function (id) {
       // Write code to update all the data of a specific user
   });
```

5. *Update part of the data of a resource:*
```
Route::patch('/users/{id}', function (id) {
    // Write code to update part of the data of a specific user
});
```
6. *Update part of the data of a resource:*
```
Route::delete('/users/{id}', function (id) {
    // Write code to delete the data of a specific user
});
```

During API development, it is common to have several resources you're working with, which means more routes to write. Here again, Laravel offers a way to make the job easy; it gives you a single line of code that can represent all these routes together. The code is shown in Listing 3-7.

Listing 3-7. A Single Line of Code that Covers All the Routes of a Resource

```
Route::apiResource('users', UserController::class);
```

Now when a client visits any of the six routes stated earlier, this single line of code knows how to direct the client's request to the appropriate method in the UserController class to handle the request.

Named Routes

In Laravel, named routes allow you to assign a unique name to a route. This makes it easier to refer to that route in your application, especially when generating URLs or redirects. Named routes improve the readability and maintainability of your code because you don't need to hard-code URLs throughout your application. For example, if the URL changes, you only need to update it in the route definition, not everywhere it's used.

You can define a named route by using the name method in the route definition. Listing 3-8 shows an example.

Listing 3-8. An example of how to name a route in Laravel

```
Route::get('/api/dashboard', function () {
    return 'Dashboard';
})→name('dashy');
```

In this example, the /api/dashboard route is assigned the name dashy. You can thus use dashy instead of the full URL (/api/dashboard).

Accessing Named Routes

Once a route is named, you can use the name to generate URLs or redirects.

Generating URLs

You can use the route() helper to generate a URL for the named route, as shown in Listing 3-9.

Listing 3-9. Example of how to access a route using its name

```
$url = route('dashy');
echo $url;
// Output: http://your-app-url/api/dashboard
```

Redirecting to Named Routes

You can use the name of a route rather than the full URL for redirection, as shown in Listing 3-10.

Listing 3-10. Redirecting to a route using the route's name

```
return redirect()→route('dashy');
```

Models

A *model* in Laravel is a class that interacts with the corresponding database table where the data about your API resources are stored. It provides a structured and efficient way to retrieve, insert, update, and delete data. By default, models are stored in the app/Models directory, and they use Laravel's Eloquent ORM (Object-Relational Mapping) to interact with the database.

The major role of a model is to centralize the logic associated with a specific database table. For example, if your application includes a users table, you would typically create a User model to manage all interactions and operations involving that table.

When building RESTful APIs, models serve as the backbone for managing resource data. They not only interact with the database, but also provide a convenient structure to define relationships, enforce data integrity, and implement business rules.

Creating a Model

To create a model in Laravel, you can use the Artisan command-line tool. For example, to create a model for a `products` table, you would execute the command in Listing 3-11.

Listing 3-11. An Artisan command for creating a model

```
php artisan make:model Product -a --api
```

This command creates a `Product` model in the `app/Models` directory as well as a controller named `ProductController`. It will also create other files for migration, seeding, policy, and so on. You can see the model generated with the Artisan command in Listing 3-12.

Listing 3-12. The Model Generated Using the Preceding Command.

```php
<?php

namespace App\Models;

use Illuminate\Database\Eloquent\Factories\HasFactory;
use Illuminate\Database\Eloquent\Model;

class Product extends Model
{
    /** @use HasFactory<\Database\Factories\ProductFactory> */
    use HasFactory;
}
```

With the preceding Artisan command, you can generate basic code for your `Product` model, and then you can modify it as needed to meet your needs.

Migrations

In the preceding section, you saw how to generate a model using Artisan. This action also generated other files, including a *migration* file. The migration file is located in the `database\migrations\` directory. The migration filename always includes a timestamp,

73

which is used to ensure migrations run in the correct order. The name of the migration file generated in this instance is 2025_01_19_123650_create_products_table.php; yours will be different because of the timestamp. See Listing 3-13.

Listing 3-13. The Generated Migration File: 2025_01_19_123650_create_products_table.php

```php
<?php

use Illuminate\Database\Migrations\Migration;
use Illuminate\Database\Schema\Blueprint;
use Illuminate\Support\Facades\Schema;

return new class extends Migration
{
    /**
     * Run the migrations.
     */
    public function up(): void
    {
        Schema::create('products', function (Blueprint $table) {
            $table->id();
            $table->timestamps();
        });
    }

    /**
     * Reverse the migrations.
     */
    public function down(): void
    {
        Schema::dropIfExists('products');
    }
};
```

What Are Migrations

Migrations are like version-controlled blueprints for your database. They allow you to outline the layout of database tables—like columns, data types, and constraints—using PHP. This makes it simpler to manage and more adaptable than traditional SQL scripts. In Laravel, you'll find these migrations saved in the `database/migrations` folder.

Creating a Migration File

You saw earlier how you can create a migration file together with a model file using one Artisan command. You can also create just the migration file alone. To create a migration file, you use the `make:migration` Artisan command, as shown in Listing 3-14.

Listing 3-14. Artisan Command to Create a Migration File

```
php artisan make:migration create_users_table
```

This generates a new migration file in the `database/migrations` folder. As mentioned, this filename will include a timestamp.

Key Sections in a Migration File

If you look at the code in the migration file generated earlier, you'll notice that it has two methods, namely `up()` and `down()`. This section discusses what they do:

1. `up()` **method:** Defines the changes to apply when the migration runs. For example, it may specify that one or more columns be created as well as their data types.

2. `down()` **method:** Reverses the changes made in the `up()` method. If, for example, the `up()` method added some columns, this method will remove them.

Modifying an Existing Table

The migrations generated with Artisan often contain just the basics, and as such you'll probably want to modify them to include additional details (for example, more columns, constraints, and so on). For example, the migration file only contains columns for IDs and timestamps (this creates two columns: `created_at` and `updated_at`). Depending on the type of application you are building, you might want additional data about your product resource, so you may want to add columns like name, description, price, and so on. To add these fields (columns), you need to modify Schema::create() inside the up() method, as shown in Listing 3-15.

Listing 3-15. Editing a Migration File to Add More Columns

```
public function up(): void
    {
      Schema::create('products', function (Blueprint $table) {
            $table→id();
            $table→string('name');
            $table→string('description')->nullable();
            $table→integer('price');
            $table->timestamps();
        });
    }
```

This code added three more columns. The following is a description of the columns being created:

1. name: The name should be of data type string with the instruction $table→string('name').

2. description: This description column specifies that it should also be a string but can be an empty value. For this, you use this instruction: $table→string('description')→nullable().

3. price: The price column is declared as an integer, via this instruction: $table→integer('price').

Basic Column Types

This section looks at some basic column types:

1. **Integer types**: $table->integer('column_name');

    This is used to create *integer-based* columns. You can use it for fields like age or score. It supports a range of signed and unsigned integers, suitable for most numeric data without decimals.

2. **String types**: `$table->string('column_name', 255);`

   Defines a VARCHAR column with a default length of 255 characters unless otherwise specified. This is typically used for storing short textual data, such as names, email addresses, and usernames.

3. **Text types**: `$table->text('column_name');`

   Use this for storing large chunks of text, such as descriptions, articles, and comments. Unlike strings, it doesn't have a character limit.

4. **Boolean**: `$table->boolean('column_name');`

   Creates a column to store `true/false` values. This is ideal for flags like `is_active` or `has_access` to determine binary states.

5. **Date and time types**: `$table->date('column_name');`, `$table->timestamp('column_name');`

   The `date` column type is used for storing date-only values, such as birthdates, while `timestamp` includes both date and time. This is useful for fields like `created_at` or `updated_at`.

6. **Foreign keys**: `$table->foreignId('user_id')->constrained();`

   Automatically creates an integer column and establishes a foreign key relationship. This ensures referential integrity with another table, such as linking a `user_id` in a `posts` table to the `id` field in a `users` table.

Basic Column Modifiers

This section looks at some basic column modifier types:

1. **Nullable:** `$table->string('column_name')->nullable();`

   Allows a column to accept NULL values, making it optional. This is useful for fields that may not always have data, like a `middle_name` or `profile_picture`.

2. **Default values:** `$table->integer('column_name')->default(0);`

   Sets a default value for the column if no value is provided during insertion. For example, an `is_active` column could default to 0 (inactive).

3.   **Unique:** `$table->string('column_name')->unique();`

Enforces a *uniqueness constraint* on the column to ensure there are no duplicate values. This is commonly used for fields like email or username to maintain data integrity.

Running Migrations

To apply migrations to the database so that the changes specified in it are reflected in your database table, use the Artisan command in Listing 3-16.

Listing 3-16. Artisan Command for Applying the Migration

```
php artisan migrate
```

This will execute all pending migrations in the `database/migrations` folder.

Rolling Back Migrations

If you need to undo a migration, you can use the `migrate:rollback` command, as shown in Listing 3-17.

Listing 3-17. Artisan Command for Reversing (Rolling Back) the Effect of a Migration

```
php artisan migrate:rollback
```

This command rolls back the last batch of migrations. To roll back multiple steps, use the `--step` option, as shown in Listing 3-18.

Listing 3-18. Artisan Command for Rolling Back Step by Step

```
php artisan migrate:rollback --step=2
```

Eloquent ORM

One of Laravel's standout features is Eloquent, its Object-Relational Mapping (ORM) system, which simplifies database interactions. When building RESTful APIs, Eloquent becomes an invaluable tool, enabling developers to manipulate database records effortlessly and intuitively. Eloquent facilitates smooth interaction with relational databases. It abstracts complex SQL queries into simple and intuitive PHP methods, allowing developers to focus more on business logic than database intricacies. Eloquent models serve as an active record implementation, enabling each model to correspond to a database table, where each instance represents a single row in the table. For example, defining a User model linked to a users table is as simple as giving your model a name of User (the singular form of the table's name), as shown in the code in Listing 3-19.

Listing 3-19. A Model Called User Linked to a Table Called Users

```
namespace App\Models;

use Illuminate\Database\Eloquent\Model;

class User extends Model
{
    // Add your code here.
}
```

The next section covers some of the basic Eloquent methods that can be used for RESTful API development.

Basic Eloquent Methods

This section looks at basic eloquent methods with examples.

1. **Retrieving data:** Retrieving data from the database is fundamental to any API. Eloquent provides several methods to query the database:

   - **Retrieving all records**

     The all() method retrieves all rows from a table:

     ```
     use App\Models\Post;
     $posts = Post::all();//Retrieves all post
     ```

   - **Finding a specific record**

     The find() method retrieves a record by its primary key:

     ```
     $post = Post::find(1); // Fetch the record with ID 1
     ```

79

Alternatively, you can write it as:

```
$post = Post:: findOrFail(1)
// findOrFail(1) throw a ModelNotFoundException
// if the record doesn't exist
```

This is useful when designing APIs that return error responses for missing resources.

- **Retrieving the first record**

  Use the first() *method to retrieve the first record matching the query:*

```
$firstPost = Post::where('status', 'published')
            →first();
// Retrieves the first record
//that matches our condition
```

2. **Query-builder methods:** Eloquent allows you to chain query methods for more complex filtering. Here are some common examples:

   - **Filtering and sorting**

     Filtering by status and sorting by creation date:

```
$posts = Post::where('status', 'published')
      →orderBy('created_at', 'desc')
      →get();
//This retrieves all posts where the status is
// "published," sorted by the newest entries first.
```

     Using multiple conditions:

```
$posts = Post::where('status', 'published')
      ->where('author_id', 5)
      →get();
//This retrieves posts where the status is "published"
// and the author_id is 5.
```

Using logical operators:

```
$posts = Post::where('views', '>', 100)
      ->orWhere('likes', '>=', 50)
      →get();
//This retrieves posts where either the views are
//greater than 100 or the likes are at least 50.
```

Limiting results:

```
$posts = Post::where('status', 'published')
      ->limit(5)
      →get();
//This retrieves only the first 5 posts that match
//the criteria.
```

Fetching specific columns:

```
$posts = Post::where('status', 'published')
        ->orderBy('created_at', 'desc')
        ->get(['id', 'title', 'author_id']);
//This retrieves only the id, title, and author_id
// columns for the matching posts, reducing unnecessary
//data retrieval.
```

3. **Creating data:** Eloquent offers an easy way to insert data into the database.

- **Creating a new instance**

    Using the save() *method:*

    ```
    $post = new Post;
    $post->title = 'New Post';
    $post->content = 'This is the content of the post.';
    $post→save();
    //Creates a new post.
    ```

Using the create() *method:*

```
$post = Post::create([
        'title' => 'New Post',
        'content' => 'This is the content of the post.',
]);
//Creates a new post.
```

4. **Updating data**

Using the save() *method:*

```
$post = Post::find(1);
$post->title = 'Updated Title';
$post→save();
//the save() method can also be used for updating
```

Using the save() *method:*

```
Post::where('id', 1)->update(['title' => 'Updated
Title']);
//updates the post with id = 1
```

5. **Deleting data**

Deleting a record by instance:

```
$post = Post::find(1);
$post→delete();
//deletes a post with id = 1
```

Deleting directly with a query:

```
Post::destroy(1);
//deletes post with id = 1
Post::destroy([1, 2, 3]);
//deletes 3 posts with id = 1,2,3 simultaneously
```

6. **Soft deletes:** Soft deletes allow you to delete a record without permanently removing it from the database. To enable soft deletes, follow these steps:

a. **Update the database migration:** Add a deleted_at column to the table. This is necessary for tracking soft-deleted records:

Updating your migration file for soft deletes:

```
Schema::table('posts', function (Blueprint $table) {
  $table->softDeletes();
});
```

b. **Enable soft deletes in the model:** Include the SoftDeletes trait in your model:

Enabling soft delete in your model:

```
use Illuminate\Database\Eloquent\SoftDeletes;

class Post extends Model
{
    use SoftDeletes;
    protected $dates = ['deleted_at'];
}
```

c. **Soft delete a record:** Use the delete() method to soft-delete a record:

Using the delete() method for a soft delete:

```
$post = Post::find(1);
$post->delete(); // Marks the record as deleted
//without removing it from the database
```

d. **Retrieve soft-deleted records**

Use withTrashed() *to retrieve both deleted and non-deleted records:*

```
$allPosts = Post::withTrashed()→get();
```

Use onlyTrashed() *to retrieve only the soft-deleted records:*

```
$trashedPosts = Post::onlyTrashed()→get();
```

e. **Restore soft-deleted records:** Restore soft-deleted records using the restore() method:

Restoring soft-deleted records:

```
$post = Post::withTrashed()->find(1);
$post->restore(); // Undoes the soft delete
```

f. **Force-delete a record:** To permanently delete a record, use the forceDelete() method:

Force-deleting records:

```
$post = Post::withTrashed()->find(1);
$post->forceDelete();
// Permanently removes the record from the database
```

The next section looks at how mass assignment works.

Mass Assignment

Mass assignment allows you to create or update a model instance (a database record) using an array of attributes in one step. While this feature is convenient, it can lead to security vulnerabilities if it's not handled correctly. Laravel addresses this with the concept of *fillable* and *guarded* attributes.

The fillable property defines the attributes that are allowed to be mass-assigned. For instance, if you set the fillable property of a model, as shown in Listing 3-20, only the title and content fields can be assigned value via mass assignment.

Listing 3-20. Setting the Model's Fillable Property to Define Which Fields Can Be Mass Assigned

```
protected $fillable = ['title', 'content'];
```

You can then create or update a record using the code in Listing 3-21.

Listing 3-21. Creating or Updating a Record Using Fields That Can Be Mass Assigned

```
$post = Post::create([
    'title' => 'My First Post',
    'content' => 'This is the content of the post.',
]);
```

If you try to mass assign any attribute not listed in the `fillable` property, Laravel will ignore it, protecting against unauthorized field updates.

Alternatively, you can use the `guarded` property to specify which attributes should not be mass assigned, as shown in the code in Listing 3-22.

Listing 3-22. Using the Guarded Property to Exclude Fields That Should Not Be Mass Assigned

```
protected $guarded = ['id'];
```

In this case, all fields except `id` can be mass assigned. However, it's generally recommended to use `fillable` for better clarity and control.

This approach is critical for securing APIs, especially when dealing with user-provided input in JSON data. Without this safeguard, malicious users could inject unintended fields, such as setting an `is_admin` flag on a user.

The next section looks at accessors and mutators.

Accessors and Mutators

Eloquent enables you to define custom logic for modifying data being retrieved (*accessors*) or stored (*mutators*) in your model, allowing for a cleaner and more expressive way to handle data transformations within your models.

These functions are defined in your model class, typically under the properties section, making them easily accessible and central to the model's behavior.

Accessors are used to transform attributes when retrieving their values. To define an accessor, create a GET-prefixed method followed by the attribute name in StudlyCase and append `Attribute`. For example, to always capitalize a user's name when it is accessed, you can implement an accessor as shown in the code in Listing 3-23.

Listing 3-23. Creating an Accessor Method That Capitalizes a User's Name When It Is Accessed

```
namespace App\Models;

use Illuminate\Database\Eloquent\Model;

class User extends Model
{
    // Define the accessor for the 'name' attribute
```

```
    public function getNameAttribute($value)
    {
        return ucfirst($value);
    }
}
```

This accessor will automatically apply whenever the name attribute is accessed, say in the controller, as shown in the code in Listing 3-24.

Listing 3-24. Accessing the User's Name to Which an Accessor Method Has Been Attached

```
$user = User::find(1);
echo $user->name; // Outputs: John
```

Mutators, on the other hand, allow you to modify the value before it is saved to the database. To define a mutator, create a SET-prefixed method followed by the attribute name in StudlyCase and append Attribute. For instance, if you want to ensure all names are stored in lowercase, the code in Listing 3-25 shows how to do it.

Listing 3-25. Creating a Mutator Method in the Model

```
namespace App\Models;

use Illuminate\Database\Eloquent\Model;

class User extends Model
{
    // Define the mutator for the 'name' attribute
    public function setNameAttribute($value)
    {
        $this->attributes['name'] = strtolower($value);
    }
}
```

You can set the name attribute, as shown in the code in Listing 3-26.

Listing 3-26. Testing out the Mutator

```
$user = new User();
$user→name = 'JOHN DOE';
$user→save();
```

By centralizing this logic in the model, accessors and mutators ensure seamless data formatting when retrieving and saving attributes, improving code readability and reducing duplication.

Up next, you'll learn how to use resource classes to structure your API response in line with your app's needs.

Laravel Resources Class

Laravel resources act as a layer between your Eloquent models and JSON responses. They ensure that API consumers receive only the necessary data, formatted as per your requirements.

Creating a Resource

To create a resource, run the following Artisan command (see Listing 3-27) to generate the resource class.

Listing 3-27. Artisan Command for Generating a Resource Class

```
php artisan make:resource UserResource
```

This will create a UserResource class in the app/Http/Resources directory. You can then edit the newly created UserResource class to define how the data should be transformed. The code in Listing 3-28 shows an example.

Listing 3-28. Editing the Resource Class Such That Only Specified Fields Are Returned In Response to a User's Request

```
namespace App\Http\Resources;

use Illuminate\Http\Resources\Json\JsonResource;
```

```php
class UserResource extends JsonResource
{
    /**
     * Transform the resource into an array.
     *
     * @param  \Illuminate\Http\Request  $request
     * @return array
     */
    public function toArray($request)
    {
        return [
            'id' => $this->id,
            'name' => $this->name,
            'email' => $this->email,
            'created_at' => $this->created_at->toDateTimeString(),
        ];
    }
}
```

This example returns a simplified JSON structure containing only the essential user fields—id, name, email, and created_at.

Pagination

For APIs handling large datasets, Eloquent's built-in pagination is invaluable. With a single line of code, you can paginate results and return a JSON response with pagination metadata. Listing 3-29 shows how to paginate.

Listing 3-29. Using the paginate() Method to Fetch Ten Users

```php
$users = User::paginate(10);
```

The result includes not only the data but also the metadata, like the total number of items, the current page, and the last page, which is especially useful for client-side applications. A typical API response for paginated results looks like what's shown in Listing 3-30.

Listing 3-30. A Typical API Response for Paginated Results

```json
{
    "current_page": 1,
    "data": [
        {
            "id": 1,
            "name": "John Doe",
            "email": "johndoe@example.com"
        },
        {
            "id": 2,
            "name": "Jane Smith",
            "email": "janesmith@example.com"
        }
    ],
    "first_page_url": "http://api.example.com/users?page=1",
    "from": 1,
    "last_page": 5,
    "last_page_url": "http://api.example.com/users?page=5",
    "next_page_url": "http://api.example.com/users?page=2",
    "path": "http://api.example.com/users",
    "per_page": 10,
    "prev_page_url": null,
    "to": 10,
    "total": 50
}
```

This structure allows API consumers to easily implement pagination controls on the client side, such as Next and Previous buttons or page numbers.

Controllers

In the section on routes, you used closures (nameless functions) when defining the routes. However, there is another option, which is the use of controllers. In Laravel, controllers and closures are two different ways to define the behavior of your application's routes. Though closures give you a quick way to define simple route logic, especially when building simple applications, controllers are usually preferred because they allow you to build applications that are easier to scale and maintain.

A *controller* is a dedicated class that groups related route logic together. Instead of defining the logic directly in the route, you point the route to a method in the controller. Controllers help handle incoming requests and return appropriate responses. They serve as a central hub for application logic, making code more organized and maintainable. Instead of defining all the request handling logic in the routes/api.php files, you can delegate this responsibility to controllers, ensuring separation of concerns.

For RESTful APIs, Laravel simplifies the process by providing tools to create resourceful controllers. These controllers link standard HTTP verbs (GET, POST, PUT, and DELETE) to actions like retrieving, creating, updating, or deleting resources.

Listing 3-31 shows an example of a route definition using a controller.

Listing 3-31. A Route Definition Using a Controller Instead of a Closure or Anonymous Function

```
use App\Http\Controllers\WelcomeController;
use Illuminate\Support\Facades\Route;

Route::get('/welcome', [WelcomeController::class, 'show']);
```

WelcomeController is the name of the controller class, and show represents the method to be called when the route is visited. Listing 3-2 shows the code that defines the controller.

Listing 3-32. Defining the Controller

```
namespace App\Http\Controllers;

use Illuminate\Http\Request;

class WelcomeController extends Controller
{
    public function show()
    {
        return 'Welcome to Laravel!';
    }
}
```

Creating Controllers for RESTful APIs

Laravel provides an Artisan command to create controllers. To create a controller suitable for RESTful APIs, you can use the command in Listing 3-33.

Listing 3-33. An Artisan command for creating a Controller

```
php artisan make:controller ProductController --api
```

This generates a controller file (ProductController.php) in the app/Http/Controllers directory with predefined methods corresponding to RESTful actions:

- **index():** Retrieves a list of resources (e.g., GET /products).

- **show():** Retrieves a specific resource by ID (e.g., GET /products/{id}).

- **store():** Creates a new resource (e.g., POST /products).

- **update():** Updates an existing resource (e.g., PUT or PATCH /products/{id}).

- **destroy():** Deletes a resource (e.g., DELETE /products/{id}).

The code contained in the generated controller file is shown in Listing 3-34.

Listing 3-34. The Complete Code of the Controller Generated Using Artisan

```php
<?php

namespace App\Http\Controllers\Api;

use App\Http\Controllers\Controller;
use Illuminate\Http\Request;

class DogController extends Controller
{
    /**
     * Display a listing of the resource.
     */
    public function index()
    {
        //
```

```php
    }

    /**
     * Store a newly created resource in storage.
     */
    public function store(Request $request)
    {
        //
    }

    /**
     * Display the specified resource.
     */
    public function show(string $id)
    {
        //
    }

    /**
     * Update the specified resource in storage.
     */
    public function update(Request $request, string $id)
    {
        //
    }

    /**
     * Remove the specified resource from storage.
     */
    public function destroy(string $id)
    {
        //
    }
}
```

Routing for RESTful Controllers

Once you have a resource controller, defining routes for it is straightforward. In the routes/api.php file, you can register the controller as a resource route, as shown in Listing 3-35.

Listing 3-35. Registering a resource route

```
use App\Http\Controllers\ProductController;

Route::apiResource('products', ProductController::class);
```

This code handles all the routes needed for the standard RESTful API operations, calling the appropriate method when a given URI and HTTP verb method combination is visited—see Table 3-1.

Table 3-1. *HTTP Verb Methods, URIs, and Controller Methods*

HTTP Verb Method	URI	Controller Method
GET	/api/users	index()
POST	/api/users	store()
GET	/api/users/{id}	show($id)
PUT/PATCH	/api/users/{id}	update($request, $id)
DELETE	/api/users/{id}	destroy($id)

Requests

When a client interacts with a RESTful API, for example, by issuing a GET request to retrieve data or a POST request to create a new resource, Laravel automatically creates an object of the Illuminate\Http\Request class. This object holds all the data from the HTTP request sent by the client, such as query parameters, form inputs, headers, cookies, files, and so on. You can get the Request object in controllers, middleware, or route closures by either adding it as a parameter or by using the request() helper function; see Listing 3-36.

Listing 3-36. Accessing the Request Object as a Parameter to a Method

```
use Illuminate\Http\Request;

public function store(Request $request)
{
    // Access request data here
}
```

Accessing Request Data

Laravel's Request object provides multiple methods to access different types of data. Some key methods include:

- **Using the `input` method**

  The input method allows you to retrieve data from the request payload by specifying the key:

  ```
  $value = $request→input('key');
  ```

  You can also provide a default value that will be returned if the key is not present:

  ```
  $value = $request->input('key', 'default');
  ```

- **Working with** query **method**

  Query parameters appended to a URL can be accessed using the same input method or the query *method:*

  ```
  $page = $request->query('page', 1); // Default value is 1 if
  'page' is not present
  ```

  To retrieve all query parameters:

  ```
  $queryParams = $request→query();
  ```

- **Handling JSON payloads**

  You can access JSON data using the same input method:

  ```
  $jsonValue = $request->input('json_key');
  ```

Alternatively, you can use the json *method for more explicit handling:*

```
$data = $request->json()->all();
$specificValue = $request->json('key');
```

- **Retrieving specific data types**

    Laravel provides specialized methods for retrieving data of specific types:

    ```
    $request→boolean('key'); //boolean
    ```

    ```
    $request→integer('key'); //integer
    ```

    ```
    $request->input('key', []); //array
    ```

- **Accessing headers**

    HTTP headers can be accessed via the header *method:*
    ```
    $headerValue = $request->header('Authorization');
    ```

    To retrieve all headers, use this:

    ```
    $headers = $request->headers->all();
    ```

- **Handling file uploads**

    For file uploads, the file method can be used to retrieve an uploaded file instance:

    ```
    $file = $request→file('uploaded_file');
    ```

    You can then perform operations like validation, storage, or retrieval of file details:

    ```
    $path = $file->store('uploads');
    $originalName = $file->getClientOriginalName();
    ```

- **Checking for the existence of data**

  You can check if a specific key exists in the request using the has *or* filled *methods:*

  ```
  if ($request->has('key')) {
      // Key exists in the request
  }

  if ($request->filled('key')) {
      // Key exists and is not null or empty
  }
  ```

- **Interacting with HTTP methods**

  Laravel provides methods to inspect the HTTP verb used in the request:

  ```
  $request→isMethod('post'); //Check if the method is POST.

  $request→method(); //Retrieve the HTTP method as a string.
  ```

Validating Client Sent Data

When a client submits a request to the API server for actions such as updating or creating a new resource, it typically includes the necessary data for these operations. The challenge lies in ensuring that this data adheres to the specifications and aligns with the type of information required by the application to process the request safely. Validation is the solution to this issue.

Implementing Validation in Laravel RESTful APIs

Laravel provides various methods to perform validation effectively. Let's look at two of them:

1. **Validation using the `validate` method**
   The simplest way to validate input in Laravel is by using the validate method directly within a controller. Listing 3-37 shows an example.

Listing 3-37. Using the Validate Method Directly Within a Controller

```
use Illuminate\Http\Request;

class UserController extends Controller
{
    public function store(Request $request)
    {
        $validatedData = $request->validate([
            'name' => 'required|string|max:255',
            'email' => 'required|email|unique:users,email',
            'password' => 'required|string|min:8',
        ]);

        // Proceed with creating the user
        $user = User::create($validatedData);

        return response()->json(['message' => 'User created successfully.',
        'user' => $user], 201);
    }
}
```

The $request->validate() method ensures that the input data meets certain criteria, as outlined here:

- name: Required, must be a string, and can have a maximum of 255 characters.

- email: Required, must be a valid email address, and must be unique in the users table under the email column.

- password: Required, must be a string, and must have a minimum length of eight characters.

This method is suitable for straightforward validation scenarios. It throws a ValidationException if the validation fails, returning a JSON response with the validation errors when used in an API context. However, if the validation succeeds, the rest of the code is executed.

2. **Validation using form request classes**

   For more complex or reusable validation logic, *form request classes* are recommended. These classes encapsulate validation logic, keeping controllers clean and manageable. To create a form request class, use the Artisan command in Listing 3-38.

Listing 3-38. Artisan Command for Creating a Form Request Class

```
php artisan make:request StoreUserRequest
```

The generated class can be customized, as shown in Listing 3-39, to get a similar validation as in the example used in the first method.

Listing 3-39. A Form Request Class

```
namespace App\Http\Requests;

use Illuminate\Foundation\Http\FormRequest;

class StoreUserRequest extends FormRequest
{
    public function authorize()
    {
        return true;
    }

    public function rules()
    {
        return [
            'name' => 'required|string|max:255',
            'email' => 'required|email|unique:users,email',
            'password' => 'required|string|min:8',
        ];
    }

    public function messages()
    {
        return [
            'name.required' => 'The name field is mandatory.',
```

```
            'email.required' => 'We need your email address.',
            'password.min' => 'The password must be at least 8
            characters long.',
        ];
    }
}
```

You can then inject the StoreUserRequest class into your controller for validation, as shown in Listing 3-40.

Listing 3-40. A Controller Using the Form Request class for Validation

```
use App\Http\Requests\StoreUserRequest;

class UserController extends Controller
{
    public function store(StoreUserRequest $request)
    {
        $user = User::create($request->validated());

        return response()->json(['message' => 'User created successfully.',
        'user' => $user], 201);
    }
}
```

The next section looks at common validation rules with examples of how they can be used.

Common Validation Rules in Laravel

Laravel offers a wide array of built-in validation rules that cater to various data validation scenarios. This section is an overview of the most commonly used rules, with examples shown in Listings 3-41 to 3-47.

1. **Basic rules:**

   - **required:** Ensures the field is present and not empty.

   - **nullable:** Allows the field to be null.

   - **sometimes:** Validates the field only if it is present in the input.

Listing 3-41. Basic Validation Rules Examples

```
$request->validate([
    'name' => 'required|string',
    'email' => 'required|email',
    'age' => 'nullable|integer',
]);
```

2. **String rules:**

- **string:** Validates that the field is a string.

- **max:<value>:** Ensures that the string does not exceed the specified length.

- **min:<value>:** Ensures that the string is at least the specified length.

- **regex:<pattern>:** Validates the field against a given regular expression.

Listing 3-42. Basic String Rules Examples

```
$request->validate([
    'username' => 'required|string|max:50|regex:/^[a-zA-Z0-9_]+$/',
    'bio' => 'nullable|string|max:255',
]);
```

3. **Numeric rules:**

- **numeric:** Ensures the field is a number.

- **integer:** Ensures the field is an integer.

- **between:<min>,<max>:** Validates that the field is within the specified range.

Listing 3-43. Basic Numeric Rules Examples

```
$request->validate([
    'price' => 'required|numeric|min:0',
    'quantity' => 'required|integer|between:1,100',
]);
```

4. **Date rules:**

- **date:** Ensures the field is a valid date.

- **before:<date>:** Ensures the date is before a specified date.

- **after:<date>:** Ensures the date is after a specified date.

Listing 3-44. Basic Date Rules Examples

```
$request->validate([
    'start_date' => 'required|date|after:today',
    'end_date' => 'required|date|after:start_date',
]);
```

5. **Array rules:**

- **array:** Validates that the field is an array.

- **in:<values>:** Ensures the value exists in the specified set.

- **not_in:<values>:** Ensures the value does not exist in the specified set.

Listing 3-45. Basic Array Rules Examples

```
$request->validate([
    'tags' => 'required|array',
    'tags.*' => 'string|distinct',
]);
```

6. **File rules:**

- **file:** Validates that the field contains an uploaded file.

- **image:** Ensures the file is an image.

- **mimes:<types>:** Restricts the file type by MIME types.

- **max:<size>:** Restricts the file size in kilobytes.

Listing 3-46. Basic File Rules Examples

```
$request->validate([
    'avatar' => 'nullable|image|mimes:jpeg,png,jpg|max:2048',
]);
```

7. **Email and URL rules:**

   - **email:** Ensures the field contains a valid email address.

   - **url:** Validates that the field contains a valid URL.

   - **active_url:** Ensures the field contains a valid, active URL.

Listing 3-47. Basic Email and URL Rules Examples

```
$request->validate([
    'website' => 'nullable|url',
    'contact_email' => 'required|email',
]);
```

Creating Custom Validation Rules

Custom rules can be defined for specific scenarios. To create a rule, use the Artisan command in Listing 3-48.

Listing 3-48. Artisan Command for Creating a Custom Rule

```
php artisan make:rule CustomRule
```

Replace CustomRule with the name of the rule you want to create. A file named /app/Rules/CustomRule.php will be created inside your Laravel installation folder. Open the file in your code editor. You can see the code in Listing 3-49.

Listing 3-49. The /app/Rules/CustomRule.php File in Your Laravel Folder

```
<?php

namespace App\Rules;

use Closure;
use Illuminate\Contracts\Validation\ValidationRule;
```

```
class CustomRule implements ValidationRule
{
    /**
     * Run the validation rule.
     *
     * @param  \Closure(string, ?string=): \Illuminate\Translation\
     PotentiallyTranslatedString  $fail
     */
    public function validate(string $attribute, mixed $value, Closure
    $fail): void
    {
        //add your validation code here
    }
}
```

Add your custom validation logic inside the validate method. Let's say you want to create a custom validation rule that checks if the value entered is an integer greater than 200. You can adjust the validate method as shown in Listing 3-50.

Listing 3-50. Adding a Custom Validation Rule to the Validation Method

```
public function validate(string $attribute, mixed $value, Closure
$fail): void
    {
        //add your validation code here
        if(!is_int($value) & $value > 200){
            $fail('The :attribute must be Integer and greater than 200');
        }
    }
```

You can now use the validation rule inside the yourrequest→validate() method by using new CustomRule() as a rule. See the example in Listing 3-51.

Listing 3-51. Using Your Custom Rule

```
$request->validate([
    'number' => ['required', new CustomRule()],
]);
```

Controllers are generally desirable because they enable you to create flexible, tidy, and easily scaled and maintained Laravel applications.

Summary

This chapter looked at several topics, including Artisan commands, routes, named routes, route parameters, route binding, models, migration, eloquent ORMs, mass assignments, accessors, mutators, resource classes, request objects, pagination, controllers, and validations.

## CHAPTER 4

Laravel for API Development: Further Steps

This chapter covers additional concepts in Laravel for API development. First, it looks at sending email, and then it explore topics such as handling events, jobs and queues, authentication, authorization, and views. This chapter covers these topics in relation to API development.

Sending Emails in Laravel

Laravel provides an easy and flexible way to send emails using the built-in `Mailable` class. This allows developers to create well-structured and reusable email templates. The following section explores how to send emails in Laravel using the `Mailable` class.

Setting Up the Mailable Class

To create a mailable class in Laravel, you can use the Artisan command shown in Listing 4-1.

Listing 4-1. Artisan Command to Creating a Mailable Class

```
php artisan make:mail WelcomeMail
```

© Adegoke Akintoye 2025
A. Akintoye, *API Development with Laravel*, https://doi.org/10.1007/979-8-8688-1576-8_4

This command generates a mailable class called WelcomeMail, located in the app/Mail directory. To create a mailable class with a different name, simply replace WelcomeMail with the name you want. The generated class extends Mailable and includes traits such as Queueable and SerializesModels to handle queueing and serialization efficiently. See Listing 4-2.

Listing 4-2. The WelcomeMail Class Generated with an Artisan Command

```php
namespace App\Mail;

use Illuminate\Bus\Queueable;
use Illuminate\Contracts\Queue\ShouldQueue;
use Illuminate\Mail\Mailable;
use Illuminate\Mail\Mailables\Content;
use Illuminate\Mail\Mailables\Envelope;
use Illuminate\Queue\SerializesModels;

class WelcomeMail extends Mailable
{
    use Queueable, SerializesModels;

    /**
     * Create a new message instance.
     */
    public function __construct()
    {
        //
    }

    /**
     * Get the message envelope.
     */
    public function envelope(): Envelope
    {
        return new Envelope(
            subject: 'Welcome Mail',
        );
    }
```

```
/**
 * Get the message content definition.
 */
public function content(): Content
{
    return new Content(
        view: 'view.name',
    );
}

/**
 * Get the attachments for the message.
 *
 * @return array<int, \Illuminate\Mail\Mailables\Attachment>
 */
public function attachments(): array
{
    return [];
}
}
```

Understanding the WelcomeMail Class

The WelcomeMail class generated in Listing 4-2 defines how email should be structured and sent. The following sections explain this class in detail.

The Constructor Method

The constructor method is used to pass dynamic data to other methods of the Mailable class as well as to the email template. This allows you to customize email content based on specific user information.

For example, instead of hard-coding email addresses, you can pass them in through the constructor as strings; or pass in an object that contains the email address as well as any other data you want to use in the email. See Listing 4-3 as an example.

Listing 4-3. Constructor Method Accepting Parameters That Can Be Used in Other Parts of the Mailable Class and in the Template File

```
public function __construct(public User $user, public string $message)
{

}
```

The information contained in the $user object, as well as in $message, can now be used from within this code and in the template file later.

The Envelope Method

This method sets the configuration details about the mail—the sender, subject, and metadata. The envelope method is shown in Listing 4-4.

Listing 4-4. The envelope() Method

```
public function envelope(): Envelope
{
    return new Envelope(
        subject: 'Welcome Mail',
    );
}
```

Using the subject parameter, Listing 4-4 specifies the subject of the email.

Additional parameters for customizing the envelope() constructor include the from: Address, the bcc: Address, the replyTo: Address, the tags: array, and the metadata: array. Each of these is explained in more detail next.

from: Address specifies the sender's name and email address, representing the author of the email. See Listing 4-5.

Listing 4-5. Example Code for the from Parameter

```
from:new Address("sender@website.com", "sender's name")
```

cc: Address adds recipients who will receive a carbon copy (CC) of the email. See Listing 4-6.

Listing 4-6. Example Code for the `cc` Parameter

```
cc:new Address("receiver@website.com", "receiver's name")
```

bcc: `Address` adds recipients who will receive a blind carbon copy (BCC) of the email, meaning that other recipients won't see their addresses. See Listing 4-7.

Listing 4-7. Example Code for the `bcc` Parameter

```
bcc:new Address("receiver@website.com", "receiver's name")
```

replyTo: `Address` specifies the email address to which replies should be sent. See Listing 4-8.

Listing 4-8. Example Code for the `replyTo` Parameter

```
replyTo:new Address("receiver@website.com", "receiver's name")
```

tags: `array` sets the tags, if relevant, for your email sender. See Listing 4-9.

Listing 4-9. Example Code for the `tags` Parameter

```
tags: ["promotion", "newsletter", "customer-engagement"]
```

metadata: `array` sets the metadata, if relevant, for your email sender. See Listing 4-10.

Listing 4-10. Example Code for the `metadata` Parameter

```
metadata: {
    "campaign_id": "12345",
    "user_id": "67890"
}
```

The content() Method

This method defines the email's contents using a Blade view template. Listing 4-11 shows a `content` method of a mailable class specifying `emails.welcome` as the Blade template to render the email message.

Note   A Blade view template is simply a PHP file that specifies how email will be displayed.

Listing 4-11. The content() Method

```php
public function content(): Content
{
    return new Content(
        view: 'emails.welcome',
    );
}
```

In addition to specifying the Blade template, you can also specify data to be passed into your blade view using the with parameter, as shown in Listing 4-12.

Listing 4-12. Specifying Data to be Passed into the Blade View Using the with Parameter

```php
public function content()
    {
        return new \Illuminate\Mail\Mailables\Content(
            view: 'emails.orders.shipped',
            with: [
                'orderNumber' => $this->order->number,
                'shippingDate' => $this->order->shipped_at,
            ]
        );
    }
```

In Listing 4-12, the view parameter specifies the Blade template as emails.orders. shipped. In addition, the with parameter is also used to specify an array of data— namely orderNumber and shippingDate—to be passed to the Blade template.

The attachments() Method

If needed, you can modify this method to include file attachments. Listing 4-13 shows various ways to attach files to your email in Laravel.

Listing 4-13. The `attachments()` Method

```
use Illuminate\Mail\Mailables\Attachment;

public function attachments(): array {
    return [
        // Attach from default disk
        Attachment::fromStorage('/path/to/file'),
        // Attach from custom disk
        Attachment::fromStorageDisk('s3', '/path/to/file'),
        // Attach a file using the local filename
        Attachment::fromPath('/absolute/path/to/file'),
        // Attach a file passing the raw data
        Attachment::fromData(fn() => file_get_contents($this->pdf),
            'whitepaper.pdf')
        ->withMime('application/pdf'),
    ];
}
```

Laravel provides different options for attaching files to email from within the `Mailable attachment()`, method as shown in Listing 4-13.

Sending Emails

Once the `Mailable` class has been modified to suit your needs, you can then send emails using the `Mail` facade, as shown in Listing 4-14.

Listing 4-14. Sending Mail

```
use App\Mail\WelcomeMail;
use Illuminate\Support\Facades\Mail;

Mail::to('recipient@example.com')->send(new WelcomeMail($user, $message));
```

The email address is passed to the to() method and an instance of the Mailable class is passed to the send() method (which in this case is the WelcomeMail class). You must not forget to pass whatever parameters the WelcomeMail class constructor needs as well.

To queue the email for asynchronous sending, use the code in Listing 4-15, replacing the send() method with the queue() method.

Listing 4-15. Replace the send() Method with the queue() Method

```
Mail::to('recipient@example.com')->queue(new WelcomeMail($user, $message));
```

Events

Events in Laravel follow the Observer pattern, where an *event* represents an action that has occurred in the application, and *listeners* execute predefined logic (e.g., sending a confirmation email, updating logs, and so on) in response to the event. This pattern enhances the modularity and reusability of the code. Events are especially useful in RESTful APIs, as they help handle background tasks like sending notifications, logging activities, and running asynchronous operations efficiently.

Implementing Events in a Laravel

The steps involved in implementing an event include defining the event and its corresponding listeners, registering the event and its listeners, and then triggering the event at an appropriate point in the code so that the listener can be triggered. The following sections look at these steps in turn.

Creating an Event

To create an event, use the Artisan command shown in Listing 4-16.

Listing 4-16. Artisan Command to Create an Event

```
php artisan make:event UserRegistered
```

UserRegistered is the name of the event being created. To use a different name, simply replace UserRegistered with the name you want. This generates an event class in app/Events/UserRegistered.php. Listing 4-17 shows the code for the UserRegistered event class.

Listing 4-17. Example Event Class

```
namespace App\Events;

use Illuminate\Broadcasting\Channel;
use Illuminate\Broadcasting\InteractsWithSockets;
use Illuminate\Broadcasting\PresenceChannel;
use Illuminate\Broadcasting\PrivateChannel;
use Illuminate\Contracts\Broadcasting\ShouldBroadcast;
use Illuminate\Foundation\Events\Dispatchable;
use Illuminate\Queue\SerializesModels;

class UserRegistered
{
    use Dispatchable, InteractsWithSockets, SerializesModels;

    /**
     * Create a new event instance.
     */
    public function __construct(public User $user)
    {
        //
    }

    /**
     * Get the channels the event should broadcast on.
     *
     * @return array<int, \Illuminate\Broadcasting\Channel>
     */
    public function broadcastOn(): array
    {
        return [
            new PrivateChannel('channel-name'),
        ];
    }
}
```

Creating a Listener

To create a *listener*, run the Artisan command shown in Listing 4-18.

Listing 4-18. Artisan Command to Create a Listener

```
php artisan make:listener SendWelcomeEmail --event=UserRegistered
```

SendWelcomeEmail is the name of the listener; notice that this code also specifies the event being targeted (UserRegistered). This creates app/Listeners/SendWelcomeEmail.php, as shown in Listing 4-19.

Listing 4-19. Example Listener Class

```
namespace App\Listeners;

use App\Events\UserRegistered;
use Illuminate\Contracts\Queue\ShouldQueue;
use Illuminate\Queue\InteractsWithQueue;

class SendWelcomeEmail
{
    /**
     * Create the event listener.
     */
    public function __construct()
    {
        //
    }

    /**
     * Handle the event.
     */
    public function handle(UserRegistered $event): void
    {
        //
    }
}
```

Registering Events and Listeners

Open app/Providers/AppServiceProvider.php and register the event and the listener inside the boot() method, using the listen() method of the Event class, as shown in Listing 4-20.

Listing 4-20. Example that Registers an Event and the Corresponding Listener

```php
namespace App\Providers;

use Illuminate\Support\ServiceProvider;
use Illuminate\Support\Facades\Event;
use App\Events\UserRegistered;
use App\Listeners\SendWelcomeEmail;

class AppServiceProvider extends ServiceProvider
{
    /**
     * Register any application services.
     */
    public function register(): void
    {
        //
    }

    /**
     * Bootstrap any application services.
     */
    public function boot(): void
    {
        //
        Event::listen(
            UserRegistered::class,
            SendWelcomeEmail::class,
        );
    }
}
```

Dispatching an Event

Listing 4-21 gives an example of how to trigger an event in a controller (e.g., when a new user registers).

Listing 4-21. Triggering an Event in a Controller

```
use App\Events\UserRegistered;
use App\Models\User;

public function register(Request $request)
{
    $user = User::create($request->all());
    event(new UserRegistered($user));
    return response()->json(['message' => 'User registered
successfully'], 201);
}
```

To trigger this event, you simply pass an instance of the event class (UserRegistered) as a parameter to the event() helper function.

Jobs and Queues

Laravel's queue system allows time-consuming tasks (jobs) to run in the background, improving API performance. This helps handle tasks like sending emails, processing payments, and generating reports efficiently without slowing down responses.

What Is a Queue?

A *queue* is a mechanism that allows tasks to be executed in the background instead of running immediately. Laravel supports multiple queue drivers, including database, Redis, Amazon SQS, and Beanstalkd.

Configuring the Queue Driver

Laravel's queue configuration file is located at `config/queue.php`. You can set the default queue driver in the `.env` file located in your Laravel's project's directory. Listing 4-22 shows an example of setting the queue driver to use `database` in the `.env` file.

Listing 4-22. Setting the Queue Driver to Use `database` in the `.env` File

```
QUEUE_CONNECTION=database
```

Other supported connections include `redis`, `sqs`, `beanstalkd`, and `sync` (which runs jobs immediately and is useful for testing).

Running the Queue Worker

To start processing the queued jobs, run the command shown in Listing 4-23.

Listing 4-23. Running the Queue Worker

```
php artisan queue:work
```

What Is a Job?

A *job* is a specific task that is pushed onto a queue for later execution. Jobs are defined as classes that implement logic for a queued task.

Creating a Job Class

To create a new job, use the Artisan command shown in Listing 4-24.

Listing 4-24. Artisan Command to Create a New Job

```
php artisan make:job ProcessUserRegistration
```

This will generate a new job class in `app/Jobs/ProcessUserRegistration.php`. Listing 4-25 shows the generated job class.

Listing 4-25. The Job Class Generated by the Command in Listing 4-24

```
namespace App\Jobs;

use Illuminate\Contracts\Queue\ShouldQueue;
use Illuminate\Foundation\Queue\Queueable;

class ProcessUserRegistration implements ShouldQueue
{
    use Queueable;

    /**
     * Create a new job instance.
     */
    public function __construct()
    {
        //
    }

    /**
     * Execute the job.
     */
    public function handle(): void
    {
        //
    }
}
```

Assume that you want to create a job that sends a welcome email whenever a user is newly registered. To do this, you can modify the job class, as shown in Listing 4-26, where the job (sending email in this case) is added to the handle method of the job class.

Listing 4-26. Adding a Job

```
namespace App\Jobs;

use Illuminate\Contracts\Queue\ShouldQueue;
use Illuminate\Foundation\Queue\Queueable;

class ProcessUserRegistration implements ShouldQueue
```

```
{
    use Queueable;

    /**
     * Create a new job instance.
     */
    public function __construct(public User $user)
    {
        //
    }

    /**
     * Execute the job.
     */
    public function handle(): void
    {
        // Perform background processing, e.g., send a welcome email
        Mail::to($this->user->email)->send(new WelcomeEmail($this->user));
    }
}
```

The job (code) to be executed in the background is added to the handle() method.

Dispatching Jobs

Jobs can be dispatched (activated) from within controllers, event listeners, and service classes. You can dispatch a job synchronously—that is, the job is activated to run immediately—as shown in Listing 4-27.

Listing 4-27. Dispatching a Job

```
ProcessUserRegistration::dispatch($user);
```

Listing 4-28 shows how to add a delay when dispatching a job.

Listing 4-28. Adding a Time Delay When Dispatching a Job

```
ProcessUserRegistration::dispatch($user)→delay(now()->addMinutes(5));
```

Authentication

Authentication ensures that only permitted users can access certain resources or parts of your application, adding a layer of security to your application. In the context of RESTful APIs, this typically involves validating users through tokens rather than through traditional session-based authentication.

Sanctum

One way to implement authentication in Laravel based API is using Sanctum. It provides a straightforward way to authenticate using tokens.

Installing Sanctum

If you haven't already created the api.php routes file, then, while connected to the Internet, run the commands shown in Listing 4-29 to create it.

Listing 4-29. Installing Sanctum

```
php artisan install:api
php artisan vendor:publish --provider="Laravel\Sanctum\
SanctumServiceProvider"
php artisan migrate
```

Next, add the HasApiTokens trait to the User model, as shown in Listing 4-30.

Listing 4-30. Adding the HasApiTokens Trait to the User Model

```
use Laravel\Sanctum\HasApiTokens;

class User extends Authenticatable
{
    use HasApiTokens, Notifiable;
    // Rest of your model code
}
```

Generating Tokens with Sanctum

Notice that in Listing 4-30, the User model class extends the Authenticatable class; this makes the createToken() method available to the User model class. Because of this, you can generate tokens for your users by calling the createToken() method on any given authenticated User object. Tokens are usually created and assigned to users who signed up to use your API. Listing 4-31 shows how to generate tokens for a user.

Listing 4-31. Generating Authentication Tokens for a User

```
$token = $user->createToken('api-token')->plainTextToken;
```

This list explains the code in Listing 4-31:

1. $user is an instance of your authenticated User model.

2. createToken('api-token') creates a new token with the given name (api-token in this case). You can name it anything you like.

3. ->plainTextToken returns the token string that you send back to the client.

Tokens are typically generated inside a login controller or route, after authenticating the user. As you'll learn later in this book, when developing the Payment Processor mimicking API project, you'll use this method to create tokens for your user.

Securing Routes

This section explains how to protect your routes using Sanctum.

Attaching Middleware to Your Route

To secure a route, add the auth:sanctum middleware directly to your route definition, as shown in Listing 4-32, where the /logout route is protected and can only be accessed by authenticated users. The other routes—/register and /login—do not require authentication to be visited.

Listing 4-32. Protecting a Route with auth:sanctum Middleware

```
use App\Http\Controllers\AuthController;

Route::post('/register', [AuthController::class, 'register']);
Route::post('/login', [AuthController::class, 'login']);
Route::post('/logout', [AuthController::class, 'logout'])→middleware('auth
:sanctum');
```

Listing 4-33 shows how to add the auth:sanctum middleware to the apiResource() route.

Listing 4-33. Securing a apiResource() Route

```
Route::middleware('auth:sanctum')->apiResource('posts',
PostController::class);
```

Every route pointed to by apiResource() in Listing 4-33 will now require authentication to be accessed.

Using the middleware() Method

You can also add auth:sanctum middleware to a route by specifying it from within the controller pointed to by the route. You do this using the middleware() method rather than adding it directly to the route definition, as shown in Listing 4-34.

Listing 4-34. Protecting a Route Using the middleware() Method

```
namespace App\Http\Controllers\Api;

use App\Http\Controllers\Controller;
use Illuminate\Http\Request;
use Illuminate\Routing\Controllers\HasMiddleware;
use Illuminate\Routing\Controllers\Middleware;

class DogController extends Controller implements HasMiddleware
{
    /**
     * Register middleware for the controller.
     */
```

```
public static function middleware(): array
{
    return [
        new Middleware('auth:sanctum')
    ];
}
}
```

By returning an array containing new `Middleware('auth:sanctum')`, as in Listing 4-34, every route connected to this controller will now require authentication to work.

Exempting Routes from Authentication

As explained in the last section, all the routes in Listing 4-34 pointed to by the `apiResource()` will now require authentication. However, you can exempt some routes by making slight modifications. You do this by adding the `except` parameter to the new `Middleware('auth:sanctum')` declaration, as shown in Listing 4-35.

Listing 4-35. Exempting Routes from Requiring Authentication

```
public function middleware()
{
    return[
        new Middleware('auth:sanctum', except:['index','show'])
    ];
}
```

In Listing 4-35, new `Middleware('auth:sanctum')` was modified by passing an extra parameter, called `except`, whose value is an array containing the actions (methods) to omit from authentication.

Another way to exempt some routes from requiring authentication is by doing it in the route definition directly inside the `api.php` route file. Listing 4-36 shows an example of how this can be done.

Listing 4-36. Another Method of Exempting Routes from Authentication

```
use App\Http\Controllers\PostController;

Route::apiResource('posts', PostController::class)-
>middleware('auth:sanctum');

// Exempt certain actions (e.g., 'index' and 'show') from authentication
Route::get('posts', [PostController::class, 'index']);
Route::get('posts/{post}', [PostController::class, 'show']);
```

In Listing 4-36, index and show will be exempted from authentication.

Authorization

Authorization determines what an authenticated user can do within an application. Laravel provides various ways to handle authorization:

1. **Gates:** Simple closures (anonymous functions or functions without name) that check user abilities. Gates are ideal for actions that aren't directly tied to a specific Eloquent model.

2. **Policies:** Classes that encapsulate authorization logic for individual models or resources. Policies help keep your controllers thin and your authorization logic well organized.

3. **Sanctum token abilities:** Sanctum tokens can also be used for authorization when you attach abilities to them.

Gates

Gates offer a closure-based approach to authorization. They are typically defined in the boot() method of your App\Providers\AuthServiceProvider class and always receive the current user as their first parameter automatically by default. You can, optionally, pass in additional parameters if you want. For example, Listing 4-37 shows how to define a gate that checks if the current user is the owner of the post model passed to it and determine if the user is allowed to make changes to the post.

Listing 4-37. Defining a Gate

```
use Illuminate\Support\Facades\Gate;
use App\Models\Post;
use App\Models\User;

public function boot(): void
{
    Gate::define('update-post', function (User $user, Post $post) {
        return $user->id === $post->user_id;
    });
}
```

This code defines a gate using the define() method of the Gate facade, where update-post is the name of the gate. The user parameter will be automatically injected by Laravel, while you have to manually pass in the post parameter at the point in the code, say inside the controller, where you need to perform the authorization.

Using Gates: Authorizing Actions

You can use the allows() or denies() methods provided by the Gate facade to determine if a user has permission to access or modify a resource. Listing 4-38 shows an example of how to use the gate defined earlier in a controller.

Listing 4-38. Using the Gate

```
namespace App\Http\Controllers;

use App\Http\Controllers\Controller;
use App\Models\Post;
use Illuminate\Http\RedirectResponse;
use Illuminate\Http\Request;
use Illuminate\Support\Facades\Gate;

class PostController extends Controller
{
    /**
     * Update the given post.
     */
```

```
public function update(Request $request, Post $post): RedirectResponse
{
    if (! Gate::allows('update-post', $post)) {
        abort(403);
    }

    // Update the post...

    return redirect('/posts');
}
}
```

Notice that this example passes in the name of the gate, update-post, as well as the $post parameter to the allows() method. If the user doesn't have the permission, the request is terminated with a HTTP code of 403; otherwise, the request is granted.

Using the any() or none() methods, you can also authorize multiple actions at a time. This is shown in Listing 4-39.

Listing 4-39. Using the any() or none() Methods

```
if (Gate::any(['update-post', 'delete-post'], $post)) {
    // The user can update or delete the post...
}

if (Gate::none(['update-post', 'delete-post'], $post)) {
    // The user can't update or delete the post...
}
```

Policies

Policies provide a structured way to group authorization logic related to a model. You can generate a policy using Artisan commands, like the one shown in Listing 4-40. Just replace PostPolicy with the name of your policy in the Artisan command.

Listing 4-40. Generating a Policy

```
php artisan make:policy PostPolicy
```

This will generate an empty policy called app/Policies/PostPolicy.php that you can edit and add the appropriate logic to. Listing 4-41 shows the generated policy.

Listing 4-41. The Generated Policy

```
namespace App\Policies;

use App\Models\User;

class PostPolicy
{
    /**
     * Create a new policy instance.
     */
    public function __construct()
    {
        //
    }
}
```

You can then add methods for each action you want to authorize. For example, let's say you want to define a policy that determines if a given user can update a given post. You start by defining a method in the generated policy, with a name of your choice, and add then add the appropriate code. Listing 4-42 creates a method inside the PostPolicy.php file called update(). Inside the update() method, there is logic that checks if the post belongs to the user who wants to update it (in order to determine if the user is allowed to update the post).

Listing 4-42. Updating the Generated Policy

```
namespace App\Policies;

use App\Models\Post;
use App\Models\User;

class PostPolicy
{
    /**
```

```
 * Create a new policy instance.
 */
public function __construct()
{
    //
}

/**
 * Determine if the given post can be updated by the user.
 */
public function update(User $user, Post $post): bool
{
    return $user->id === $post->user_id;
}
}
```

Using Policies: Authorizing Actions

To use your policy, say in your controller, you can use the Gate facade's authorize()
method, as shown in Listing 4-43.

Listing 4-43. Using the Policy

```
namespace App\Http\Controllers;

use App\Http\Controllers\Controller;
use App\Models\Post;
use Illuminate\Http\RedirectResponse;
use Illuminate\Http\Request;
use Illuminate\Support\Facades\Gate;

class PostController extends Controller
{
    /**
     * Update the given blog post.
     *
     * @throws \Illuminate\Auth\Access\AuthorizationException
     */
```

```
public function update(Request $request, Post $post): RedirectResponse
{
    Gate::authorize('update', $post);

    // The current user can update the blog post...

    return redirect('/posts');
}
}
```

To authorize an action from within your controller using the policy method created earlier, you simply pass the name of the policy method (in this case, update), and any other parameter the policy method expects (in this case, $post), to the authorize() method.

Sanctum Token Abilities

Sanctum's token abilities are a neat way to give your API tokens a set of permissions or "scopes" so you can fine-tune what each token is allowed to do. In Laravel 12, this feature comes in super handy for RESTful API development, where you might want different tokens for different purposes—say, one token with the ability to read data and another that can update or delete it.

Implementing Token Abilities

This section explains how to work with token abilities.

Note   In Laravel Sanctum, abilities are just strings you define yourself—they don't exist automatically. You decide what they're called and what they mean in your app. There's no built-in list; it's all up to you.

Issuing Tokens with Abilities

To create a token with abilities using Sanctum, you can pass an array of strings representing its abilities. For example, Listing 4-44 creates a token with two abilities using the server:update and orders:place strings. You are free to use any string you want.

Listing 4-44. Issuing Tokens with Abilities

```
$token = $user->createToken('my-token', ['server:update', 'orders:place'])
->plainTextToken;
```

This token can now be distinguished from others using the strings attached to it during its creation.

Checking Abilities in Requests

This section looks at how to determine the abilities attached to a token when handling an incoming request authenticated by Sanctum.

Using the tokenCan() or tokenCant() Methods

In your controllers or middleware, you can use the tokenCan() or tokenCant() method to check if a token has the required ability. This is shown in Listing 4-45, which checks for two abilities—namely update-profile and view-profile.

Listing 4-45. Checking Abilities in Tokens

```
if ($request->user()->tokenCan('update-profile')) {
    // Process the update
} else if($request->user()->tokenCan('view-profile')) {
    // Only Show the Profile
} else {
    // Return an unauthorized response
}
```

Listing 4-46 shows how to use the tokenCant() method.

Listing 4-46. Using the tokenCant() Method

```
if ($user->tokenCant('server:update')) {
    // Return an unauthorized response
}
// Allow server to be updated
```

Using Token Ability Middleware

Middleware can also be used to check that an incoming request is authenticated with a token that has been granted a given ability.

To get started, however, you need to first define the following middleware aliases in your application's bootstrap/app.php file. Open the file and update it, as shown in Listing 4-47.

Listing 4-47. Using Token Ability Middleware

```
use Laravel\Sanctum\Http\Middleware\CheckAbilities;
use Laravel\Sanctum\Http\Middleware\CheckForAnyAbility;

->withMiddleware(function (Middleware $middleware) {
    $middleware->alias([
        'abilities' => CheckAbilities::class,
        'ability' => CheckForAnyAbility::class,
    ]);
})
```

You can now assign the abilities middleware to a route to verify that the incoming request's token has all of the listed abilities, as shown in Listing 4-48.

Listing 4-48. Assigning the abilities Middleware to a Route

```
Route::get('/orders', function () {
    // Token has both "check-status" and "place-orders"
    //abilities...
})->middleware(['auth:sanctum', 'abilities:check-status,place-orders']);
```

You can also assign the ability middleware to a route to verify that the incoming request's token has at least one of the listed abilities, as shown in Listing 4-49.

Listing 4-49. Assigning the ability Middleware to a Route

```
Route::get('/orders', function () {
    // Token has the "check-status" or "place-orders" ability...
})->middleware(['auth:sanctum', 'ability:check-status,place-orders']);
```

View

A View in Laravel is simply a file that contains HTML (and sometimes a bit of PHP) to display content to the users. Think of it like the frontend of your application — the part people actually see. Laravel stores its view files in the `resources/views` folder.

Note   Strictly speaking, APIs do not require Laravel view to function since they use for machine-to-machine communication (for example, a client-server communication) and views are essentially human interfaces to an application. However, let's take a quick look at view in Laravel, since you'll be creating a dashboard (user interface) that'll enable your API users to manage their experiences (like managing tokens, viewing transaction history, making withdrawals, and so on). These can be done using the API alone; however, creating a dashboard for them makes life much easier for the human user.

Each view is usually a `.blade.php` file, because Laravel uses a templating engine called Blade.

Creating a Simple View

Let's say you want to create a page called `hello.blade.php`.

1. Go to `resources/views/`.

2. Create a file named `hello.blade.php`.

3. Add HTML that defines the page you want to create. Listing 4-50 shows an example.

Listing 4-50. Adding HTML to Define the Page

```
<!-- resources/views/hello.blade.php -->
<!DOCTYPE html>
<html>
<head>
    <title>Hello Page</title>
</head>
```

```
<body>
    <h1>Hello, Laravel!</h1>
</body>
</html>
```

Returning a View from a Route

Now that you have a view, how do you show it in your app? To display the contents of a view file, you need to create a route that leads to code that allows the view file to be loaded and displayed when that route is visited by a client, say a web browser. Listing 4-51 shows an example of a route that returns a view file.

Listing 4-51. A Route that Returns a view File

```
Route::get('/hello', function () {
    return view('hello');
});
```

Notice that this listing uses view('hello'). Laravel automatically looks for a file named hello.blade.php in the resources/views folder.

Passing Data to a View

You can also pass data from your route to your view. Listing 4-52 gives an example of how this can be done.

Listing 4-52. Passing Data from a Route to a View

```
Route::get('/greet', function () {
    $name = 'John';
    return view('hello', ['name' => $name]);
});
```

In the route in Listing 4-52, an associative array passes a variable called name and sets its value to John. To use this variable, you can modify the hello.blade.php file, as shown in Listing 4-53, to use the variable as $name.

133

Listing 4-53. Modifying the `hello.blade.php` File

```
<!-- resources/views/hello.blade.php -->
<!DOCTYPE html>
<html>
<head>
    <title>Hello Page</title>
</head>
<body>
    <h1>Hello, {{ $name }}!</h1>
</body>
</html>
```

Now, when you visit the /hello route, it will display `Hello, John!`

Blade Templating: Making Views Dynamic

Blade lets you use simple, readable syntax for things like:

1. Echoing data, as shown in Listing 4-54.

Listing 4-54. Echoing Data

```
{{ $name }}
```

2. If statements, as shown in Listing 4-55.

Listing 4-55. Creating `if` Statements

```
@if($name == 'John')
    <p>Welcome back, John!</p>
@else
    <p>Hello, stranger!</p>
@endif
```

3. Loops, as shown in Listing 4-56.

Listing 4-56. Creating Loops

```
@foreach($users as $user)
    <p>{{ $user }}</p>
@endforeach
```

Using Layouts with @yield and @section

When your website has a consistent structure—like a shared header, footer, or sidebar—you can create a layout file and reuse it across multiple pages. This helps keep your code organized and reduces repetition. The following steps explain how you can do this.

1. **Create a layout file:** Create a base layout file in, for example, `resources/views/layouts/main.blade.php`. See Listing 4-57.

Listing 4-57. Creating a Base Layout File

```
<!-- layouts/main.blade.php -->
<html>
<head>
    <title>@yield('title')</title>
</head>
<body>
    <div class="content">
        @yield('content')
    </div>
</body>
</html>
```

2. **Extend the layout in a view:** Now create a view that uses the layout in, for example, `resources/views/about.blade.php`. See Listing 4-58.

Listing 4-58. Creating a View That Uses the Layout

```
<!-- about.blade.php -->
@extends('layouts.main')

@section('title', 'About Page')

@section('content')
    <h1>About Us</h1>
    <p>This is the about page.</p>
@endsection
```

By using layouts, you avoid repeating the same HTML on every page. It keeps your views clean, consistent, and easier to maintain.

Summary

You have reached the end of this chapter, where you learned about topics such as sending emails, using events, jobs, and queues, authentication, authorization, and using views.

PART II

Payment Processor API Development

## CHAPTER 5

Implementing The Authentication System and Dashboard

In this chapter, you start building the book project, an API that mimics a payment processor platform. First, the chapter explains what a payment processor API is. Then you'll learn how the API will handle payment. Finally, you'll put in place the user authentication system called Magic Link, as well as the user dashboard.

Payment Processor API

A payment processor API allows businesses, or any organization for that matter, to receive payments or donations online via their websites, web apps, mobile apps, desktop apps, and so on. The way it works is that these businesses register to use the API and, with the help of their developers, they will integrate the API into their business application. That way, prospective clients can pay for goods and services or make donations, depending on the organization's line of business.

The Payment Processor API Usage Flow

This section explains how a typical user of a payment processor is likely to interact with it, beginning with the typical steps of interaction.

© Adegoke Akintoye 2025
A. Akintoye, *API Development with Laravel*, https://doi.org/10.1007/979-8-8688-1576-8_5

Registration

Users are required to register before they can use the API in their application. To register, they must provide an email address. Immediately after registration, users are directed to a page that tells them to check for an email. They need to follow the email instructions to verify the email address and to log in.

Verification

By receiving and being able to access the login link, users are verified as owning the email address.

Logging In

By clicking the login link, users can be verified and then logged in if the link is valid. Once logged in, users are directed to the Dashboard page. The Dashboard page allows users to generate and manage tokens, bank account details, webhooks, view transaction history, and so on.

Making Payments

Once a user has been able to log in and create tokens, they can start receiving payments from their customers using the Payment API. The next section takes a deeper look at the payment process.

Tokens

To use this API, users need to use tokens. They need to be logged in to create tokens. This API uses two types of tokens—*secret key* and *public key* tokens. The difference between these is that they have different abilities attached to them when created. The *public key*, which can be used from the frontend of the application consuming the API, can be used to view a list of transactions. The *secret key,* which can be used to do additional and more sensitive operations, should only be used from the server side of the client application and should not be made public. The secret key can be used to list transactions, initiate payments, verify payments, approve payments, and so on.

Payment Flow

To receive payments, the app must take the following steps.

Collecting Customer and Transaction Details

When a customer visits a website or uses an app, and the website or app wants to collect payment from the customer, the app must first collect the details of the customer and the transaction. This information can be retrieved from the database, from the session data, or through the use of an HTML form. The information to be collected includes the transaction amount, the user's email, first name, last name, and callback_url (the web address to direct the user to once payment is successful or terminated), and optionally the user's phone number,

Initializing the Transaction

The next step is for the app or website to forward these details to the payment initialization endpoint of the API via a POST request.

If the API call is successful, a response will be sent back to the app containing, among other things, an authorization URL, which the app will redirect to. This URL displays a web page for the customer to input their payment information, such as credit or debit card details, in order to complete the transaction.

Of course, an unsuccessful initialization API call will result in an error response from the server.

Verifying the Transaction

If the payment was successful or terminated (canceled), the API will redirect the customer to the provided callback_url, appending the transaction reference as a URL encoded parameter. See Listing 5-1 for an example.

Listing 5-1. The `callback_url` with the Transaction Reference Appended

```
http://payment_receiving_website.com/payment_ended_callback.
html?reference=YOUR_REFERENCE
```

There are two methods of payment verification by the API.

Verification by Calling the Verification Endpoint

The app will need to extract the reference from the callback_url and use it to call the API verification endpoint. The response obtained from calling the Verification API endpoint can be used to determine if the payment was successful or not.

Verification by Webhook

A *webhook* is a URL, a web address, made available by the users of the API via the user dashboard. It usually points to a server-side script. Whenever an event occurs, say a transaction becomes successful, a transaction fails, and so on, the API will visit this webhook to notify the API user of this event. This way, the event can be noted and the right action can be taken—actions like indicating notification and the payment made, sending email, and so on. Of course, this script should contain code that performs the required action when a given event occurs in the API.

Therefore, by using webhooks, users can determine the state of an initiated payment transaction.

Transaction Notification

For every payment made successfully, the API sends an email to notify the API user that they've been paid. Optionally, it can also email the customer about the payment they made.

Logging Out

Users will be able to log out from the dashboard once they are done. However, logging out from the dashboard does not log them out of using the API. As long as they have generated their tokens, they can continue to interact with the API and receive payment via the app by using their token.

Dashboard Management Code and UI Design

The Dashboard API allows users to manage tokens, bank account details, and webhooks, view transaction history, make withdrawals, and so on. However, to use the dashboard and the API, users must first register. Users should also be able to log in to and log out from the dashboard. This section explains how to put this dashboard in place. It also includes the registration, email verification, login, logout, and other processes using a concept referred to as a *Magic Link*.

You'll soon start looking at creating the pages that make up the user dashboard experience. However, you'll first look at the Blade file used or extended by all the other Blade files used by the pages you'll be creating later. Thereafter, you'll install Sanctum and make the appropriate adjustments to the user model (the users table).

Note   The source code for this book is available on GitHub via the book's product page, located at `https://github.com/Apress/API-Development-with-Laravel`.

The Base View (Blade) File

This Blade file holds the contents common to all the other dashboard blade files you'll be working with later in this chapter. The code for this Blade file is shown in Listing 5-2.

Listing 5-2. The `resources/views/dashboard/base.blade.php` Blade File Extended by Other View Files Discussed Later in this Section

```
//resources/views/dashboard/base.blade.php
<!DOCTYPE html>
<html lang="en">
    <head>
        <link rel="icon" href="https://via.placeholder.com/70x70">
        <link rel="stylesheet" href="{{ asset('css/dashboard/classless.
        css') }}">
        <link rel="stylesheet" href="{{ asset('css/dashboard/tabbox.
        css') }}">
        <meta charset="utf-8">
        <meta name="description" content="My description">
        <meta name="viewport" content="width=device-width, initial-
        scale=1.0">
        <title>@yield('title') - Dexy Payment Proccessing API</title>
    </head>
```

```
<body>
   <header>
      <nav>
         <ul>
            <li><img alt="Logo" src="{{ asset('img/dexypay4.png') }}"
            height="40"></li>
            <li class="float-right sticky"><a href="@yield('url')">@
            yield('sign')</a></li>
            <li><a href="#">Home </a></li>
            <li>
               <a href="#">Developer ▼</a>
               <ul>
                  <li><a href="#">Documentation</a></li>
                  <li><a href="#">Integrate Our API</a></li>
               </ul>
            </li>
            <li><a href="#">About Us </a></li>
            <li><a href="#">Contact Us </a></li>
         </ul>
      </nav>
   </header>
   <main>
   <div  class="float-right "> Welcome <em>@yield('name')</em></div>
      <br/>
      @yield('content')
   </main>
   <footer>
      <hr>
      <div id="copyright"align="center"></div>
   </footer>
   <script>
      const d = new Date();
      let year = d.getFullYear();
      let elem = document.getElementById("copyright");
```

```
      elem.innerHTML = "<b>Dexy Pay</b> &copy; All Rights Reserved
      2024 - "+year;
    </script>
  </body>
</html>
```

Note the following in Listing 5-2:

1. The code is located in `resources/views/dashboard/base.blade.php`.

2. The `asset()` function is used to add the assets—CSS, JavaScript, and image files. The assets must be placed relative to the `public` folder of your Laravel project.

3. The `@yield()` directives are placeholders for content from the extending view files. You see how this is done when you extend this Blade file from other Blade files later in this section.

Note   To style the dashboard, you'll use a CSS library called `classless.css` with slight modifications. The CSS, JavaScript, and image files are located in the `public` folder of the Laravel project.

Sanctum

If you haven't installed Sanctum yet, it's time to do so. To install Sanctum, run the Artisan command shown in Listing 5-3 from the command-line terminal from inside your project folder.

Tip   Keep your Internet on while running this command.

Listing 5-3. Installing Sanctum

```
php artisan install:api
php artisan vendor:publish --provider="Laravel\Sanctum\
SanctumServiceProvider"
```

Updating the User Model

Next you'll be updating the user model so that you can use Sanctum. Listing 5-4 shows the user model (app/models/user.php). The changes are shown in bold.

Listing 5-4. Updating the User Model app/models/user.php

```php
<?php

//app/models/user.php

namespace App\Models;

use Illuminate\Database\Eloquent\Factories\HasFactory;
use Illuminate\Foundation\Auth\User as Authenticatable;
use Illuminate\Notifications\Notifiable;
use Illuminate\Support\Str;
use Laravel\Sanctum\HasApiTokens;
use Illuminate\Database\Eloquent\Model;

class User extends Authenticatable
{
    /** @use HasFactory<\Database\Factories\UserFactory> */
    use HasApiTokens, HasFactory, Notifiable;

    /**
     * The attributes that are mass assignable.
     *
     * @var list<string>
     */
    protected $fillable = [
        'name',
        'email',
        'balance',
    ];

    /**
     * Get the attributes that should be cast.
     *
     * @return array<string, string>
```

```php
 */
protected function casts(): array
{
    return [
        'email_verified_at' => 'datetime',
    ];
}

    // Each user has many transactions
public function transaction()
{
    return $this->hasMany(Transaction::class);
}

    // Each user has many withdrawals
public function withdrawal()
{
    return $this->hasMany(Withdrawal::class);
}

    // Each user has one bankDetail
public function bankDetail()
{
    return $this->hasOne(BankDetail::class);
}

    // Each user has one setting
public function setting()
{
    return $this->hasOne(Setting::class);
}

}
```

Listing 5-4 added the HasApiTokens trait as well as the balance field, which is required for the API to operate. The HasApiTokens trait will enable you to work with tokens using Sanctum. The listing also added relationships for the Transaction, Withdrawal, BankDetail, and Setting models.

Next, you'll starting creating the pages for the dashboard.

Implementing the Welcome Page

The Welcome page can be accessed by anyone, without the need to register or be logged in. For this reason, the page is relatively easy to implement. Let's implements its view file first.

View (Blade File) Definition

The view file of the Welcome page is shown in Listing 5-5.

Listing 5-5. The Code for the Welcome Page Is Located in the resources/views/ dashboard/welcome.blade.php File

```
<!--resources/views/dashboard/welcome.blade.php-->
@extends('dashboard.base')
@section('title', 'Welcome Page')
@section('sign', $sign)
@section('name', $name)
@section('url', $url)
@section('content')
<section>
    <p><b> Dexy Pay<sup>TM</sup></b> Payment Processing API makes receiving
payments online super simple. </p>
    <button type="button">Get Started</button>
    <img src="{{ asset('img/dashboard-hero.jpg') }}" alt="An image">
    <div class="row">
        <div class="col">
            <div class="card">
                <img src="{{ asset('img/multi-device1.jpg') }}">
                <p>Let's help you recieve payments via your online channels -
                website, web app, android & ios app, desktop app etc.</p>
                <button type="button">Get Started</button>
            </div>
        </div>
        <div class="col">
            <div class="card">
                <img src="{{ asset('img/secure-payment1.jpg') }}">
```

```
        <p>A Secure Payment Processing System you can Trust</p>
        <button type="button">Get Started</button>
      </div>
    </div>
  </div>
  <div class="row">
    <div class="col">
      <div class="card">
        <img src="{{ asset('img/easy-integration.jpg') }}">
        <p>Dexy Pay API is Easy to Integrate.</p>
        <button type="button">Get Started</button>
      </div>
    </div>
    <div class="col">
      <div class="card">
        <img src="{{ asset('img/dev-community.jpg') }}">
        <p>Our API is Well Documented and backed by A Friendly
        Developer Community</p>
        <button type="button">Get Started</button>
      </div>
    </div>
  </div>
</section>
@endsection
```

Note the following in Listing 5-5:

1. The code is located in the resources/views/dashboard/welcome.
   blade.php file.

2. The asset() function is used to add the image asset files. Be sure
   to place your images relative to the public folder of your Laravel
   project folder.

3. The @section() directives contain contents to be passed to the
   corresponding @yield() directives of the extended view file
   (base.blade.php) so that the content can be displayed.

The Welcome Page Route Definition

Now that you've put together the view file of the Welcome page, the next thing to do is to define the route for the page. The route code will be added to the routes/web.php file in your Laravel application folder, as shown in Listing 5-6.

Listing 5-6. The route Definition for the Welcome Page

```php
<?php

//routes/web.php
//For the Welcome page
Route::get('/', function () {
    return view('dashboard.welcome', ['sign' => 'Login', 'name' => 'Guest',
'url' => route('display.auth')]);
})->name('welcome');
```

This list explains the code in Listing 5-6:

1. The code is located in the routes/web.php file.

2. You use the get() method to specify that any request sent to the base or root URL be handled by this route. The URL attached to this route is the base URL (/). This means that whoever visits this website will be taken to this page, unless a different page is specified in the URL.

3. The second parameter is a closure (an anonymous function) that Laravel will execute when a request is made to the specified URL (/).

4. Inside the closure, the view() helper function is called. This helper returns a view, which is a template that usually contains HTML and Blade directives.

5. The view being returned is named dashboard.welcome. This corresponds to the resources/views/dashboard/welcome.blade. php file.

6. The second argument to the view() function is an associative array that passes data to the view.

The keys of this array are turned into variables of the same name ($sign,$name, $url). These variables can then be accessed within the Blade template to display dynamic contents.

If you visit the route (/) attached to this method, say in your web browser, you'll see the page shown in Figure 5-1. In local development mode, the URL is localhost. This is true if you are using the local development environment you set up in Chapter 2. However, if you've changed the port, it will be localhost:port. In live server mode, assuming you are using www.my-url.com as your base URL, this will be the URL of the Welcome page.

Figure 5-1. *The Welcome page from which, among other things, users can proceed to register for or log in to manage the API*

Next, you learn how to implement the Registration/Login page of the API dashboard.

Magic Link-Based Authentication Implementation

In this section, you'll be implementing the Magic Link-based authentication system.

What Is a Magic Link?

A *Magic Link* is a way to log in without having to remember or use a password. Instead of typing in a password, you just enter your email address, and the website sends you a unique link. When you click that link, it proves that you own the email and lets you log in automatically—like having a one-time secret key that only works for a short period. It's a simple, secure, and hassle-free way to get access. You'll be using it to determine access to the dashboard pages that require protection.

The next section explains how to implement this Magic Link authentication system.

Creating Models and Migration Files

In this section, you implement the models needed by the Magic Link system.

Updating the User Migration and Model Files

In this section, you modify the default users table migration in `database/migrations/xxxx_xx_xx_xxxxxx_create_users_table.` php in line with the changes made to the model file earlier in this chapter. Open the file in your code editor and replace its contents with those shown in Listing 5-7.

Listing 5-7. Modifying the Default Users Table

```php
<?php

use Illuminate\Database\Migrations\Migration;
use Illuminate\Database\Schema\Blueprint;
use Illuminate\Support\Facades\Schema;

return new class extends Migration
{
    /**
     * Run the migrations.
     */
    public function up(): void
    {
        Schema::create('users', function (Blueprint $table) {
            $table->id();
```

```
        $table->string('name')->nullable();
        $table->string('email')->unique();
        $table->timestamp('email_verified_at')->nullable();
        $table->decimal('balance', 17, 2)->default(0.00);
        $table->timestamps();
    });

    Schema::create('sessions', function (Blueprint $table) {
        $table->string('id')->primary();
        $table->foreignId('user_id')->nullable()->index();
        $table->string('ip_address', 45)->nullable();
        $table->text('user_agent')->nullable();
        $table->longText('payload');
        $table->integer('last_activity')->index();
    });
}

/**
 * Reverse the migrations.
 */
public function down(): void
{
    Schema::dropIfExists('users');
    Schema::dropIfExists('password_reset_tokens');
    Schema::dropIfExists('sessions');
}
};
```

To reflect the changes made to the user model file, I've added one additional field—balance.

After ensuring the contents are updated and the file is saved, you need to run the Artisan command in Listing 5-8 from the terminal. The change will then be reflected in the users database.

Listing 5-8. The Artisian Command to Reflect the Change in the Users Database

```
php artisan migrate:refresh
```

Creating the Magic Link (Token) Table

Next, you'll create the migration file for the database table so it can store Magic Link tokens. To do this, run the Artisan command shown in Listing 5-9.

Listing 5-9. The Artisan Command to Create the Migration File

```
php artisan make:migration create_magic_links_table
```

Open the generated migration file (database/migrations/xxxx_xx_xx_xxxxxx_create_magic_links_table.php) and modify it by adding the required database fields to it. See Listing 5-10. The code you should add is shown in bold.

Listing 5-10. Migration File for the magic-links Table

```php
<?php

use Illuminate\Database\Migrations\Migration;
use Illuminate\Database\Schema\Blueprint;
use Illuminate\Support\Facades\Schema;

return new class extends Migration
{
    /**
     * Run the migrations.
     */
    public function up(): void
    {
        Schema::create('magic_links', function (Blueprint $table) {
            $table->id();
            $table->foreignId('user_id')->constrained()-
            >onDelete('cascade');
            $table->string('token')->unique();
            $table->timestamp('expires_at');
            $table->timestamps();
        });
    }
```

```
    /**
     * Reverse the migrations.
     */
    public function down(): void
    {
        Schema::dropIfExists('magic_links');
    }
};
```

Three fields were added here—user_id, token, and expires_at. Next, enter the command in Listing 5-11 via the command-line to run the migration and add the fields to magic_links.

Listing 5-11. The Artisan Command to Make the Changes Dictated in the Migration File

```
php artisan migrate
```

Note   By convention, Laravel uses singular StudlyCase names for models. So, for a table named magic_links, the model should be MagicLink.

Creating the MagicLink Model

Now that you have a database table for the Magic Link, you'll create the corresponding model. Run the Artisan command in Listing 5-12 to generate the model's file—app/Models/MagicLink.php.

Listing 5-12. The Artisan Command to Create the MagicLink Model

```
php artisan make:model MagicLink
```

Open the generated file, app/Models/MagicLink.php, in your code editor and replace its contents with Listing 5-13. Then save it.

Listing 5-13. Updated app/Models/MagicLink.php File

```php
<?php

namespace App\Models;

use Illuminate\Database\Eloquent\Factories\HasFactory;
use Illuminate\Database\Eloquent\Model;
use Illuminate\Support\Carbon;

class MagicLink extends Model
{
    use HasFactory;

    protected $fillable = ['user_id', 'token', 'expires_at'];

    public function user()
    {
        return $this->belongsTo(User::class);
    }

    public function isExpired(): bool
    {
        return Carbon::now()->greaterThan($this->expires_at);
    }
}
```

The model defined in Listing 5-13 contains the logic related to the MagicLink model—including which fields are assignable, its relationship to the user, and a helper method to determine if the link has expired. This helps keep the business logic organized and easily reusable.

Creating the HiToken Table and Model

When users visit the Manage Keys (Tokens) sub-page of the home page, they should be able to generate tokens. To support this functionality, you need to create a new model called HiToken and its corresponding database table hi_tokens, which will store tokens in encrypted form. This will enable users to access their tokens through the dashboard interface while ensuring proper security. By encrypting and saving this token, you make it easy for users to retrieve it at any time while adding some level of security using encryption.

Note   While Sanctum generates tokens in plain text format, it does not store them as such for security purposes. Instead, Laravel stores only the hashed version of each token in the database. The plain text token must be captured and stored securely immediately upon generation, as it cannot be retrieved later—hash values cannot be converted back to their original plain text form. Since API users require the plain text token for authentication, you need to store these tokens using encryption to maintain security standards. The key point is that token storage must occur at the moment of generation, as this represents the only opportunity to preserve the plain text format needed for API access.

Hashing is a one-way process that converts data into a fixed-length string that cannot be reversed, making it ideal for password storage and data verification. *Encryption*, on the other hand, is a two-way process that transforms data using a key; the key can be decrypted back to its original form when needed.

To create the HiToken model and the corresponding migration file, run the Artisan command shown in Listing 5-13a from the command-line terminal.

Listing 5-13a.

```
php artisan make:model HiToken --migration
```

Running this command will generate the app/Models/HiToken.php file containing your model inside your Laravel project folder. It will also generate a corresponding migration file, called database/migrations/xxxx_xx_xx_xxxxxx_create_hi_tokens_table.php, inside your project folder. Next, you'll modify these two files to better match your needs.

Open the model file and update it as shown in Listing 5-13b.

Listing 5-13b. Updating the Model File

```php
<?php

//app/Models/HiToken.php

namespace App\Models;

use Illuminate\Database\Eloquent\Model;

class HiToken extends Model
{
    /**
     * The attributes that are mass assignable.
     *
     * @var list<string>
     */
    protected $fillable = [
        'user_id',
        's_token',
        'p_token',
    ];

    public function user()
    {
        return $this->belongsTo(User::class);
    }

    /**
     * Get the attributes that should be cast.
     *
     * @return array<string, string>
     */
    protected function casts(): array
    {
        return [
            's_token' => 'encrypted',
            'p_token' => 'encrypted',
```

```
    ];
  }
}
```

Note the following from the code in Listing 5-13b:

- The $fillable **property**: This array defines which attributes of the model can be mass assigned. Mass assignment allows you to create or update a model using an array of attributes. By specifying the fields (user_id, s_token, and p_token), you protect the model from accidental assignment of any fields that should not be modified in bulk.

- **The** user() **method**: This method defines a relationship between the HiToken model and the User model. The belongsTo() method indicates that each instance of HiToken is associated with one user. This allows you to easily retrieve the user related to a token (e.g., $hiToken→user).

- **The** casts **method**: This method returns an associative array that maps certain attributes (s_token and p_token) to an encrypted cast type. The encrypted cast indicates that these attributes should be automatically encrypted when saved to the database and decrypted when retrieved. This is a useful security measure to protect sensitive token data.

Next, open the generated migration file in database\migrations\xxxx_xx_ xx_xxxxxx_create_hi_tokens_table.php and update it using the code shown in Listing 5-13c.

Listing 5-13c. Updating the Migration File

```
<?php

/*database/migrations/xxxx_xx
_xx_xxxxxx_create_hi_tokens_table.php*/

use Illuminate\Database\Migrations\Migration;
use Illuminate\Database\Schema\Blueprint;
use Illuminate\Support\Facades\Schema;
```

```
return new class extends Migration
{
    /**
     * Run the migrations.
     */
    public function up(): void
    {
        Schema::create('hi_tokens', function (Blueprint $table) {
            $table->id();
            $table->foreignId('user_id')->constrained()->
            onDelete('cascade');
            $table->mediumText('s_token');
            $table->mediumText('p_token');
            $table->timestamps();
        });
    }

    /**
     * Reverse the migrations.
     */
    public function down(): void
    {
        Schema::dropIfExists('hi_tokens');
    }
};
```

Notice that this code includes three new fields in the hi_tokens database table.

1. The user_id field represents the user the tokens are assigned to.

2. The s_token and p_token fields will hold the encrypted versions of the secret and public key (tokens), respectively.

To add the hi_tokens table and the fields defined in the migration file, run the command shown in Listing 5-13d from your command-line terminal.

Listing 5-13d. Artisan Command to Add the New Table and Fields

```
php artisan migrate
```

If the Artisan command in Listing 5-13d is successful, the hi_tokens table and its fields should be created and added to the database.

Implementing the Mail and Controllers Classes

This section explains how to implement the email class and the authentication controller for the Magic Link system.

Implementing the Email Class

The Magic Link system needs to be able to send email. In this section, you'll start putting together the code to get this done. First, you need to generate a mail class to send the Magic Link. You do this by running the Artisan command shown in Listing 5-14.

Listing 5-14. The Artisan Command to Generate a Mail Class

```
php artisan make:mail MagicLinkMail
```

This Artisan command will generate a mail class in app/Mail/MagicLinkMail.php. Open the file and replace its contents with Listing 5-15. Don't forget to save the changes.

Listing 5-15. Updated app/Mail/MagicLinkMail.php File

```php
<?php

//app/Mail/MagicLinkMail.php
namespace App\Mail;

use Illuminate\Bus\Queueable;
use Illuminate\Mail\Mailable;
use Illuminate\Queue\SerializesModels;

class MagicLinkMail extends Mailable
{
    use Queueable, SerializesModels;

    public string $link;
```

```php
    public function __construct(string $link)
    {
        $this->link = $link;
    }

    public function build()
    {
        return $this->subject('DexyPay: Your Login Link')
            ->view('emails.magic-link')
            ->with(['link' => $this->link]);
    }
}
```

This class helps you construct the login/authentication mail sent to the email address submitted by your users when they are trying to access the dashboard. It receives the authentication link (URL) and then specifies the mail subject (DexyPay: Your Login Link), the view file (emails.magic-link), and the variable to be passed to the view ($link). This mail class will be used in the AuthController controller in the next section to send the Magic Link.

Tip   The location of the view file (emails.magic-link) is resources/view/ emails/magic-link.blade.php. This file will be created later; you are only referencing it here.

Implementing the AuthController Controller Class

Next, you'll put together the authentication controller, called AuthController. This controller will contain the logic for processing the request for Magic Link generation, as well as for logging in and logging out the dashboard users. Run the Artisan command in Listing 5-16 to generate the controller file.

Listing 5-16. The Artisan Command to Generate a Controller File

```
php artisan make:controller Auth/AuthController
```

Running this command will generate the controller file called app/Http/
Controllers/Auth/AuthController.php. Open the file and update its code to match
Listing 5-17a.

Listing 5-17a. The AuthController Class Code

```php
<?php

//app/Http/Controllers/Auth/AuthController.php
namespace App\Http\Controllers\Auth;

use App\Http\Controllers\Controller;
use App\Models\MagicLink;
use App\Models\User;
use Illuminate\Http\Request;
use Illuminate\Support\Carbon;
use Illuminate\Support\Facades\Mail;
use Illuminate\Support\Facades\URL;
use Illuminate\Support\Str;

class AuthController extends Controller
{
    //
    public function requestLink(Request $request)
    {
        $request->validate([
            'email' => 'required|email',
        ]);

        // Find or create user
        $user = User::firstOrCreate(['email' => $request->email]);

        // Generate a magic link token
        $token     = Str::random(64);
        $expiresAt = Carbon::now()->addMinutes(15); // Link valid for
        15 minutes

        // Store token in database
        MagicLink::create([
```

```
            'user_id'    => $user->id,
            'token'      => $token,
            'expires_at' => $expiresAt,
    ]);

    // Generate login link
    $link = URL::temporarySignedRoute(
        'auth.login',
        $expiresAt,
        ['token' => $token]
    );

    // Send email
    Mail::to($user->email)->send(new \App\Mail\MagicLinkMail($link));
    //
    $masked_email = substr_replace($user->email, '****', 0, 3);
    return redirect()->route('sent_email_notifier', ['email' =>
    $masked_email]);
}

public function login(Request $request, $token)
{
    // Validate token
    $magicLink = MagicLink::where('token', $token)->first();

    if (! $magicLink || $magicLink->isExpired()) {
        return response()->json(['message' => 'Invalid or expired
        link.'], 401);
    }
    $user = $magicLink->user;
    // Log in the user
    auth()->login($user);
    return redirect()->route('home.pages.page', ['page' =>
    'transactions']);
}
```

```
public function logout()
{
    auth()->logout();
    //return response()->json(['message' => 'Logged out
    successfully']);
    return redirect()->route('do.auth');

}
}
```

The AuthController class facilitates passwordless authentication using Magic Links through three primary methods:

1. requestLink(Request $request): Handles the process of generating and sending a magic login link to the user's email.

2. login(Request $request, $token): Manages user authentication upon clicking the Magic Link, verifying their validity and logging the users in.

3. logout(): Logs out the authenticated user from the application.

These methods collectively enable a seamless, passwordless authentication experience for users.

Implementing the DashboardPagesController Controller Class

Next, you'll create the DashboardPagesController controller class. It is used to manage the Home sub-pages, including the Manage Keys (Tokens) page. Run the Artisan command shown in Listing 5-17b to generate the controller file.

Listing 5-17b. The Artisan Command to Generate a Controller File

```
php artisan make:controller DashboardPages/DashboardPagesController
```

Running the command in Listing 5-17b will generate the controller file called app/ Http/Controllers/DashboardPages/DashboardPagesController.php. Open that file and update its code to that shown in Listing 5-17c.

Listing 5-17c. Updating the Controller File

```php
<?php

/*app/Http/Controllers/DashboardPages/DashboardPagesController.php*/

namespace App\Http\Controllers\DashboardPages;

use App\Http\Controllers\Controller;
use App\Models\HiToken;
use App\Models\Transaction;
use App\Models\BankDetail;
use App\Models\Withdrawal;
use App\Models\Setting;

//use App\Models\User;
use Illuminate\Http\Request;

class DashboardPagesController extends Controller
{
    //
    public function index(Request $request, $page, ?string $action = '')
    {

        \Log::info('amt2withdraw : '.$request->amt2withdraw);

        $request->validate([

            //IBAN code
            'iban'   => 'alpha_num|min:8|max:34',

            //SWIFT Code
            'swift'   => 'alpha_num|min:8|max:11',

            'amt2withdraw'   => 'decimal:2|max:1000000000.00|min:20.00',

            'webhook_url' =>  'url',

            'webhook_secret' => 'string',

        ]);
```

```php
    $this->request = $request;
    $dPage        = '';
    $data         = [];
    if ($page == 'transactions') {
        $data = $this->transactions($action);
    } elseif ($page == 'tokens') {
        $data = $this->tokens($action, $page);
    } elseif ($page == 'bank') {
        $data = $this->bank($action);
    } elseif ($page == 'withdrawal') {
        $data = $this->withdrawal($action);
    } elseif ($page == 'settings') {
        $data = $this->settings($action);
    }
    $arr   = ['user' => auth()->user()->id, 'page' => $page];
    $sign  = 'Logout';
    $name  = auth()->user()->email;
    $url   = route('auth.logout');
    $paged = ['name' => $page, 'data' => $data];

    return view('dashboard.home', compact('sign', 'name', 'url',
    'paged'));
}

private function transactions($action)
{
    $txns = auth()->user()->transaction();
    $txns = $txns->simplePaginate(30)->withPath('/home/pages/
    transactions/get'); // Get 30 transactions per page

    return ['txns' => $txns, 'cnt' => 0, 'bal' => auth()->user()-
    >balance, 'currency' => 'USD'];


}
```

```php
private function tokens($act, $pg)
{
    $userid = auth()->user()->id;

    if ($act === 'regen' && $this->request->isMethod('post')) {

        //delete old tokens
        auth()->user()->tokens()->delete();

        //delete existing encrypted tokens
        HiToken::where('user_id', $userid)->delete();

        //generate array of new tokens
        $newToken = $this->generateToken($userid);

        //return the new tokens
        return $newToken;
    }

    //Try to reteieve user's tokens
    $retToken = HiToken::firstWhere('user_id', $userid);

    //if the user already has token in the database
    if ($retToken) {
        //return retrieved tokens
        return ['public' => $retToken->p_token, 'secret' =>
        $retToken->s_token];

    } else {

        //generate array of new tokens
        $newToken = $this->generateToken($userid);

        //return the new tokens
        return $newToken;
    }

}
```

```php
private function bank($act)
{

    \Log::info("bank: " . $this->request->iban.' and
    '.$this->request->swift);

    $uid = auth()->user()->id;

    if($act === "post" && $this->request->iban && $this->
    request->swift){
        //Store the user bank details in database
        BankDetail::updateOrCreate(
        [
            'user_id' => $uid,
        ],
        [
            'iban' => $this->request->iban,
            'swift' => $this->request->swift,
        ]);

        return ['iban' => $this->request->iban, 'swift' => $this->
        request->swift];
    }

    //Reteieve user's bank details
    $bankDetails = BankDetail::firstWhere('user_id', $uid);

    //if the user already has token in the database
    if ($bankDetails) {
        //return retrieved tokens
        return ['iban' => $bankDetails->iban, 'swift' =>
        $bankDetails->swift];

    }

    return ['iban' => '', 'swift' => ''];
}
```

```php
private function withdrawal($act)
{

    $balance = (float)auth()->user()->balance;
    $amt2with = (float)$this->request->amt2withdraw;

    \Log::info($balance.' bal > a2w  '.$amt2with);

    if($act === "post" && $this->request->amt2withdraw && $amt2with
    <= $balance){

        //Credit the merchant
        auth()->user()->decrement('balance', $amt2with);

        //record withdrawal
        $this->recordWithdrawal();

    }

    $withdrawals = auth()->user()->withdrawal();
    $withdrawals = $withdrawals->simplePaginate(30)->withPath('/home/
    pages/withdrawal/get'); // Get 30 withdrawals per page

    return ['withdrawals' => $withdrawals, 'cnt' => 0, 'bal' =>
    auth()->user()->balance, 'currency' => 'USD'];

}

private function settings($act)
{
    \Log::info("settings: " . $this->request->webhook_url.'
    and  '.$this->request->webhook_secret);

    $uid = auth()->user()->id;

    if($act === "post" && ($this->request->webhook_url || $this->
    request->webhook_secret)){
        //Store the user bank details in database
        Setting::updateOrCreate(
        [
```

```php
            'user_id' => $uid,
        ],
        [
            'webhook_url' => $this->request->webhook_url,
            'webhook_secret' => $this->request->webhook_secret,
        ]);

        return ['webhook_url' => $this->request->webhook_url,
         'webhook_secret' => $this->request->webhook_secret];
    }

    //Reteieve user's bank details
    $settings = Setting::firstWhere('user_id', $uid);

    //if the user already has token in the database
    if ($settings) {
        //return retrieved tokens
        return ['webhook_url' => $settings->webhook_url, 'webhook_
        secret' => $settings->webhook_secret];

    }

    return ['webhook_url' => '', 'webhook_secret' => ''];
}

private function generateToken(int $uid)
{
    //generate new tokens
    $p_token = auth()->user()->createToken(
        'public', ['public']
    );
    $s token = auth()->user()->createToken(
        'secret', ['secret']
    );

    //Store the encrypted tokens in database
    HiToken::create([
        'user_id' => $uid,
        'p_token' => $p_token->plainTextToken,
```

```php
            's_token' => $s_token->plainTextToken,
        ]);

        return ['public' => $p_token->plainTextToken, 'secret' =>
        $s_token->plainTextToken];

    }

    private function recordWithdrawal()
    {
        Withdrawal::create([
            'user_id' => auth()->user()->id,
            'amount'  => $this->request->amt2withdraw,
            'status'  => 'successful',
        ]);
    }

}
```

This list explains the code in Listing 5-17c:

1. The index() method detects which page is being visited and calls
   the appropriate methods to process the request.

2. The tokens($act, $pg) method first checks if the value passed
   through the route parameter, $act, is equal to the regen string.
   It also checks if the route method used is POST. If these two
   conditions are met, new public and private keys (tokens) are
   created by calling the generateToken(int $uid) method with
   the ID of the current user passed in as an argument. Apart from
   generating new keys, the generateToken(int $uid) method
   also saves the newly created keys to the hi_tokens database
   table. After logging in to the dashboard, if you visit a URL such as
   http://localhost/home/pages/tokens/regen, a new set of keys
   (tokens) will be generated and displayed on the Manage Keys
   (Tokens) page, as shown in Figure 5-2a. If on the other hand, you
   visit a URL such as http://localhost/home/pages/tokens, the if
   ($act === 'regen' && $this->request->isMethod('post'))
   part of the tokens($act, $pg) method will not be executed.

The remaining code will execute such that if the user already has tokens saved in the database, they will be retrieved and displayed, as shown in Figure 5-2b. If no token can be retrieved for the user, new tokens will be generated, saved, and displayed on the Manage Keys (Tokens) page, as shown in Figure 5-2b.

3.   The code creates the generateToken(int $uid) method used in Step 2.

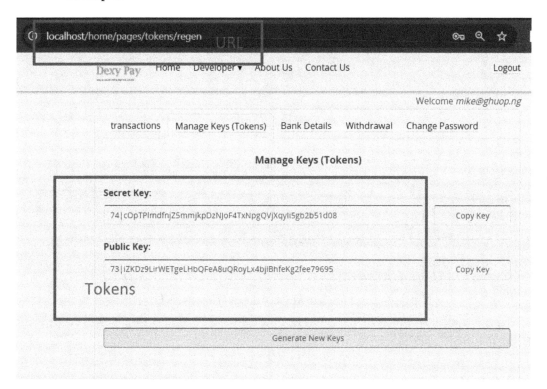

Figure 5-2a.   *The Manage Keys (Tokens) page accessed via the http://localhost/ home/pages/tokens/regen URL (POST)*

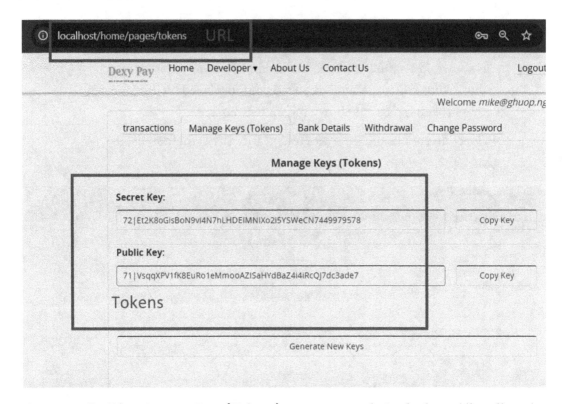

Figure 5-2b. *The Manage Keys (Tokens) page accessed via the http://localhost/home/pages/tokens/ URL*

The API users can now manage the keys (tokens) they need to connect to the API. Next, you'll start building the payment processor API. These tokens will come handy during testing it. Let's go.

Implementing Pages

In this section, you implement the various pages used by the Magic Link system. This is in addition to the Welcome page you created earlier in this chapter.

Creating the Auth Page

The Auth page allows the API users to submit their email addresses to the Magic Link authentication system. They will then retrieve a login link via the requestLink() method in the AuthController class that you created earlier. Create a view file in resources/views/dashboard/auth.blade.php and add the code in Listing 5-18 to it.

Listing 5-18. The auth.blade.php View File

```
<!--resources/views/dashboard/auth.blade.php-->
@extends('dashboard.base')
@section('title', 'Sign Up Page')
@section('sign', $sign)
@section('name', $name)
@section('url', $url)
@section('content')
<section>
   <div class="row">
      <div class="col-3"></div>
      <div class="col-6">
         <h4 align ="center" >Get Started</h4>
         <br/>
         <form action = "{{route('do.auth')}}" method = "post">
            @csrf
            <label for="email">Email</label>
            <input id="email" type="text" placeholder="Enter your email to
            Start?" name = "email" required>
            @error('email')
              {{$message}}
            @enderror
            <br/>
            <input id="submit" type="submit" value="Submit">
         </form>
      </div>
      <div class="col-3"></div>
   </div>
</section>
@endsection
```

The auth view file defined in Listing 5-18 will be displayed, as shown in Figure 5-3. This will allow users to enter an email address in order to log in to the dashboard.

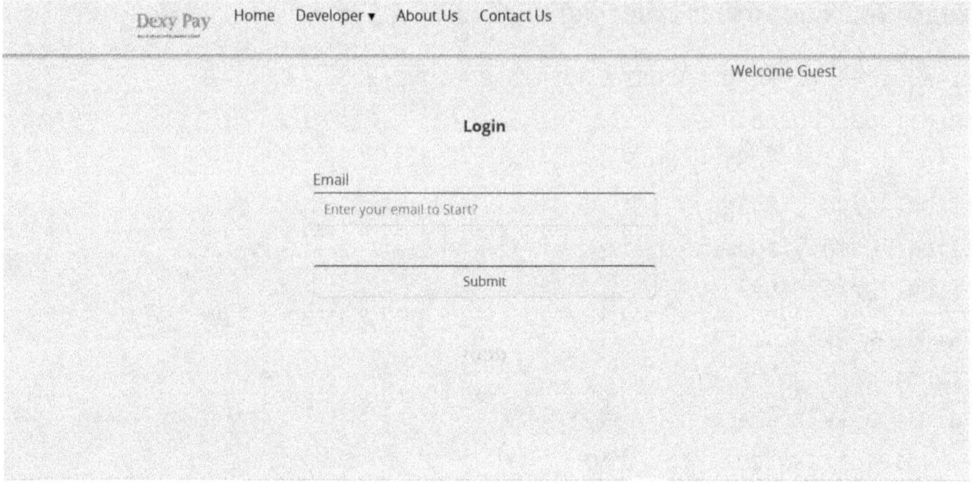

Figure 5-3. *The Login page*

Creating the Sent Email Notifier Page

The code for the Sent Email Notifier page is shown in Listing 5-19. Create a file called resources/views/dashboard/sent_email_notifier.blade.php in your Laravel project and save the code in Listing 5-19 to it.

Listing 5-19. The sent_email_notifier.blade View File

```
<!--resources/views/dashboard/sent_email_notifier.blade.php-->
@extends('dashboard.base')
@section('title', 'Email Verification Required')
@section('sign', $sign)
@section('name', $name)
@section('url', $url)
@section('content')
    <section>
        <h5 align="center">You're Almost There!</h5>
        <p>A login link has been sent to <b>{{$masked_email}}</b>.
        To resend the link, click <u><a href="{{route('display.
        auth')}}">here</a></u>.</p>
    </section>
@endsection
```

The sent_email_notifier view file defined in Listing 5-19 will be displayed as shown in Figure 5-4 to the user of the message sent to the email address submitted for login.

Figure 5-4. *The Sent Email Notifier page*

Creating the Home Page

Once the login link has been sent to your email address, clicking this link should call the login() method of the AuthController class shown in Listing 5-17a. This method will, among other things, determine if the login link is valid and not expired. If the login link is found to be valid, the API user will be logged in and redirected to the home page. The home page enables users to carry out sensitive operations involving tokens, banking details, passwords, and so on, so the users need to be authenticated and logged in to access it. For this reason, as you'll see later when you create the route for the home page, you need to add the auth middleware to its route.

The code for the home page view file (resources/views/dashboard/home.blade.php) is shown in Listing 5-20.

Listing 5-20. The Home Page View File

```
<!--resources/views/dashboard/home.blade.php-->
@extends('dashboard.base')
@section('title', 'Home Page')
@section('sign', $sign)
```

```
@section('name', $name)
@section('url', $url)
@section('content')
<div class="tabs">
    <input type="radio" name="tabs" id="tabone" @if($paged['name'] ==
    'transactions')checked="checked"@endif>
    <label for="tabone"><a href="/home/pages/transactions/
    get">Transactions</a></label>
    <div class="tab">
        <h4 style = "color:green;" >Balance: <em> @if(isset($paged['data']
        ['bal'])) {{$paged['data']['currency']}} {{ number_
        format($paged['data']['bal'], 2) }} @endif</em></h4>
        <h4  align ="center" >Transactions</h4>
        <br>
        @isset($paged['data']['txns'])
            <table>
            <thead>
            <tr>
              <th>SN.</th>
              <th>Email</th>
              <th>Amount</th>
              <th>Status</th>
              <th>Date</th>
            </tr>
            </thead>
            <tbody>

        @foreach ($paged['data']['txns'] as $txn)
            <tr>
              <td>{{ ++$paged['data']['cnt'] }}</td>
              <td>{{ $txn->email}}</td>
              <td>USD {{ number_format($txn->amount, 2) }}</td>
              <td>{{ $txn->status }}</td>
              <td>{{ $txn->updated_at }}</td>
            </tr>
        @endforeach
```

```
            </tbody>
        </table>
        {{ $paged['data']['txns'] }}
    @endisset
    @if(!isset($paged['data']['txns']))
    <p align ="center" >No Transaction Yet</p>
    @endif

</div>
<input type="radio" name="tabs" id="tabtwo" @if($paged['name'] ==
'tokens')checked="checked"@endif>
<label for="tabtwo"><a href="/home/pages/tokens">Manage
Keys (Tokens)</a></label>
<div class="tab">
    <h4 align ="center" >Manage Keys (Tokens)</h4>
    <br/>
    <section>
        <b>Secret Key: </b><br/>
        <div class="row">
            <div class="col"><input id="skey" type="text" placeholder="No
            secret key Generated Yet" disabled @isset($paged['data']
            ['secret']) value="{{$paged['data']['secret']}}"@
            endisset ></div>
            <div class="col-3">
                <input type="reset" id="copyskey" value="Copy Key" >
            </div>

        </div>
        <hr>
        <b>Public Key: </b><br/>
        <div class="row">
            <div class="col"><input id="pkey" type="text" placeholder="No
            public key Generated Yet" disabled  @isset($paged['data']
            ['secret']) value="{{$paged['data']['public']}}"@
            endisset ></div>
            <div class="col-3">
```

```
                <input type="reset" id="copypkey" value="Copy Key" >
            </div>

        </div>
        <br><br>
        <div class="row" >
            <div class="col">
                <form  action = "/home/pages/tokens/regen" method = "post">
                @csrf
                    <a ><input id="submitskey" type="submit" value="Generate
                    New Keys">
                    </a>

                </form>
            </div>
        </div>
    </section>
</div>
<input type="radio" name="tabs" id="tabthree" @if($paged['name'] ==
'bank')checked="checked"@endif >
<label for="tabthree"><a href="/home/pages/bank/get">Bank Details</a>
</label>
<div class="tab">
    <h4 align ="center" >Bank Details</h4>
    <br/>
    <section>
        <div class="row">
            <div class="col-3"></div>
            <div class="col-6">
                <form    action = "/home/pages/bank/post" method = "post">
                @csrf
                    <label ></label>
                    <label for="iban">IBAN Code</label>
                    <input id="iban" type="text"  name="iban"
                    placeholder="your IBAN code?" value = "@
                    isset($paged['data']['iban']) {{$paged['data']['iban']}}
                    @endisset" >
```

```html
            <label for="swift">SWIFT Code</label>
            <input id="swift" type="text"  name="swift"  placeholder=
            "your SWIFT code?" value = "@isset($paged['data']
            ['swift']) {{$paged['data']['swift']}} @endisset">
            <br/><br/>
            <input id="submitbank" type="submit" value="Save">
        </form>
      </div>
      <div class="col-3"></div>
    </div>
  </section>
</div>
<input type="radio" name="tabs" id="tabfour" @if($paged['name'] ==
'withdrawal')checked="checked"@endif >
<label for="tabfour"><a href="/home/pages/withdrawal/get">Withdrawal
</a></label>
<div class="tab">
  <h4 style = "color:green;" >Balance: <em> @if(isset($paged['data']
  ['bal'])) {{$paged['data']['currency']}} {{ number_
  format($paged['data']['bal'], 2) }} @endif</em></h4>

  <section>
    <div class="row">
        <div class="col-3"></div>
        <div class="col-6">
          <form    action = "/home/pages/withdrawal/post" method
          = "post">
          @csrf
            <label ></label>
            <label for="amt2withdraw">Amount To Withdraw</label>
            <input id="amt2withdraw" type="text"  name="amt2withdraw"
            inputmode="decimal" pattern="^(?:(?:\d{1,3}(?:,\d{3})+)|\
            d+)\.[0-9]{2}$" placeholder="5,678.99">

            <br/><br/>
            <input id="withdraw" type="submit" value="Withdraw">
```

```
            </form>
          </div>
          <div class="col-3"></div>
      </div>
    </section>

    <h4 align ="center" >Withdrawals</h4>
    <br>
    @isset($paged['data']['withdrawals'])
        <table>
        <thead>
        <tr>
          <th>SN.</th>
          <th>Amount</th>
          <th>Status</th>
          <th>Date</th>
        </tr>
        </thead>
        <tbody>
      @foreach ($paged['data']['withdrawals'] as $withdrawal)
          <tr>
            <td>{{ ++$paged['data']['cnt'] }}</td>
            <td>USD {{ number_format($withdrawal->amount, 2) }}</td>
            <td>{{ $withdrawal->status }}</td>
            <td>{{ $withdrawal->updated_at }}</td>
          </tr>
      @endforeach
        </tbody>
      </table>
        {{ $paged['data']['withdrawals'] }}
    @endisset
    @if(!isset($paged['data']['withdrawals']))
    <p align ="center" >No Withdrawal Yet</p>
    @endif
</div>
```

```
<input type="radio" name="tabs" id="tabfive" @if($paged['name'] ==
'settings')checked="checked"@endif>
<label for="tabfive"><a href="/home/pages/settings">Settings</a></label>
<div class="tab">
    <h4 align ="center" >Settings</h4>
    <section>
        <div class="row">
            <div class="col-3"></div>
            <div class="col-6">
                <form  action = "/home/pages/settings/post" method = "post">
                @csrf
                    <label ></label>
                    <label for="webhook_url">Enter Your Web-Hook URL <span
                    data-tooltip="URL pointinting to a script on your server
                    that will be called and passed relevant data whenever you
                    are paid.">ⓘ</span></label>
                    <input id="webhook_url" name="webhook_url"  type="url"
                    placeholder="https://my-webhook-url.com/my-webhook-scrip.
                    php"  value = "@isset($paged['data']['webhook_url'])
                    {{$paged['data']['webhook_url']}} @endisset">
                    <label for="webhook_secret">Enter Your Web-Hook secret
                    <span data-tooltip="Any alpha-numeric string that'll
                    be used as a secret for securing your Web-Hook.">ⓘ</
                    span></label>
                    <input id="webhook_secret" name="webhook_secret"
                    type="text" placeholder="my-webhook-secret"  value =
                    "@isset($paged['data']['webhook_secret'])
                    {{$paged['data']['webhook_secret']}} @endisset">
                    <br/><br/>
                    <input id="submit" type="submit" value="Save">
                </form>
            </div>
            <div class="col-3"></div>
        </div>
    </section>
```

```
    </div>
</div>
@endsection
```

This view file is a bit more complex than the previous ones you've looked at. However, as you'll see, it's also easy to understand. Note the following points in Listing 5-20:

1. The file begins with `@extends('dashboard.base')`, which means it uses the base layout located at `resources/views/dashboard/base.blade.php`. This layout contains the overall HTML structure (head, header, footer, etc.) that wraps around unique page content.

2. The template sets several sections using the `@section` directive:

   `@section('title', 'Home Page')` sets the page title.

   `@section('sign', $sign)`, `@section('name', $name)`, and `@section('url', $url)` pass dynamic data (coming from the associated `GET /home/{user}` route) into corresponding placeholders in the base layout.

3. Finally, `@section('content')` begins the main content block that will be inserted into the base layout wherever `@yield('content')` is declared.

4. It contains the five tabs:

   Transactions tab: Displays payment transactions.

   Manage Keys (Tokens) tab: Manages API tokens.

   Bank Details tab: Adds banking details.

   Withdrawal tab: Displays information about withdrawals.

   Settings tab: Provides a form to manage application settings.

When a user is successfully authenticated via this Magic Link authentication system, they will be redirected to the page represented by this view file. That page is shown in Figure 5-5.

Figure 5-5. *This home page is loaded once a user has successfully logged in*

Creating the Email Message Base Page

In this section, you create a blade file that'll hold content common to all the email pages. This base file will be extended by the other email pages. The code for the base email blade file is shown in Listing 5-21a.

Listing 5-21a. The Base Email Blade File

```
<!--resources/views/emails/base.blade.php-->
<!DOCTYPE html>
<html>
<head>
  <meta charset="UTF-8" />
  <meta name="viewport" content="width=device-width, initial-scale=1" />
  <title> @yield('title')</title>
</head>
<body style="margin:0; padding:0; font-family: Arial, sans-serif;
background-color: #f7f7f7;">
  <table width="100%" cellpadding="0" cellspacing="0" bgcolor="#f7f7f7">
    <tr>
      <td align="center">
```

```
<table width="600" cellpadding="0" cellspacing="0"
bgcolor="#ffffff" style="margin: 30px auto; border-radius: 8px;
overflow: hidden;">

  <!-- Header -->
  <tr style="background-color: #004aad;">
    <td align="center" style="padding: 20px;">
      <img src="{{ asset('img/dexy-pay-logo.png') }}" alt="Company
      Logo" width="150" style="display: block; margin-bottom:
      10px;" />
      <h1 style="color: #ffffff; margin: 0; font-size: 24px;">@
      yield('subject')</h1>
    </td>
  </tr>

  <!-- Body -->

   @yield('content')

  <!-- Footer -->
  <tr style="background-color: #f1f1f1;">
    <td align="center" style="padding: 20px; font-size: 12px;
    color: #888888;">
      <p style="margin: 5px 0;">&copy; 2025 Dexy Pay. All rights
      reserved.</p>
      <p style="margin: 5px 0;">
        <a href="#" style="color: #888888; text-decoration:
        underline;">Unsubscribe</a> |
        <a href="#" style="color: #888888; text-decoration:
        underline;">Privacy Policy</a>
      </p>
    </td>
  </tr>

</table>
    </td>
  </tr>
```

```
    </table>
</body>
</html>
```

Creating the Login (Sign Up) Email Message Page

The email message for sending the Magic Link requires a view blade file. Create a new email template in resources/views/emails/magic-link.blade.php and add the contents in Listing 5-21b to it.

Listing 5-21b. The magic-link.blade View File

```
<!--resources/views/emails/magic-link.blade.php-->
@extends('emails.base')
@section('title','Login Request')
@section('subject', 'Secure Login')
@section('content')
        <tr>
            <td style="padding: 30px; color: #333333;">
            <p style="font-size: 16px;">Hello,</p>
            <p style="font-size: 16px;">
              Use the link below to log in securely to your account. This
              link is valid for one-time use only and will expire in 15
              minutes.
            </p>
            <p style="text-align: center; margin: 30px 0;">
              <a href="{{ $link }}" style="background-color: #007BFF;
              color: #ffffff; padding: 14px 28px; text-decoration:
              none; border-radius: 6px; display: inline-block; font-
              weight: bold;">
                Log In Now
              </a>
            </p>
            <p style="font-size: 14px; color: #666;">
              If you did not request this login, please ignore
              this email.
            </p>
```

```
            </td>
        </tr>
@endsection
```

An example of the login email message page generated with the code in Listing 5-21b is shown in Figure 5-6.

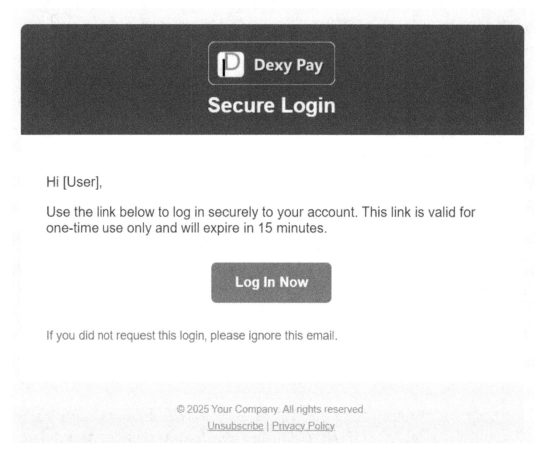

Figure 5-6. *The email message powered by the* `magic-link.blade` *view file*

Defining Routes

In this section, you create the routes that'll power the Magic Link system/user dashboard experience. You'll create the following routes:

1. A route that opens the Welcome page defined in Figure 5-6. This route was defined when you created the Welcome page.

2. A second route that links to the Auth (view) page. It contains the form to enter an email address (see Listing 5-22).

3. A third route that allows the entered email, via the form on the Auth page, to be submitted to the requestLink() method of the AuthController class, so that a login link can be sent to the email address. See Listing 5-22.

4. A fourth route that links to the Sent Email Notifier page, which is shown to the API users after they submit an email address. It informs the users that an email containing a login link has been sent to their email address. See Listing 5-22.

5. A fifth route that allows the clicking of the login link sent to the API user's email address to trigger the login() method of the AuthController class. This verifies the link and determines whether the user should be logged. See Listing 5-22.

6. A sixth route that leads to the home page. This page is only accessible to logged-in users because it contains sensitive information and allows the performance of sensitive actions involving tokens, banking details, passwords, and so on. This route will therefore be protected using the Laravel's built-in Auth middleware.

7. And, finally, a seventh route which, when visited, triggers the logout() method of the AuthController class and logs the user out. Users must be logged in before they can visit this route or they can't access it. This route will also be protected using Laravel's built-in Auth middleware.

All these routes are implemented in the routes/web.php file, as shown in Listing 5-22.

Listing 5-22. The route definition for the Page

```php
<?php

//routes/web.php
use App\Http\Controllers\Auth\AuthController;
use App\Models\User;
use Illuminate\Support\Facades\Route;
use App\Http\Controllers\DashboardPages\DashboardPagesController;
use Illuminate\Http\Request;
use Illuminate\Http\RedirectResponse;

//For the Welcome page
Route::get('/', function () {
    return view('dashboard.welcome', ['sign' => 'Login', 'name' => 'Guest',
'url' => route('display.auth')]);
})->name('welcome');

//For the Auth page
Route::get('/auth', function () {
    return view('dashboard.auth', ['sign' => 'Login', 'name' => 'Guest',
    'url' => route('display.auth')]);
})->name('display.auth');

//For sending email address to the requestLink()method
Route::post('/auth', [AuthController::class, 'requestLink'])->
name('do.auth');

//For connecting the login link when clicked to the
//login() method for authentication
Route::get('/login/{token}', [AuthController::class, 'login'])->name('auth.
login');

//Alias for display.auth route
Route::get('/login-alias', function () {
    return redirect()->route('display.auth',['sign' => 'Login', 'name' =>
    'Guest', 'url' => route('display.auth')]);
})->name('login');
```

```
//For the sent_email_notifier page
Route::get('/sent_email_notifier/{email}', function ($email = 'abc@
def.ghi') {
    return view('dashboard.sent_email_notifier', ['sign' => 'Login', 'name'
    => 'Guest', 'masked_email' => $email, 'url' => route('display.auth')]);
})->name('sent_email_notifier');

//The Auth middleware applied to a group of two routes
Route::middleware('auth')->group(function () {

    //Triggers the logout() method for logging user out
    Route::post('/logout', [AuthController::class, 'logout'])->name('auth.
    logout');

    //Targets the Home page. The page where logged in
    //user are redirected to
    Route::get('/home/{user}', function (User $user) {
        return view('dashboard.home', ['sign' => 'Logout', 'name' =>
        $user->email, 'url' => route('auth.logout')]);
    })->name('home');

    //Can be used to open any of the Dashboard sub pages (Transactions,
    Manage Keys(Tokens), Transfer, Bank Details, Settings)
    Route::match(['get', 'post'], '/home/pages/{page}/{action?}', [Dashboar
    dPagesController::class, 'index'])->name('home.pages.page');

});


Route::get('/payment/form', function (Request $request) {
    //$amt     = $request->query('amt');

    $transaction_ref = $request->query('tx_ref');
    $amount          = $request->query('amt');
    return view(
        'payment.form',
        compact(
            'transaction_ref',
            'amount'
```

```
        )
    );
})->name('payment.form')->middleware('signed');
```

Test-Driving the API Dashboard

Now that the dashboard and the accompanying Magic Link authentication system are in place, it's time to take a test drive. First, you'll test the web browser and then you'll implement some feature tests.

Tip   To run these tests, be sure that your Apache and MySQL servers are running. See Chapter 2 for more information.

Offline Email Testing

To test this Magic Link system and the dashboard, you also need to test the email sending functionality of the app. The good news is that you can also test this offline. To do this, you can use an application called *MailHog*. It's very simple to use and available for all major operating systems. To download version 1.0.0 (the latest version as the time of writing this book), go to `https://github.com/mailhog/MailHog/releases/v1.0.0` Scroll down the page to download a suitable installer (32- or 64-bit) for your computer. Since I'm working on Windows (64-bit), I downloaded the 64-bit version installer; see Figure 5-7a.

After downloading the proper version, locate the file and double-click it to launch the application. This will open a command-line window as well as a Windows Security Alert. Click the Allow Access button to continue; see Figure 5-7b.

This PC › Downloads › Programs › new				⌄ ↻	Search new
Name	Date modified	Type	Size		
🔳 MailHog_windows_amd64	02/06/2025 11:20	Application	11,013 KB		

Figure 5-7a. *MailHog installer*

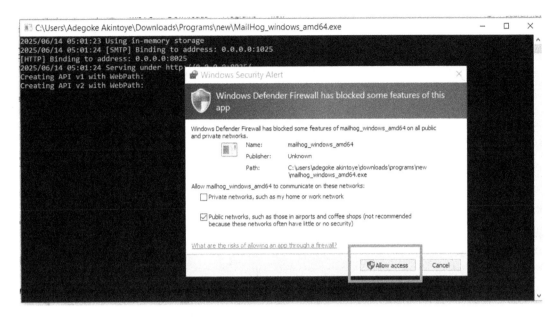

Figure 5-7b. *Windows security alert*

Visit `http://localhost:8025/` in your web browser to open a page where you can access sent mails from your application; see Figure 5-7c.

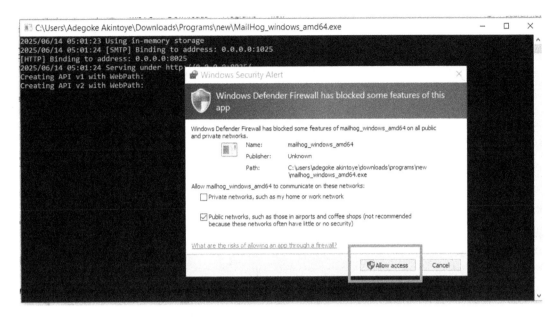

Figure 5-7c. *Your mail will be displayed here*

Configuring Mail Settings

Update the .env file with the MailHog mail settings shown in Listing 5-23.

Listing 5-23. MailHog Mail Settings

```
MAIL_MAILER=smtp
MAIL_HOST=127.0.0.1
MAIL_PORT=1025
MAIL_USERNAME=null
MAIL_PASSWORD=null
MAIL_FROM_ADDRESS=no-reply@dexypay.com
MAIL_FROM_NAME="Dexy Pay"
```

Browser-Based Testing

Use the following steps to test the dashboard and its accompanying Magic Link authentication system.

Step 1: Open the Welcome Page

Visit the base URL (localhost for local development) in your browser—see Figure 5-8.

Figure 5-8. Address bar of a web browser

Visiting the base URL should open the Welcome page shown in Figure 5-9.

Figure 5-9. *The Welcome page from which, among other things, usesr can proceed to register for or log in to manage the API*

Step 2: Open the Login Page

Click the Login button located on the top-right side of the Welcome page in Figure 5-9. This should load the Auth page, as shown in Figure 5-10.

Figure 5-10. *The Auth page for registering/logging in users*

Step 3: Enter Your Email Address

Enter your email into the Auth page (see Figure 5-10) and click the Submit button. A login link will be sent to you.

If the email address submission was successful, you'll be redirected to the Sent Email Notifier page shown in Figure 5-11.

Figure 5-11. *The sent email notification page*

Step 4: Check Your Email for a Login Link

Open the MailHog web interface shown in Figure 5-12a. Locate the email and click to open it, as shown in Figure 5-12b.

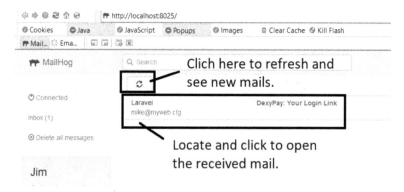

Figure 5-12a. *The MailHog web interface showing the received email*

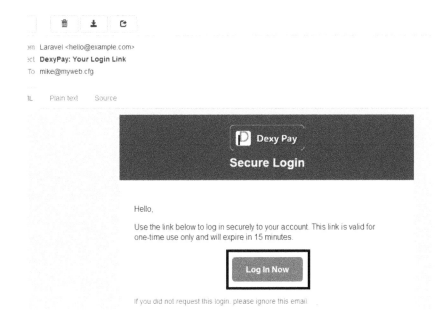

Figure 5-12b. *The MailHog web interface showing the email with the login link*

Clicking the Log In Now button or the link will redirect you to the home page (see Figure 5-12c) if the link is valid. If the link is not verified, you won't be logged in and will be redirected to the Login page (see Figure 5-12d).

Dexy Pay	Home	Developer ▾	About Us	Contact Us		Logout

Welcome *sdew@wr45r.lk*

Transactions   Manage Keys (Tokens)   Bank Details   Withdrawal   Settings

Dexy Pay © All Rights Reserved 2024 - 2025

Figure 5-12c. *The home page*

Figure 5-12d. *The Login page*

Feature Tests Implementation

In this section, you write a Laravel feature test for the Magic Link system. The test will cover three main scenarios:

1. **Requesting a Magic Link:** This submits an email request to generate a Magic Link, asserts that the user and Magic Link record are created, and verifies that the email was queued.

2. **Logging in with a valid Magic Link:** This creates a user and an associated Magic Link with a valid (non-expired) token, then asserts that a GET request to the login endpoint logs the user in, deletes the token from the database, and returns the expected JSON response.

3. **Handling an expired Magic Link:** This creates a user and a Magic Link with an expired token, then asserts that the login attempt fails and returns an appropriate error message.

Generating the Test File

Open your terminal in your Laravel project directory and run the Artisan command in Listing 5-24.

Listing 5-24. The Artisan Command to Generate the File Containing the
MagicLinkTest Test Class

```
php artisan make:test MagicLinkTest
```

This command creates a new test file called tests/Feature/MagicLinkTest.php.
Open the newly created file and paste the Magic Link test code in Listing 5-25 into it.

Listing 5-25. The Code for the MagicLinkTest Test Class

```php
<?php

//tests/Feature/MagicLinkTest.php
namespace Tests\Feature;

use App\Mail\MagicLinkMail;
use App\Models\MagicLink;
use App\Models\User;
use Illuminate\Foundation\Testing\RefreshDatabase;
use Illuminate\Support\Carbon;
use Illuminate\Support\Facades\Mail;
use Tests\TestCase;

class MagicLinkTest extends TestCase
{
    use RefreshDatabase;

    /**
     * Test that requesting a magic link creates a user, stores a
     magic link,
     * and queues an email.
     */
    public function test_magic_link_request_sends_email_and_creates_token()
    {
        // Fake the mail so no actual email is sent.
        Mail::fake();

        // Post a request to get a magic link.
        $response = $this->post('/auth', [
```

```php
        'email' => 'test@example.com',
    ]);

    // Assert the user record was created.
    $this->assertDatabaseHas('users', [
        'email' => 'test@example.com',
    ]);

    // Assert a magic link record was created.
    $this->assertDatabaseCount('magic_links', 1);

    // Assert that the MagicLinkMail was sent to the expected recipient
    Mail::assertSent(MagicLinkMail::class, function ($mail) {
        return $mail->hasTo('test@example.com');
    });
}

/**
 * Test that a valid magic link allows the user to log in.
 */
public function test_valid_magic_link_allows_login()
{
    // Create a user using a factory or manually.
    $user = User::factory()->create([
        'email' => 'user@example.com',
    ]);

    // Create a valid magic link token for the user.
    $token     = 'valid-token';
    $expiresAt = Carbon::now()->addMinutes(15);

    MagicLink::create([
        'user_id'    => $user->id,
        'token'      => $token,
        'expires_at' => $expiresAt,
    ]);

    // Simulate the GET request to the magic link login route.
    $response = $this->get('/login/' . $token);
```

```
    // Assert the magic link was deleted after use.
    $this->assertDatabaseMissing('magic_links', [
        'token' => $token,
    ]);

    // Assert that the user is now authenticated.
    $this->assertAuthenticatedAs($user);
}

/**
 * Test that an expired magic link does not allow login.
 */
public function test_expired_magic_link_fails_login()
{
    // Create a user.
    $user = User::factory()->create([
        'email' => 'expired@example.com',
    ]);

    // Create an expired magic link token.
    $token    = 'expired-token';
    $expiresAt = Carbon::now()->subMinutes(1);

    MagicLink::create([
        'user_id'    => $user->id,
        'token'      => $token,
        'expires_at' => $expiresAt,
    ]);

    // Attempt to log in with the expired token.
    $response = $this->get('/login/' . $token);

    // Assert a 401 Unauthorized response.
    $response->assertStatus(401)
        ->assertJson([
            'message' => 'Invalid or expired link.',
        ]);
```

```
        // Ensure the expired magic link still exists in the database.
        $this->assertDatabaseHas('magic_links', [
            'token' => $token,
        ]);
    }
}
```

This list explains the code in Listing 5-25:

1. **Using** RefreshDatabase: The RefreshDatabase trait resets the database between tests for a clean slate.

2. **Faking mail**: Using Mail::fake() prevents actual emails from being sent during the test, while allowing you to assert that an email was queued.

3. **Magic Link request**: The first test submits a JSON POST request to /request-link and then checks that a user and magic link are present in the database and that the mail was queued.

4. **Valid Magic Link login**: The second test manually creates a valid Magic Link record. It then sends a GET request to /login/{token}, checks the JSON response, ensures the Magic Link is deleted after use, and confirms that the user is authenticated.

5. **Expired Magic Link**: The third test creates a Magic Link record with an expired timestamp. A GET request with that token should return a 401 response and the record remains in the database.

This test suite ensures that your Magic Link system behaves as expected.

Setting Up Your Testing Environment

Make sure your .env.testing file (or your test environment settings) is configured properly and run any pending migrations if necessary. See the Artisan command in **Listing 5-26**.

Listing 5-26. Running Any Pending Migrations

```
php artisan migrate --env=testing
```

Running the Tests

Execute your tests from the terminal while in your project folder, using the Artisan command in Listing 5-27.

Listing 5-27. Artisan Command for Running Tests

```
php artisan test
```

Running the Artisan command in Listing 5-27 will produce output similar to Figure 5-13 if the test is successful.

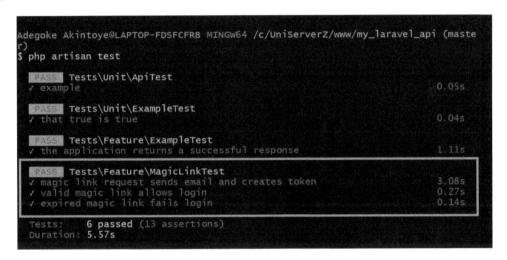

Figure 5-13. *Typical command-line output for running the feature test specified in Listing 5-27*

Enhancing Security and Performance

This section contains suggestions on how to make the Magic Link system more secure and perform more efficiently.

Utilizing UUIDs for Primary Keys

Using Universally Unique Identifiers (UUIDs) as primary keys instead of auto-incrementing integers can enhance security by making it more difficult for malicious users to predict resource identifiers.

Queuing Emails for Asynchronous Processing

Sending emails synchronously can slow down your application, leading to a poor user experience. Laravel 11's built-in queue system allows you to send emails asynchronously, enhancing performance.

Committing Your Changes

Commit your changes to Git by running the command in Listing 5-28.

Listing 5-28. Comitting Your Changes

```
git add . && git commit -m "Chapter 5"
```

Conclusion

In this chapter, you started building the API that mimics a payment processor platform. You learned what a payment processor API is and then learned how the API you build in this book will handle payments. Finally, you put in place the user authentication system called Magic Link.

In the next chapter, you'll continue building this project.

## CHAPTER 6

Implementing Endpoints and Generating Documentation

In the last chapter, you put in place the Magic Link authentication system. It allows your API users to log in to the API dashboard using just their email without the need for password. You also put in place a dashboard for your API users. In this chapter, you'll start building the Payment Processor API. You will implement the API models, migration files, controllers, and routes. You'll also learn about Scramble, which is used for documentation generation and basic API testing.

Note The source code for this book is available on GitHub via the book's product page, located at `https://github.com/Apress/API-Development-with-Laravel`.

Creating Models and Migrations

You'll start by creating four new models—`Transaction`, `Payment`, `BankDetail`, `Setting`, and `Withdrawal`—and you'll also modify the `User` model. To create these models and their migration files, run the Artisan command in Listing 6-1.

Tip To run the following command, you may have to press the Enter key twice.

© Adegoke Akintoye 2025
A. Akintoye, *API Development with Laravel*, https://doi.org/10.1007/979-8-8688-1576-8_6

Listing 6-1. Creating Four New Models

```
php artisan make:model BankDetail -m;\
php artisan make:model Transaction -m;\
php artisan make:model Payment -m;\
php artisan make:model Withdrawal -m;\
php artisan make:model Setting -m;\
```

The -m flag automatically generates a migration file for each model. Models represent the data and business logic, while migration, also called the database schema, specifies the database table and its components. Running the command in Listing 6-1 will create the following model files inside your Laravel project folder:

1. app/Models/BankDetail.php

2. app/Models/Transaction.php

3. app/Models/Payment.php

4. app/Models/Setting.php

5. app/Models/Withdrawal.php

In addition, the following corresponding migration files will be generated for you.

1. database/migrations/xxxx_xx_xx_xxxxxx_create_bank_
   details_table.php

2. database/migrations/xxxx_xx_xx_xxxxxx_create_
   transactions_table.php

3. database/migrations/xxxx_xx_xx_xxxxxx_create_payments_
   table.php

4. database/migrations/xxxx_xx_xx_xxxxxx_create_settings_
   table.php

5. database/migrations/xxxx_xx_xx_xxxxxx_create_
   withdrawals_table.php

Next, you learn to update these files.

Updating the Migration Files

This section explains how to update the migration files generated in the last section.

The BankDetail Migration File

This migration file contains the instructions for creating the bank_details database table. This table contains data needed for withdrawals to be made from accumulated payments received by the API users via their website or app. Open the file and modify it as shown in Listing 6-2.

Listing 6-2. The BankDetail Migration File Modifications

```php
<?php

/*database/migrations/xxxx_xx_xx_xxxxxx_create_bank_details_table.php*/

use Illuminate\Database\Migrations\Migration;
use Illuminate\Database\Schema\Blueprint;
use Illuminate\Support\Facades\Schema;

return new class extends Migration
{
    /**
     * Run the migrations.
     */
    public function up(): void
    {
        Schema::create('bank_details', function (Blueprint $table) {
            $table->id();
            $table->foreignId('user_id')->constrained()-
            >onDelete('cascade');
            $table->string('iban')->nullable();
            $table→string('swift')->nullable();
            $table->timestamps();
        });
    }
```

```php
/**
 * Reverse the migrations.
 */
public function down(): void
{
    Schema::dropIfExists('bank_details');
}
};
```

As you can see, this code has added some new columns:

1. The user_id field will hold the ID of the user who owns the bank details.

2. The iban field will contain the International Bank Account Number (IBAN) of the merchant.

3. The swift field stores the Bank Identifier Code (BIC) of the merchant.

The Transaction Migration File

The Transaction migration file is used to create the Transactions database table. This table contains data that describes each initiated payment transaction. Open the file and modify it as shown in **Listing 6-3**.

Listing 6-3. The Transaction Migration File Modifications

```php
<?php

/*database/migrations/xxxx_xx_xx_xxxxxx_create_transactions_table.php*/

use Illuminate\Database\Migrations\Migration;
use Illuminate\Database\Schema\Blueprint;
use Illuminate\Support\Facades\Schema;

return new class extends Migration
{
    /**
     * Run the migrations.
     */
```

```php
public function up(): void
{
    Schema::create('transactions', function (Blueprint $table) {
        $table->id();
        $table->foreignId('user_id')->constrained()->
        onDelete('cascade');
        $table->uuid('transaction_ref')->unique();
        $table->string('email', 150);
        $table->string('currency', 5);
        $table->string('redirect_url', 500);
        $table->decimal('amount', 10, 2);
        $table->decimal('fee', 10, 2)->default(0.00);
        $table->string('status', 15)->default('pending');
        $table->boolean('pass_charge');
        $table->timestamps();
    });
}

/**
 * Reverse the migrations.
 */
public function down(): void
{
    Schema::dropIfExists('transactions');
}
};
```

The Payment Migration File

The Payment table stores the payment method (e.g., credit card) used in making payment as well as the payment status. You'll use the Payment migration file to create the Payments table. Open the file and modify it as shown in Listing 6-4.

Listing 6-4. The Payment Migration File Modifications

```php
<?php

/*database/migrations/xxxx_xx_xx_xxxxxx_create_payments_table.php*/

use Illuminate\Database\Migrations\Migration;
use Illuminate\Database\Schema\Blueprint;
use Illuminate\Support\Facades\Schema;

return new class extends Migration
{
    /**
     * Run the migrations.
     */
    public function up(): void
    {
        Schema::create('payments', function (Blueprint $table) {
            $table->id();
            $table->uuid('transaction_id');
            $table->foreign('transaction_id')
            ->references('transaction_ref')
            ->on('transactions')
            ->onDelete('cascade');
            //$table->foreignId('transaction_id')->constrained()->
            onDelete('cascade');
            $table->string('payment_method');
            $table->string('payment_status')->default('pending');
            $table->timestamps();
        });
    }

    /**
     * Reverse the migrations.
     */
    public function down(): void
    {
        Schema::dropIfExists('payments');
```

```
    }
};
```

The Withdrawals Migration File

Lastly, you need to update the Withdrawals migration file to create the `Withdrawals` table. The `Withdrawals` table records when a user withdraws funds. Open the withdrawals migration file and modify it as shown in Listing 6-5a.

Listing 6-5a. The Withdrawals Migration File Modifications

```php
<?php

//database/migrations/xxxx_xx_xx_xxxxxx_create_withdrawals_table.php

use Illuminate\Database\Migrations\Migration;
use Illuminate\Database\Schema\Blueprint;
use Illuminate\Support\Facades\Schema;

return new class extends Migration
{
    /**
     * Run the migrations.
     */
    public function up(): void
    {
        Schema::create('withdrawals', function (Blueprint $table) {
            $table->id();
            $table->foreignId('user_id')->constrained()-
            >onDelete('cascade');
            $table->decimal('amount', 10, 2);
            $table->string('status')->default('pending');
            $table->timestamps();
        });
    }

    /**
     * Reverse the migrations.
     */
```

```
    public function down(): void
    {
        Schema::dropIfExists('withdrawals');
    }
};
```

The Settings Migration File

This migration file contains the instruction for creating the Settings database table. This table contains data like webhook URLs, webhook secrets, and so on. (Webhooks are discussed in Chapter 8.). Open the file and modify it as shown in Listing 6-5b.

Listing 6-5b. The Settings Migration File Modifications

```php
<?php

/*database/migrations/xxxx_xx_xx_xxxxxx_create_settings_table.php*/

use Illuminate\Database\Migrations\Migration;
use Illuminate\Database\Schema\Blueprint;
use Illuminate\Support\Facades\Schema;

return new class extends Migration
{
    /**
     * Run the migrations.
     */
    public function up(): void
    {
        Schema::create('settings', function (Blueprint $table) {
            $table->id();
            $table->foreignId('user_id')->constrained()-
            >onDelete('cascade');
            $table->string('webhook_url')->nullable();
            $table->string('webhook_secret')->nullable();
            $table->timestamps();
        });
    }
```

```
    /**
     * Reverse the migrations.
     */
    public function down(): void
    {
        Schema::dropIfExists('settings');
    }
};
```

Next, run the command shown in Listing 6-5c to execute the instructions in the added migration files so that the corresponding tables can be created.

Listing 6-5c. Artisan Command to Execute the Instructions in the Migration Files

```
php artisan migrate
```

Running the Artisan command in Listing 6-5c will create the bank_details, transactions, payments, settings, and withdrawals database tables.

Setting Up Model Relationships

In this section, you'll be modifying the model files generated earlier to achieve the API's objective.

The BankDetail Model

This model can be used to access and manipulate the bank_details table. To modify the model, open the file and make the changes indicated in bold in Listing 6-6.

Listing 6-6. Modifying the BankDetail Model

```
<?php
```

//app/Models/BankDetail.php

```
namespace App\Models;
```

```
use Illuminate\Database\Eloquent\Model;
```

```php
class BankDetail extends Model
{
    /**
     * The attributes that are mass assignable.
     *
     * @var list<string>
     */
    protected $fillable = [
        'user_id',
        'iban',
        'swift',
    ];

    public function user()
    {
        return $this->belongsTo(User::class);
    }   //
}
```

The Transaction Model

This model makes it possible to create, retrieve, or update a transaction in the Transactions table. Open the Transaction model file and make the changes in bold in shown Listing 6-7.

Listing 6-7. Modifying the Transaction Model

```php
<?php

//app/Models/Transaction.php

namespace App\Models;

use Illuminate\Database\Eloquent\Factories\HasFactory;
use Illuminate\Database\Eloquent\Model;

class Transaction extends Model
{
```

```php
use HasFactory;

protected $fillable = [
    'user_id',
    'amount',
    'fee',
    'status',
    'transaction_ref',
    'email',
    'currency',
    'redirect_url',
    'pass_charge',
];

/**
 * The attributes that should be hidden for serialization.
 *
 * @var list<string>
 */
protected $hidden = [
    'id',
    'user_id',
    'checkout_url',
];

// Each transaction belongs to a user
public function user()
{
    return $this->belongsTo(User::class);
}

// Each transaction has one payment
public function payment()
{
    return $this->hasOne(Payment::class);
}
}
```

The Payment Model

This model makes it possible to create, retrieve, or update a payment in the Payments table. Open the Payment model file and make the changes in bold shown in Listing 6-8.

Listing 6-8. Modifying the Payment Model

```php
<?php

//app/Models/Payment.php

namespace App\Models;

use Illuminate\Database\Eloquent\Factories\HasFactory;
use Illuminate\Database\Eloquent\Model;

class Payment extends Model
{
    use HasFactory;

    protected $fillable = [
        'transaction_id',
        'payment_method',
        'payment_status',
        'transaction_ref',
    ];

    // A payment belongs to a transaction
    public function transaction()
    {
        return $this->belongsTo(Transaction::class);
    }
}
```

The Withdrawal Model

This model makes it possible to create, retrieve, or update withdrawals in the Withdrawal table. Open the Withdrawal model file and make the changes in bold shown in Listing 6-9a.

Listing 6-9a. Modifying the Withdrawal Model

```php
<?php

//app/Models/Withdrawal.php

namespace App\Models;

use Illuminate\Database\Eloquent\Factories\HasFactory;
use Illuminate\Database\Eloquent\Model;

class Withdrawal extends Model
{
    use HasFactory;

    protected $fillable = [
        'user_id',
        'amount',
        'status',
    ];

    // A withdrawal belongs to a user
    public function user()
    {
        return $this->belongsTo(User::class);
    }
}
```

The Setting Model

This model makes it possible to create, retrieve, or update settings data in the Setting table. Open the Setting model file and update it to reflect the code in Listing 6-9b.

Listing 6-9b. Modifying the Setting Model

```php
<?php

//app/Models/Setting.php

namespace App\Models;

use Illuminate\Database\Eloquent\Model;
```

```php
class Setting extends Model
{
    /**
     * The attributes that are mass assignable.
     *
     * @var list<string>
     */
    protected $fillable = [
        'user_id',
        'webhook_url',
        'webhook_secret',
    ];

    public function user()
    {
        return $this->belongsTo(User::class);
    }
}
```

Creating Payment Status Email Pages

For every successful payment, you need to email the merchant into whose account
the money was paid. You'll also need to send an email to the customer who made the
payment to acknowledge the receipt of their payment. This section explains how to
create the blade files that'll serve as the template for these email messages. These blade
files use the base email blade file (`resources/views/emails/base.blade.php`) that you
created in Chapter 5 (see Listing 5-21a).

Creating the Success Email Page for the Merchant

Whenever a merchant is paid, you'll use the blade file in Listing 6-9c to notify the
merchant of the successful payment.

Listing 6-9c. Blade File That Notifies the Merchant about a Successful Payment

```
<!--resources/views/emails/success-merchant.blade.php-->
@extends('emails.base')
@section('title','Payment Notification')
@section('subject', $subject)
@section('content')
            <tr>
              <td style="padding: 30px; color: #333333;">
                <p style="font-size: 16px;">Hi, {{$email}}<p>
                <p style="font-size: 16px;">
                  You just received a payment of <b> USD{{$amount}}</
                  b>.<br><br>
                  <b>Reference ID:</b> {{$refid}}<br><br>
                  <em><b>Note</b>: Please verify the payment before giving
                  value</em>
                </p>
                <p style="text-align: center; margin: 30px 0;">
                  <a href="{{ route('do.auth') }}" style="background-
                  color: #007BFF; color: #ffffff; padding: 14px 28px; text-
                  decoration: none; border-
                  radius: 6px; display: inline-block; font-weight: bold;">
                    Visit Your Dashboard
                  </a>
                </p>
                <p style="font-size: 14px; color: #666;">
                  If you have any question, please feel free to contact us:
                  merchant.emquiry@dexypay.com
                </p>
              </td>
            </tr>
@endsection
```

You specify the base blade file using the @extend keyword. Likewise, the @section keyword is used to specify the data to be passed to the base blade file.

Creating the Success Email Page for the Customer

To notify a customer that their payment was received, you'll use the blade file in Listing 6-9d .

Listing 6-9d. Blade File That Tells Customers Their Payment Was Received

```
<!--resources/views/emails/success-customer.blade.php-->
@extends('emails.base')
@section('title','Payment Receipt Notification')
@section('subject', $subject)
@section('content')
        <tr>
         <td style="padding: 30px; color: #333333;">
           <p style="font-size: 16px;">Hi, {{$email}}<p>
           <p style="font-size: 16px;">
             You have successfully made a payment of <b>
             USD{{$amount}}</b>.<br><br>
             <b>Reference ID:</b> {{$refid}}<br><br>
           </p>
           <p style="font-size: 14px; color: #666;">
             If you have any question, please feel free to contact us:
             payments.emquiry@dexypay.com
           </p>
         </td>
        </tr>
  @endsection
```

Here too, the base blade file is specified by using the @extend keyword. The data to be passed to the base blade file is also specified using the @section keyword.

Creating the Payment Form and Related Pages

Whenever a customer, using a website or app connected to the API, wants to make a payment, you can expect the website or app to send details about the payment to the API in order to initiate the payment. After receiving the payment details, you'll need to initialize the payment and store the payment details on the server. You'll then need to send a payment link (URL), among other data, back to the website or app. When the customer visits the link, it will open a payment page, where they can enter credit card details and pay. In addition to this payment page, you also need a page that will display the outcome (status) of a payment attempt. In this section, you'll be building these two pages.

Creating the Payment Form Page

The code in Listing 6-9e represents the contents of the blade file for the payment form to be used for making payments.

Note   The blade file in this section is based on the library called `payment-bank-card` and is available at `https://github.com/adnanelamghari/payment-bank-card`.

Listing 6-9e. Blade File for the Payment Form

```
<!--resources/views/payment/form.blade.php-->
<!DOCTYPE html>
<html>
<head>
 <title>Dexy Pay - Payment Form</title>
 <meta charset="utf-8">
 <meta content="width=device-width, initial-scale=1" name="viewport">
    <meta content="ie=edge" http-equiv="x-ua-compatible">

    <!-- STYLE TO IMPORT TO YOUR PROJECT -->
    <link href="{{ asset('css/paytForm/bank-card.css') }}"
    rel="stylesheet">
    <!-- STYLE TO IMPORT TO YOUR PROJECT -->

</head>
<style>
```

```
.centered-div {
    width:320px;
    margin-right: auto;
    margin-left: auto;

}
    </style>
<body>

<div  class="centered-div" >
<img alt=""   class="" src="{{ asset('img/payment/dexypay.
png')}}"  style="width:320px; height:auto; margin-right: auto;
    margin-left: auto; ">

<div  class="card">

    <p  align="center" style="color:blue; ">You Are About To Make A Payment
    To <b>{{$email}}</b></p>
    <h3  align="center" >Amount: <em style="color:green; ">USD @
    if(isset($amount)){{number_format($amount,2)}} @else 10,000 @endif</
    em></h3>
    <p  align="center" >To complete this payment, Please enter your payment
    details below and click the PAY button</p></br>
    </div>

<!-- PART TO COPY TO YOUR PROJECT -->
<div class="card">
    <div class="card-front card-part" id="card-front">
        <img alt="" class="card-front-square card-square" src="{{
        asset('assets/icons/sim-card-chip.png')}}">
        <img alt="" class="card-front-square card-square" src="{{
        asset('assets/icons/contactless-payment-white.png')}}"/>
        <img alt="" class="card-front-logo card-logo" src="{{
        asset('assets/logos/22.svg')}}">
        <p class="card-number" id="card-number">**** **** **** ****</p>
        <div class="card-space-75">
            <span class="card-label">Card holder</span>
```

```
            <p class="card-info" id="card-holder">Your name here</p>
        </div>
        <div class="card-space-25">
            <span class="card-label">Expires</span>
            <p class="card-info" id="card-expires-date">**/**</p>
        </div>
    </div>

    <div class="card-back card-part" id="card-back">
        <div class="card-black-line"></div>
        <div class="card-back-content">
            <div class="card-secret">
                <p class="card-secret--last" id="card-secret-cvc">***</p>
            </div>
            <img alt="" class="card-back-logo card-logo" src="{{
            asset('assets/logos/22.svg')}}">
        </div>
    </div>
</div>
</div>
<div>
    <form action="/api/v1/payment/charge" method = "post">
        @csrf
        <div class="row">
            <label>Card holder :</label>
            <input id="card-holder-input" placeholder="Card holder name"
            type="text"  name="card_name" required>
            @error('card_name'){{$message}}@enderror
        </div>
        <div class="row">
            <label>Card number :</label>
            <input id="card-number-input" maxlength="19" minlength="19"
            placeholder="Card number" type="text"  name="card_num"
            required>
            @error('card_num'){{$message}}@enderror

        </div>
```

```
<div class="row">
    <div class="col-50">
        <label>Expires :</label>
        <input id="card-expires-date-input" max="1299"
        maxlength="5" minlength="5" placeholder="Expires"
                type="text"  name="card_exp" required>
                @error('card_exp'){{$message}}@enderror

    </div>
    <div class="col-50">
        <label>CVC :</label>
        <input id="card-secret-cvc-input" max="999" maxlength="4"
        min="100" minlength="4" placeholder="CVC"
                type="text" name="card_secret" required>
                @error('card_secret'){{$message}}@enderror

    </div>
</div>

<input type="hidden" value="card" name="payment_method" />
<input type="hidden" value="@if(isset($amount)){{$amount}} @endif"
name="amount" />
<input type="hidden" value="@if(isset($transaction_ref))
{{$transaction_ref}} @endif" name="transaction_ref" />
<input type="hidden" value="USD" name="currency_code" />
<input type="hidden" value="0" name="direct_charge" />

@error('payment_method'){{$message}}@enderror
@error('amount'){{$message}}@enderror
@error('transaction_ref'){{$message}}@enderror
@error('currency_code'){{$message}}@enderror

</br>
    <div class="row">
        <input id="submit" value="PAY" type="submit">
    </div>

</form>
```

```
</div>
<!-- PART TO COPY TO YOUR PROJECT -->

<!-- SCRIPT TO IMPORT TO YOUR PROJECT -->
<script src="{{ asset('js/paytForm/bank-card.js')}}"></script>

<!-- SCRIPT TO IMPORT TO YOUR PROJECT -->

</div>
</body>
</html>
```

Note the following:

1. The Laravel asset() method loads the CSS, JavaScript, and image files.

2. The @csrf directive is used to prevent cross-site request forgery.

3. The @if directives are used to make logical decisions.

4. The @error directives are used to display form input validation errors.

5. The form is submitted to the /api/v1/payment/charge endpoint of the API.

Creating the Payment Status (Success or Failure) Page

The code in Listing 6-9f represents the contents of the blade file for the payment status page.

Listing 6-9f. The Blade File for the Payment Status Page

```
<!--resources/views/payment/status.blade.php-→
<!DOCTYPE html>
<html>
<head>
    <title>Dexy Pay - Payment Status</title>
    <meta charset="utf-8">
    <meta content="width=device-width, initial-scale=1" name="viewport">
    <meta content="ie=edge" http-equiv="x-ua-compatible">
```

```html
    <!-- STYLE TO IMPORT TO YOUR PROJECT -->
    <link href=" " rel="stylesheet">
    <!-- STYLE TO IMPORT TO YOUR PROJECT -->

</head>
<body>
    <style>
    .centered{
        width:400px;
        margin-left:auto;
        margin-right:auto;

    }
    .gif{
width:1oo%;
    }
    .text-centered{

    }
    </style>

<div  class = "centered">
    @if($status === "successful")
    <img class = "gif" src="{{asset('img/payment/tx_success.gif')}}"  alt =
    "Payment successful">
    <h3 class = ""  align-"center"> Please wait while you are being
    redirected .......</h3>
    @elseif($status === "failed")
    <img class = "gif" src="{{asset('img/payment/tx_failed.gif')}}"  alt =
    "Payment failed"><br>
    <h2  onclick="history.back()"  align="center" >Retry</h2>
    @endif
</div>
<script>
    @if($status === "successful")
    setTimeout(
        function(){
```

```
        window.location.replace(
            "{{$redirect_url}}"
        )
    },
    10000
  )
  @endif
</script>

</body>
</html>
```

Implementing the PaymentMail Mailable Class

Next you'll create a mailable class to send email to the merchant when they are paid and to the paying customer to acknowledge receipt of the payment. To create this class, run the command in **Listing 6-9g**, from the command-line.

Listing 6-9g. Command to Create the Mailable Class

```
php artisan make:mail PaymentMail
```

Open the file (app/Mail/PaymentMail.php) that's generated when you run the command in Listing 6-9g and update its contents to that shown in Listing 6-9h.

Listing 6-9h. Updating the app/Mail/PaymentMail.php File

```php
<?php

//app/Mail/PaymentMail.php
namespace App\Mail;

use Illuminate\Bus\Queueable;
use Illuminate\Mail\Mailable;
use Illuminate\Queue\SerializesModels;

class PaymentMail extends Mailable
```

```php
{
 use Queueable, SerializesModels;

 /**
 * Create a new message instance.
 */
 public function __construct(public $mailData)
 {
 //
 }

 public function build()
 {
 \Log::info("maildata: " . json_encode($this->mailData));

 return $this->subject($this->mailData['subject'])
 ->view($this->mailData['mailView'])
 ->with([
 'subject' => $this->mailData['subject'],
 'amount'  => $this->mailData['amount'],
 'refid'   => $this->mailData['refid'],
 'email'   => $this->mailData['email'],
 ]);
 }
}
```

An instance of this class will be created and passed an array containing the required data whenever you want to send email to the merchant or the customer.

Implementing Controllers

This section explains how to start implementing the controllers that'll power the payment API. However, since controllers hold the key to the API documentation, you'll first need to see how to write them in order to generate good documentation. To document the API, you'll be using a tool called Scramble. The next section takes a quick look at Scramble.

An Introduction to Scramble

API documentation is crucial for ensuring developers understand how to interact with your application's endpoints. However, documenting an API can be a tedious task when done manually. Scramble is a package that simplifies the process by automatically generating documentation from your Laravel codebase. It extracts route details, validation rules, sample responses, and more to produce a clear, interactive, and human-friendly documentation. Scramble is designed to work seamlessly with Laravel by reading your routes, controllers, form requests, and more.

In addition to being used as a tool for API documentation, Scramble can also be used for basic API testing.

Compared to most tools of its kind, Scramble is easy to use. It produces documentation that's both functional and good to look at. You can learn more about **Scramble** at `https://scramble.dedoc.co`. The next section walks you through how to set up Scramble and tailor it to your needs.

Installation and Setup

Scramble requires Laravel 10+ and PHP8.1+. To install Scramble, run the command shown in Listing 6-10.

Tip   Keep your Internet on while running this command.

Listing 6-10. Command to Install Scramble

```
composer require dedoc/scramble
```

Running the command in Listing 6-10 will create and add two new routes to your application, as listed here:

1. `/docs/api`: Visit this route to view the generated API documentation.

2. `/docs/api.json`: Visit this route to get a JSON description of your API in line with the Open API specification.

Publishing the Configuration

In order to customize Scramble, you need to create (publish) its configuration file, which you can do by running the Artisan command in Listing 6-11.

Tip   Keep your Internet on while running this command.

Listing 6-11. Artisan Command to Publish Scramble's Configuration File

```
php artisan vendor:publish --provider="Dedoc\Scramble\
ScrambleServiceProvider" --tag="scramble-config"
```

The command in Listing 6-11 creates the `scramble.php` file in your `config` directory, where you can adjust various options for your documentation.

Configuring Scramble

Open the `config/scramble.php` file created in the last section. Set your API's title, description, version number, and the URL of the logo for your documentation, as shown in Listing 6-12.

Listing 6-12. Configuring Scramble

```php
<?php

//config/scramble.php

use Dedoc\Scramble\Http\Middleware\RestrictedDocsAccess;

return [
    /*
     * Your API path. By default, all routes starting with this path will
     be added to the docs.
     * If you need to change this behavior, you can add your custom routes
     resolver using 'Scramble::routes()'.
     */
    'api_path'                          => 'api/v1',

    /*
```

```
 * Your API domain. By default, app domain is used. This is also a part
 of the default API routes
 * matcher, so when implementing your own, make sure you use this
 config if needed.
 */
'api_domain'                        => null,

/*
 * The path where your OpenAPI specification will be exported.
 */
'export_path'                       => 'api.json',

'info'                              => [
    /*
     * API version.
     */
    'version'     => env('API_VERSION', '0.0.1'),

    /*
     * Description rendered on the home page of the API documentation
     ('/docs/api').
     */
    'description' => 'DexyPay API enables merchants to collect payments
    from their customers via their website, web apps, mobile apps,
    desktop apps etc.',
],

/*
 * Customize Stoplight Elements UI
 */
'ui'                                => [
    /*
     * Define the title of the documentation's website. App name is
     used when this config is 'null'.
     */
    'title'                        => 'DexyPay API',

    /*
```

```
 * Define the theme of the documentation. Available options are
 'light' and 'dark'.
 */
'theme'                      => 'light',

/*
 * Hide the 'Try It' feature. Enabled by default.
 */
'hide_try_it'                => false,

/*
 * Hide the schemas in the Table of Contents. Enabled by default.
 */
'hide_schemas'               => false,

/*
 * URL to an image that displays as a small square logo next to the
 title, above the table of contents.
 */
'logo'                       => '/img/payment/dexypay_square.png',

/*
 * Use to fetch the credential policy for the Try It feature.
 Options are: omit, include (default), and same-origin
 */
'try_it_credentials_policy' => 'include',

/*
 * There are three layouts for Elements:
 * - sidebar - (Elements default) Three-column design with a
 sidebar that can be resized.
 * - responsive - Like sidebar, except at small screen sizes it
 collapses the sidebar into a drawer that can be toggled open.
 * - stacked - Everything in a single column, making integrations
 with existing websites that have their own sidebar or other
 columns already.
 */
```

```php
    'layout'                        => 'responsive',
],

/*
 * The list of servers of the API. By default, when 'null', server URL
will be created from
 * 'scramble.api_path' and 'scramble.api_domain' config variables. When
providing an array, you
 * will need to specify the local server URL manually (if needed).
 *
 * Example of non-default config (final URLs are generated using
Laravel 'url' helper):
 *
 * '''php
 * 'servers' => [
 *     'Live' => 'api',
 *     'Prod' => 'https://scramble.dedoc.co/api',
 * ],
 * '''
 */
'servers'                        => null,

/**
 * Determines how Scramble stores the descriptions of enum cases.
 * Available options:
 * - 'description' – Case descriptions are stored as the enum schema's
description using table formatting.
 * - 'extension' – Case descriptions are stored in the
'x-enumDescriptions' enum schema extension.
 *
 *    @see https://redocly.com/docs-legacy/api-reference-docs/
specification-extensions/x-enum-descriptions
 * - false - Case descriptions are ignored.
 */
'enum_cases_description_strategy' => 'description',

'middleware'                     => [
```

```
        'web',
        RestrictedDocsAccess::class,
    ],

    'extensions'                      => [],
];
```

Here is a brief description of the values that changed in the Scramble configuration file in Listing 6-12:

1. api_path: This is the path to the controllers that Scramble will use to generate the documentation. Only controllers in this path will be documented. Here, it's set to api/v1, which the location of the API controllers.

2. version: This specifies the current version of the API. I left it at 0.0.1 as we are in the first version of this API.

3. title: A short description of the API. Here, I set it to DexyPay API.

4. description: This is a detailed description of the API compared to its title. It is a summary of what it's about.

5. logo: The path to the logo you want to use for the API.

Figures 6-1 and 6-2 show how the changes look on the generated documentation. For now, the default value of the other configuration parameters will suffice.

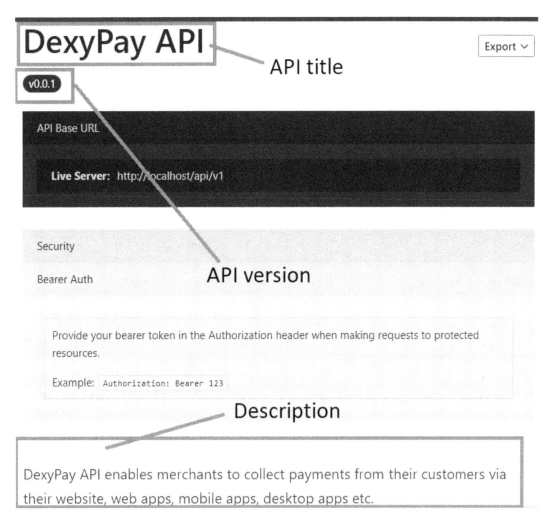

Figure 6-1. *The home page of the generated documentation using Scramble*

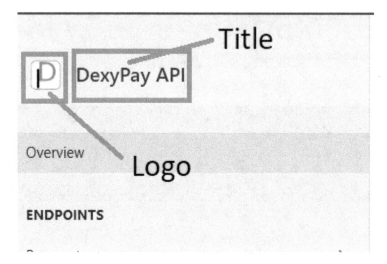

Figure 6-2. *The logo and title added via Scramble's configuration file on the documentation*

Configuring a Bearer Token for Authentication (Using Sanctum)

Since your API will use Laravel Sanctum token-based authentication, you need to tell Scramble about this. To do this, navigate to the app/Providers/ folder and open the AppServiceProvider.php file. Make the changes shown in bold in Listing 6-13. It is worth noting that other authentication methods, like JWT, OAuth, and so on, can also be configured. See Scramble's documentation for more on this.

Listing 6-13. Modifying the AppServiceProvider.php File

```php
<?php

//app/Providers/AppServiceProvider.php

namespace App\Providers;

use Dedoc\Scramble\Scramble;
use Dedoc\Scramble\Support\Generator\OpenApi;
use Dedoc\Scramble\Support\Generator\SecurityScheme;
use Illuminate\Support\ServiceProvider;

class AppServiceProvider extends ServiceProvider
{
    /**
```

```
 * Register any application services.
 */
public function register(): void
{
    //
}

/**
 * Bootstrap any application services.
 */
public function boot(): void
{
    Scramble::configure()
        ->withDocumentTransformers(function (OpenApi $openApi) {
            $openApi->secure(
                SecurityScheme::http('bearer')
            );
        });
}
}
```

Once you make the changes indicated in Listing 6-13, Scramble will document all the endpoints as requiring authentication. However, by using the @unauthenticated annotation, any route that does not use authentication can be exempted. Information about authentication and the type or form required is displayed on the documentation, as shown in Figure 6-3. Endpoints requiring authentication will have this indicated on their documentation too, as you'll see later.

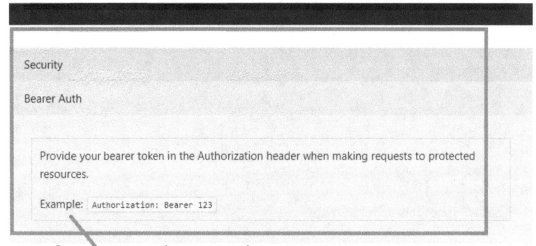

Information about authentication

Figure 6-3. *The part of the documentation that displays information concerning endpoint's authentication*

Enhancing the Generated Documentation

In most cases, Scramble can generate decent API documentation without requiring you to manually annotate or comment your code. However, there are instances when using some annotations and comments can make the generated document more comprehensive.

This section explores the use of annotations, attributes, and comments for enhancing your API documentation even further. The first section looks at examples of how you might enhance the generated documentation.

Enhancing the Documentation of a Method

The code in Listing 6-14 shows a method without any comments or annotation added and Figure 6-4 shows the corresponding generated documentation for the method.

Listing 6-14. A Method Without Comments or Annotation

```php
<?php

namespace App\Http\Controllers\Api\V1;

use App\Http\Controllers\Controller;
use App\Models\Book;
use Illuminate\Http\Request;

class BookController extends Controller
{
    public function create(Request $request)
    {
        // Validate input.
        $request->validate([
            'title'  => 'required|string|min:1|max:150',
            'author' => 'required|string|min:1|max:150',
            'price'  => 'required|decimal:2|max:1000000000',
        ]);

        $book = Book::create([
            'title'  => $request->title,
            'author' => $request->author,
            'price'  => $request->price,
        ]);

        return response()->json([
            'status'  => 201,
            'message' => 'successful',
            'data'    => $book,

        ], 201);
    }
}
```

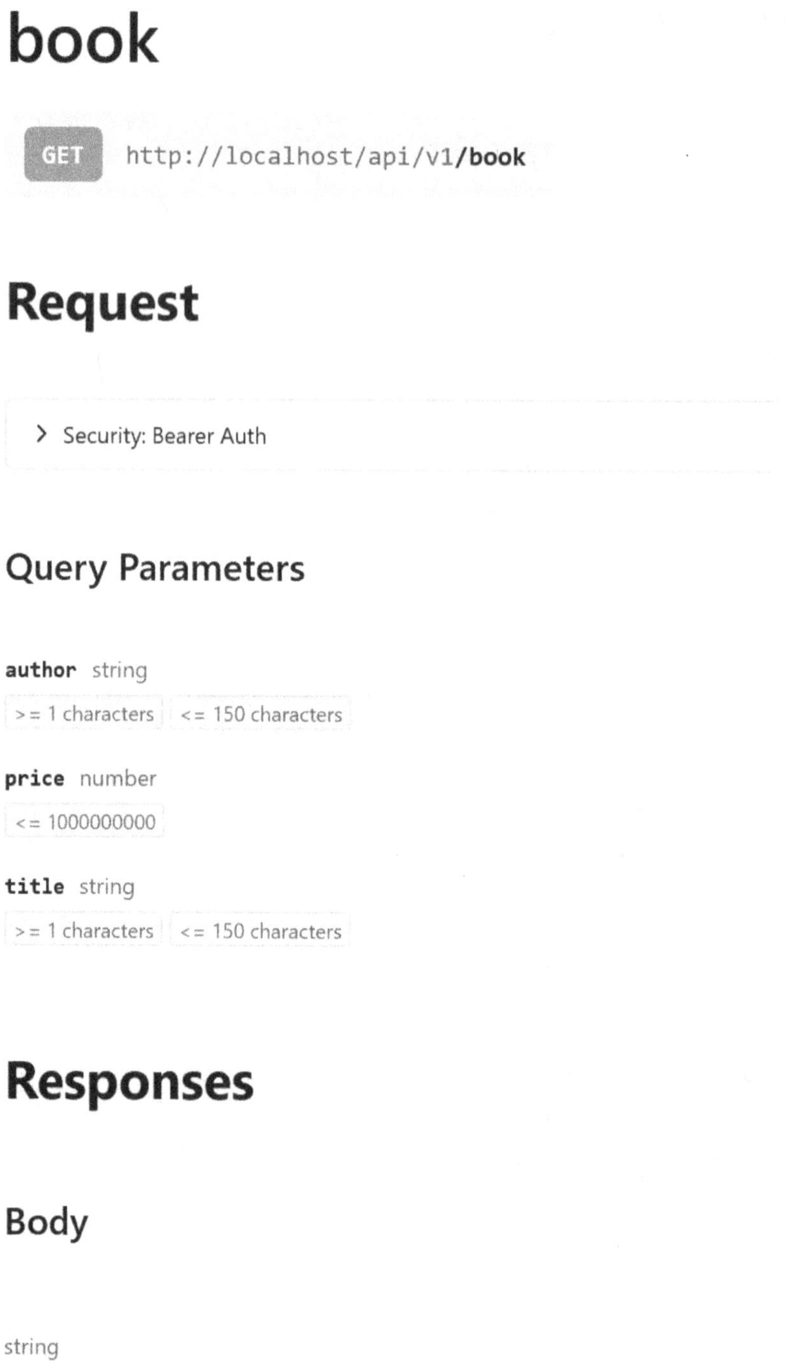

book

`GET`   `http://localhost/api/v1/book`

Request

> Security: Bearer Auth

Query Parameters

author string

| >= 1 characters | <= 150 characters |

price number

| <= 1000000000 |

title string

| >= 1 characters | <= 150 characters |

Responses

Body

string

Figure 6-4. *The documentation showing information about an endpoint with no annotation*

The same method is shown in Listing 6-15, but this time, it includes some comments and annotations. Figures 6-5a and 6-5b show the corresponding generated documentation (the figure has been split into two parts for proper display). As you can see, adding just a few lines of comments and annotation to the code enhances the documentation even further.

Listing 6-15. A Method with Comments and Annotations Added

```php
<?php

namespace App\Http\Controllers\Api\V1;

use App\Http\Controllers\Controller;
use App\Models\Book;
use Illuminate\Http\Request;

class BookController extends Controller
{
    /**
     * Creates a book
     *
     * Creates and adds a book to the database
     *
     */
    public function create(Request $request)
    {
        // Validate input.
        $request->validate([
            //The book's title. Example: Laravel API Development
            'title'  => 'required|string|min:1|max:150',
            //The author's full-name. Example: Adegoke Akintoye
            'author' => 'required|string|min:1|max:150',
```

```
    //The book's price. Example: 149.99
    'price'  => 'required|decimal:2|max:1000000000',
]);

$book = Book::create([
    'title'  => $request->title,
    'author' => $request->author,
    'price'  => $request->price,
]);
//Returns the created book
return response()->json([
    'status'  => 201,
    'message' => 'successful',
    // @body Book
    'data'     => $book,

], 201);
    }
}
```

The following is an explanation of the comments and annotation used in enhancing the documentation that Scramble generates:

1. **Summary and description**: To add a summary and description to a method, you simply add a PHPDoc style comment to the method, as shown in Listing 6-15. The first comment line (Creates a book) is used by Scramble as the method's summary and the second comment line (Creates and adds a book to the database) is used as its description. These new additions are labeled in Figure 6-5a with a 1 and 2.

2. **Request parameters**: You can enhance the documentation of the request parameters by adding comments to each of them, as shown in Listing 6-15, where a comment was added to the title, author, and price parameters. These comments are reflected/labeled in Figure 6-5a as 3 and 4, and in Figure 6-5b as 1.

3. **Response commenting**: Next, a comment (`Returns the created book`) was added to the response being returned. The effect of this on the generated documentation is shown in Figure 6-5b, labeled as 2.

4. `@body` **annotation**: Finally, the `@body` annotation tells Scramble that the value to be returned through the `$book` variable is a Book model instance. This helps Scramble decode the data structure that the `$book` variable will contain. The effect of this annotation is shown in Figure 6-5b, labeled as 4.

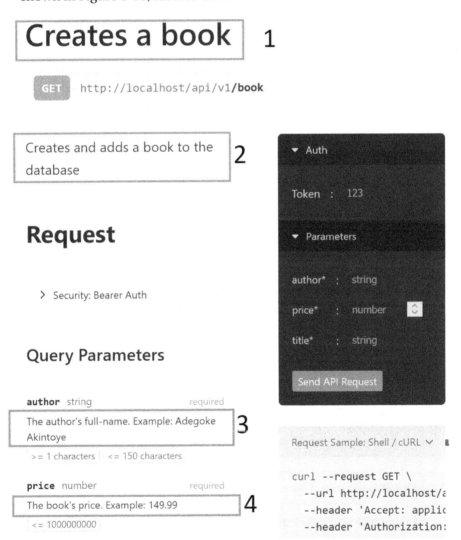

Figure 6-5a. *Using annotations results in more details in the generated documentation*

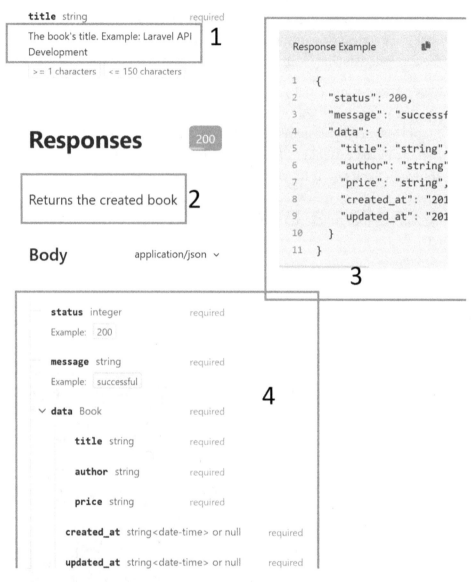

Figure 6-5b. *Using annotations results in more details in the generated documentation as well*

Grouping Endpoints

By default, all the endpoints related to a controller will be grouped under the name of the controller. However, you can change this default by using the Group attribute.
Listing 6-16 shows how to do this.

Listing 6-16. Grouping Endpoints

```
use Dedoc\Scramble\Attributes\Group;

#[Group('Book Maker')]
class BookController extends Controller
{
    // ...
}
```

Now every method within the BookController controller will be categorized and displayed in the documentation under the group named Book Maker, as shown in Figure 6-6.

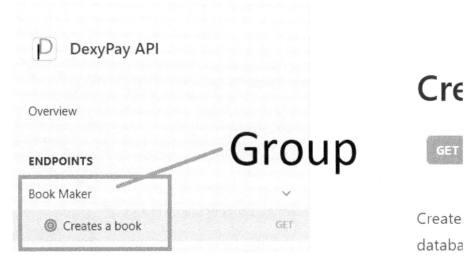

Figure 6-6. *The effect of using the Group attribute*

Documenting a Paginated Response

Scramble requires you to explicitly notify it of any paginated response you might be using through the use of appropriate annotation. Listing 6-17 returns a paginated response, so you need to add an annotation so Scramble can effectively document it. This example uses the @response annotation as well as the required use statement, shown in bold in Listing 6-17.

Listing 6-17. Documenting a Paginated Response

```
namespace App\Http\Controllers\Api\V1;

use App\Http\Controllers\Controller;
use App\Models\Book;
use Dedoc\Scramble\Attributes\Group;
use Illuminate\Http\Request;
use Illuminate\Pagination\LengthAwarePaginator;

#[Group('Book Maker')]

class BookController extends Controller
{

    /**
     * Returns a book
     *
     * Returns a book from the database given a book ID
     *
     */
    public function get(Request $request)
    {
        /**
         * @response LengthAwarePaginator<TodoItem>
         */
        return Book::where('id', 1)->paginate(10);

    }
```

With this annotation, Scramble will be able to document the paginated response. The next section explains how to create the needed controllers.

Implementing Controllers

In this section, you create the controllers. You start by using Artisan to generate some basic controller files, which you can then edit to suit your needs.

Generating Controllers

Generate the basic controllers files using the Artisan command in Listing 6-18.

Tip   To run this command, you may have to press the Enter key twice.

Listing 6-18. Generating the Basic Controllers Files

```
php artisan make:controller Api/V1/PaymentController;\
php artisan make:controller Api/V1/TransactionController;\
php artisan make:controller Api/V1/WalletController;\
php artisan make:controller Custom/FormatResponseController.php;\
php artisan make:controller Custom/AuthorizeAccessController.php;\
```

Executing the Artisan command in Listing 6-18 will generate five controller files inside your Laravel project:

1. `app/Http/Controllers/Api/V1/PaymentController.php`

2. `app/Http/Controllers/Api/V1/TransactionController.php`

3. `app/Http/Controllers/Api/V1/WalletController.php`

4. `app/Http/Controllers/Custom/FormatResponseController.php`

5. `app/Http/Controllers/Custom/AuthorizeAccessController.php`

Next, you'll start updating these controllers to get them to do what you want.

TransactionController

Open the `TransactionController.php` file and replace its code with the code shown in Listing 6-19. Save the file. The controller contains five methods, and you'll learn about these methods shortly. Notice that this code includes comments and annotations to enhance the documentation.

Listing 6-19. Modifying the TransactionController.php File

```php
<?php

//app/Http/Controllers/Api/V1/TransactionController.php

namespace App\Http\Controllers\Api\V1;

use App\Http\Controllers\Controller;
use App\Http\Controllers\Custom\FormatResponseController;
use App\Models\Transaction;
use Dedoc\Scramble\Attributes\Group;
use Dedoc\Scramble\Attributes\QueryParameter;
use Illuminate\Http\Request;
use Illuminate\Pagination\LengthAwarePaginator;
use Illuminate\Support\Carbon;
use Illuminate\Support\Facades\URL;
use Illuminate\Support\Str;

#[Group('Payment Processor Version 0.0.1', weight: 2)]

class TransactionController extends Controller
{

    /**
     * InitPayment
     *
     * It initializes payment in preparation for charging a customer.<br>
     * -Requires the use of your <b>secret key</b>.
     *
     */

    public function initTransaction(Request $request)
    {
        $user = auth()->user();

        try {
            // Validate input.
            $request->validate([
```

```
//The customer's name. Optional. Example: Peter
Parker Smith

'name'          => 'string',


//Customer's email. Required. Example: ppsmith@mail.com
'email'          => 'required|email',

//Amount to be paid. Required. Example: 55678.55
'amount'          => 'required|decimal:2|min:0.50|m
ax:1000000000.00',

//Currency of payment. Required. Only USD accepted for now.
Example: USD
'currency'        => 'required|string|size:3',

//The URL to redirect customer once payment is done.
Example: https://myapp.com
'redirect_url'  => 'url:http',

//Determines who pays, customer or merchant, the payment
processing charges. A value of 1 means customers pay. 0
means merchant pays. Example: 1
'pass_charge'   => 'boolean',

//Is payment a direct charge?. A value of 0 (false)
means you are paying via the URL (<em>checkout_url</
em>) receieved after calling this endpoint for payment
initialization. This URL when visited displays a form
provided by Dexy Pay for payment to be made. A value of 1
(true) means you are retrieving customer's card details
yourself and forwarding it with the data returned by this
endpoint to the <em>/payment/charge</em> endpoint for a
direct charge of the customer. <br> In the first case,
you are using Dexy Pay's provided payment page to collect
the customer's card details; while in the last case, you
are responsible for devising a means for collecting the
```

```php
                card detail yourself, say via a form on your website or
                app.<br><br>Example: false
                'direct_charge' => 'boolean',

        ]);
    } catch (ValidationException $e) {
        return FormatResponseController::response422($e->errors()
        . '1**');
    }

    try {

        $transaction_ref = Str::uuid();
        $amount           = $request->amount;
        //create the payment link
        $payLink = $this->getPaymentLink($transaction_ref, $amount);
        //
        $payFee = $this->getPaymentFee($amount);
        //register transaction
        $transaction = Transaction::create([
            'user_id'          => $user->id,
            'transaction_ref'  => $transaction_ref,
            'amount'           => $amount,
            'fee'              => $payFee,
            'email'            => $request->email,
            'currency'         => $request->currency,
            'redirect_url'     => $request->redirect_url,
            'checkout_url'     => $payLink,
            'pass_charge'      => $request->pass_charge,
            'status'           => 'pending',
        ]);

    } catch (QueryException $e) {

        return FormatResponseController::response500($e->getMessage()
        . '2**');
```

```php
} catch (\Exception $e) {
    return FormatResponseController::response500($e->getMessage()
    . '3**');

}

// If the transaction initiation succeeds, return a success JSON
response.

$data = [
    //Success message. <br><br>Example: 'Payment Initialized
    successfully!'
    'message'            => 'Payment Initialized successfully!',

    //Currency of payment. Only USD accepted for now.
    <br><br>Example: USD
    'currency'           => 'USD',

    //The URL to redirect customer to once payment is done.
    <br><br>Example: https://myapp.com
    'redirect_url'       => $request->redirect_url,

    //Transaction reference. Unique to each transaction.
    <br><br>Example: er43rft-8uytrettu-mjkuyt-bhgtrdsp
    'transaction_ref'    => $transaction->transaction_ref,

    //Amount to be paid. <br><br>Example: 55678.55
    'transaction_amount' => $request->amount,

    //Generated payment link. Used for indirect payment. When
    visited, displays a payment page.
    'checkout_url'       => $payLink,

    //Transaction status. It can be any of the following: pending,
    failed, or completed. <br><br>Example: completed
    'status'             => 'successful',

];
```

```
        return FormatResponseController::response200($data);

}

/**
 * GetTransactions
 *
 * Retrieves paginated transactions for a user without the need for the
 * user ID.<br> -Requires the use of either your <b>public key</b> or
 * <b>secret key</b>.
 *
 * @response LengthAwarePaginator<Transaction>
 *
 */
#[QueryParameter('page', description: 'Current page.', type: 'int',
default:1, example: 7)]
public function getTransactions()
{
    $user = auth()->user();

    $transactions = Transaction::where('user_id', $user->id)->
    paginate(10);
    return response()->json($transactions);

}

/**
 * GetTransaction
 *
 * Retrieves a transaction given a transaction ID.<br> -Replace
 * <b>txnid</b> in the endpoint URL with the ID of the transaction to be
 * retrieved. <br>-Requires the use of either your <b>public key</b> or
 * <b>secret key</b>.
 *
 * @param  string  $txnid  The transaction reference/ID of the
 * transaction to be retrieved. <br><br>Example: f15ee5cd-
 * dd0d-4ec9-8e39-922708d10f99
```

```php
 *
 */
public function getTransaction(string $txnid)
{
    try {

        $user = auth()->user();

        $transaction = Transaction::where('transaction_ref', $txnid)-
        >where('user_id', $user->id)->first();

        //return $transaction;
        $data = [
            //Amount paid
            "transaction_amount"     => $transaction->amount,

            //Transaction reference ID
            "transaction_ref"        => $transaction->transaction_ref,

            //Transaction status. It can be any of the following:
            pending, failed, or completed. <br><br>Example: completed
            "transaction_status"     => $transaction->status,

            //Payment currency. Only USD is supported
            "transaction_currency"   => $transaction->currency,

            "transaction_created_at" => $transaction->created_at,

            //Customer's email
            "email"                  => $transaction->email,
        ];

        return FormatResponseController::response200($data);

    } catch (QueryException $e) {

        return FormatResponseController::response500($e->getMessage() .
        '***1');

    } catch (\Exception $e) {
```

```php
            return FormatResponseController::response500($e->getMessage() .
            '***2');

        }

    }

    /**
     * VerifyTransaction
     *
     * Verifies a transaction given a transaction ID. <br>-Replace
     * <b>txnid</b> in the endpoint URL with the ID of the transaction to be
     * verified. <br> -Requires the use of either your <b>public key</b> or
     * <b>secret key</b>.
     *
     * @param  string  $txnid  The transaction reference/ID of the
     * transaction to be verified. <br><br>Example: f15ee5cd-
     * dd0d-4ec9-8e39-922708d10f99
     *
     */
    public function verifyTransaction(string $txnid)
    {
        return $this->getTransaction($txnid);

    }

    /**
     * @hideFromAPIDocumentation
     */
    private function getPaymentLink(string $tx_id, string $amt)
    {

        $expiresAt = Carbon::now()->addMinutes(600); // Link valid
        for 6hours

        // Generate and return a payment link
        return URL::temporarySignedRoute(
```

```
        'payment.form',
        $expiresAt,
        ['amt' => $amt, 'tx_ref' => $tx_id]
    );
}

/**
 * @hideFromAPIDocumentation
 */

private function getPaymentFee($amount)
{
    // Define the fee (flat $0.25 + 0.5%)
    return round(0.25 + ($amount * 0.005), 2);
}

}
```

This list looks at each method in turn to explains what they do:

1. `initTransaction()` **method**: This is the biggest of all these methods in terms of code volume. Its job is to help initialize payment. This is the first endpoint to be called when payment is to be made. To initialize payment using this method, a merchant will need to first register and have a *secret key,* as the secret key will be needed to access this method. Data (email, amount, currency, `redirect_url`, `pass_charge`, and `direct_charge`) about the payment to be made is passed to the method. It checks the data passed to it to be sure it's what it should be, using the `validate()` method of the `Request` object. If there is anything wrong with the data, it returns a detail of the error. On the other hand, if the data is okay, it'll save the data together with a signed URL for payment, which is generated into the `Transaction` table in the database. The recording of this data into the database accomplishes the initialization process. Note that to generate the signed payment URL, this method uses another method in this controller, the `getPaymentLink()`, which you'll look at later. Once this data has been saved, it will return some of the data it saved, including the

signed payment URL generated earlier as well as information to show that the initialization was successful. I sends this back to the merchant who initiated the payment process. Let's explore what data this method requires.

a. `email`: The email of the customer making payment. This data must be provided. It's used to communicate with this customer and also used for identification.

b. `amount`: The amount to be paid. It is required and must be in decimal form, e.g., 45678.98.

c. `currency`: The currency of payment. It is a string and is required. The only accepted value is USD.

d. `redirect_url`: The URL or web address to direct a customer to after payment. Usually, this points to a page on the website or app of the merchant using the API to receive payment.

e. `pass_charge`: This can only take a value of 1 or 0. If it's 0, then the customer pays for the payment processing fees and it'll be added to the amount to pay. Otherwise, the merchant will pay, and it'll be deducted from the amount being paid.

f. `direct_charge`: This tells the API how the merchant wants to receive payment after payment initialization. If a value of 1 is given, then the merchant will be responsible for collecting the customer's card details and forwarding them= via an HTTP request to the API charging endpoint in order for the customer to be charged. However, if a value of 0 is given, the merchant can use the signed payment URL received after initialization. The merchant's website or app can be arranged so that when the customer clicks the Payment button, the signed payment URL is activated and opens a Dexy Pay payment page for payment to be made.

2. `getTransactions()` **method**: This method allow users (merchants) of the API to retrieve a list of transactions with details on payments made to them by their customers. The user's public or secret key is required. As you can see in Listing 6-19, this is a

very simple method. All it's doing is retrieving the transactions belonging to a user via the Transaction model using the user's ID. Note that it does not require the ID to be passed via the route. You can get the ID because the user is verified via the public or secret key.

3. `getTransaction()` **method**: This method retrieves only one transaction and requires that the transaction ID (`$txn_ref`) be provided. The user's public or secret key is required. It's also a relatively simple method. It uses the transaction ID to retrieve the desired transaction and then return some fields from the returned transaction.

4. `verifyTransaction()` **method**: This is about the simplest of the five methods. As a matter of fact, it simply calls the `getTransaction()` method. These two methods are returning the same thing given the same parameter.

5. `getPaymentLink()` **method**: Unlike the other four methods in this controller, this method is private and cannot be accessed directly. It can only be used from within the controller. Notice that `@hideFromAPIDocumentation` is added to it. Therefore, it won't be included in the API documentation. Its job is to generate and return a signed route that can be used as a payment link.

6. `GetPaymentFee()` **method**: This method is used to calculate the amount you receive for each payment processed by your API.

PaymentController

Open the `PaymentController.php` file and replace its code with the code in Listing 6-20. Then save it. This controller contains just two methods. You'll look at these methods shortly. Comments and annotations have also been added to these methods to enhance the documentation.

Listing 6-20. Modifying the PaymentController.php File

```php
<?php

//app/Http/Controllers/Api/V1/PaymentController.php

namespace App\Http\Controllers\Api\V1;

use App\Http\Controllers\Controller;
use App\Http\Controllers\Custom\FormatResponseController;
use App\Jobs\SendWebhookNotification;
use App\Models\Payment;
use App\Models\Transaction;
use App\Models\User;
use Dedoc\Scramble\Attributes\Group;
use Illuminate\Http\Request;
use Illuminate\Support\Facades\DB;
use Illuminate\Support\Facades\Log;
use Illuminate\Support\Facades\Mail;

#[Group('Payment Processor Version 0.0.1', weight: 3)]
/**
 * @group Payment Processor Version 0.0.1
 *
 */
class PaymentController extends Controller
{
    /**
     * PaymentCharge
     *
     * It process payment and dispatch jobs for webhook, email, etc to
     * relay the status of the payment processed.
     *
     * @unauthenticated
     *
     */
    public function processPayment(Request $request)
    {
```

```php
// Validate input.
$request->validate([
    //Card holder's name. Example: ENIOLUWA MIKE STEVEN
    'card_name'      => 'required|string',

    //Card number. Example: 5453 8765 7654 5432
    'card_num'       => 'required|string|min:12|max:19',

    //Card expiry date. Example: 12/99
    'card_exp'       => 'required|string|size:5',

    //Card cvc. Example: 906
    'card_secret'    => 'required|string|min:3|max:4',

    //Amount to pay. Example: 10890.75
    'amount'         => 'required|decimal:2|max:1000000000|min:0.5',

    //Three letter currency code. Examples - USD
    'currency_code'  => 'required|string|size:3',

    //Transaction reference id. Example: f15ee5cd-
    dd0d-4ec9-8e39-922708d10f99
    'transaction_ref' => 'required|uuid',

    //A value of false means you are paying via the provided
    checkout_url, which when visited displays a form provided by
    Dexy Pay for payment to be made, while a value of true means
    you've retrieved customer's card details yourself and you are
    now forwarding them with the data obtained from calling the
    initialization endpoint earlier for a direct charge/payment of
    your customer. <br><br>Example: 1
    'direct_charge'  => 'required|boolean',

    //Payment method (optional). Example: card
    'payment_method' => 'string|min:1|max:10',

]);

log::info('inside processPayment');
```

```php
$direct_charge = $request->direct_charge;
$amount        = $request->amount;
$tx_id         = $request->transaction_ref;

//verify existence and validity of transaction request
$txn = Transaction::where('transaction_ref', $tx_id)->first();

if (
    ! $txn
    || $amount !== $txn->amount
    || $txn->status === 'completed') {

    if (isset($direct_charge) && ! $direct_charge) {
                    log::info('ifErr: '.$amount.' '.$txn->status);

        return FormatResponseController::responseWeb('failed');
    } else {

        return FormatResponseController::response422('Validation
        error***1');

    }

}


// Retrieve and lock the associated user record
$user = User::where('id', $txn->user_id)
    ->lockForUpdate()
    ->first();

try {

    // Wrap the transaction in a try-catch block.
    DB::transaction(function () use ($request, $txn, $user) {

        //Amount due to merchant after deducting payment fee
        $netPay = $txn->amount - $txn->fee;
        //Credit the merchant
        $user->increment('balance', $netPay);
```

```php
        //Update transaction status to completed
        $this->recordPaymentStatus($request, $txn);

        //set transaction status to completed
        $txn->status = 'completed';
        $txn->save();

    });

    if (
        isset($direct_charge) && ! $direct_charge) {

        $this->sendMail($txn);
        $this->sendWebhookNotification($user);
        return FormatResponseController::responseWeb('successful',
        $txn->redirect_url);
    } else {

        $this->sendMail($txn);
        $this->sendWebhookNotification($user);
        // If the transaction succeeds, return a success JSON
        response.
        return FormatResponseController::response200($this-
        >successData($txn));
    }

} catch (QueryException $e) {

    if (
        isset($direct_charge) && ! $direct_charge) {

        return FormatResponseController::responseWeb('failed');
    } else {

        return FormatResponseController::response500($e-
        >getMessage() . '***2');

    }

} catch (\Exception $e) {
```

```php
            if (isset($direct_charge) && ! $direct_charge) {

                return FormatResponseController::responseWeb('failed');
            } else {

                return FormatResponseController::response500('Transaction
                failed: ' . $e->getMessage() . '***3');
            }

        }

    }


    /**
     * @hideFromAPIDocumentation
     */

    private function recordPaymentStatus(Request $request, $txn)
    {
        Payment::create([
            'transaction_id' => $txn->transaction_ref,
            'payment_method'  => $request->payment_method,
            'payment_status'  => $txn->status,
        ]);
    }

    private function successData($txn)
    {

        return [
            'status'         => 'success',
            'message'        => 'Transaction completed successfully!',
            'amount'         => $txn->amount,
            'fee'            => $txn->fee,
            'amount_less_fee' => number_format($txn->amount - $txn->fee, 2,
            '.', ''),
            'transaction_ref' => $txn->transaction_ref,
        ];
```

```php
}

private function sendMail($txnn){

    $subject = 'Payment Receipt Notification';

    $mailData = [
        'mailView' => 'emails.success-customer',
        'subject'  => $subject,
        'amount'   => $txnn->amount,
        'refid'    => $txnn->transaction_ref,
        'email'    => $txnn->email,

    ];

    Mail::to($txnn->email)->send(new \App\Mail\
    PaymentMail($mailData));

    $mailData['subject'] = 'Payment Notification';

    $mailData['mailView'] = 'emails.success-merchant';

    $mailData['email']    = $txnn->user->email;

    Mail::to($txnn->user->email)->send(new \App\Mail\
    PaymentMail($mailData));

}

private function sendWebhookNotification($user){

    // Dispatch a job for the user's webhook URL using their secret

}
}
```

Let's take a look at the major methods of this controller:

1. processPayment() **method**: Once a payment has been initialized, the next step is to charge the customer, and that is what this method does. Whether using the direct or indirect charge method, a merchant will use this method to charge a customer. To charge the customer, the method must be provided with the

card details (card holder's name, card number, card expiry date, card CVC number), the ID (`transaction_ref`) of the transaction being settled, the amount to be paid, and the currency type. The method will retrieve the transaction from the database using the submitted transaction ID and check if the amount being offered for payment corresponds to the amount recorded in the database. It will also check to see if the transaction has been fulfilled. If the amount offered is the same as what's in the transaction record and the transaction has not been fulfilled, it will debit the customer's card and credit the merchant. It does this using the database transaction and record locking feature in order to guarantee the integrity of the payment recording operation.

2. `recordPaymentStatus()` **method**: This method is private and not available for use outside the controller. However, it is used within the controller by the `processPayment()` method you learned about earlier. The method records the transaction as a successful payment in the `payment` database table.

3. `sendMail($txnn)`: Sends email when a payment is successful. It will be modified later for sending email asynchronously.

4. `sendWebhookNotification($user)`: This is an empty function for now; it will be modified later to send webhook notifications asynchronously.

WalletController

Open the `WalletController.php` file and replace its code with Listing 6-21. Then save it. This controller consists of two methods. You'll be looking at these two methods shortly. Comments and annotations have also been added to these methods to enhance the documentation.

Listing 6-21. Modifying the `WalletController.php` File

```php
<?php

//app/Http/Controllers/Api/V1/WalletController.php

namespace App\Http\Controllers\Api\V1;
```

```php
use App\Http\Controllers\Controller;
use App\Http\Controllers\Custom\FormatResponseController;
use App\Models\Transaction;
use App\Models\User;
use Dedoc\Scramble\Attributes\Group;
use Illuminate\Http\Request;
use Illuminate\Support\Facades\DB;

#[Group('Payment Processor Version 0.0.1', weight: 1)]


/**
 * @group Payment Processor Version 0.0.1
 *
 */

class WalletController extends Controller
{
    /**
     * GetBalance
     *
     * Retrieves merchants wallet balance. <br> - Requires the use of
     * either your <b>public key</b> or <b>secret key</b>.
     *
     */

    public function getWalletBalance()
    {

        try {

            $user = auth()->user();

            $data = [
                'status'         => 'successful',
                'wallet_balance' => $user->balance,
                'currency_code'  => 'USD',

            ];

            return FormatResponseController::response200($data);
```

```php
    } catch (QueryException $e) {
        // Handle query exceptions specifically
        return FormatResponseController::response500($e->getMessage());
    } catch (\Exception $e) {
        // Fallback for catching other exceptions
        return FormatResponseController::response500($e->getMessage());

    }
}

/**
 * WithdrawFund
 *
 * Withdraws fund from a merchant wallet balance. <br> - Requires the
 * use of your <b>secret key</b>.
 *
 */

public function withdrawFund(Request $request)
{
    // Validate input.
    $request->validate([
        //Amount to be withdrawn. Example: 25000.56
        'amount' => 'required|decimal:2|max:500000',
    ]);

    $user = auth()->user();
    if ($user->balance < $request->amount) {
        return FormatResponseController::response422('Validation
        error');
    }

    try {
        // Wrap the transaction in a try-catch block.
        DB::transaction(function () use ($request, $user) {

            // Retrieve and lock the associated user record
            User::where('id', $user->id)
```

```
                    ->lockForUpdate()
                    ->first();

             $user->decrement('balance', $request->amount);

        });

        // If the transaction succeeds, return a success JSON response.
        $data = [

            'status'            => 'successful',
            'message'           => 'Withdrawal completed successfully!',
            'amount_withdrawn'  => $request->amount,
            'balance'           => number_format($user->balance, 2,
            '.', ''),
        ];
        return FormatResponseController::response200($data);

    } catch (QueryException $e) {
        // Handle query exceptions specifically
        return FormatResponseController::response500($e->getMessage());

    } catch (\Exception $e) {

        return FormatResponseController::response500($e->getMessage());

    }

  }

}
```

Next, let's look into the two methods in the controller in Listing 6-21.

1. `getWalletBalance()` **method**: This method retrieves the merchant's wallet balance. This balance indicates the total money paid the merchant less the total amount already withdrawn.

2. `withdrawFund()` **method**: This method transfers fund to a merchant's bank account.

FormatResponseController

This controller will be modified to operate as a helper or service class for the first three controller classes you just created. It is not used as a typical class tied to a route. Open the FormatResponseController.php file and replace the code in it with the Listing 6-22.

This controller contains six methods. Each of these methods is used to create a specific type of response sent by the API endpoints.

Listing 6-22. Modifying the FormatResponseController.php File

```php
<?php

//app/Http/Controllers/Custom/FormatResponseController.php

namespace App\Http\Controllers\Custom;

use Illuminate\Support\Facades\Log;

class FormatResponseController
{
    public static function response500($msg = 'Server error')
    {
        // Handle query exceptions specifically
        Log::error("Server error: " . $msg);
        return response()->json([
            'status'  => 500,
            'message' => $msg,
        ], 500);

    }
    public static function response422($err)
    {
        Log::error("validation errors " . $err);

        // Customize the error handling
        return response()->json([
            'status'  => 422,
            'message' => 'There were validation errors',
            'errors'  => $err,
```

```php
    ], 422);
}

public static function response401($arr = [])
{
    Log::error("Failed authentication " . $err);

    // Customize the error handling
    return response()->json([
        'status'  => 401,
        'message' => 'Unauthenticated',
        'errors'  => $err,
    ], 401);

}

public static function response403($arr)
{
    Log::error("Permission denied: " . $err);

    // Customize the error handling
    return response()->json(
        ['status' => 403,
            'message' => 'Unauthenticated',
            'errors'  => $err,
        ],
        401
    );

}

public static function response200($arr = [])
{
    return response()->json(
        ["status" => 200,
            "success" => true,
            "message" => "Success",
            "data"    => $arr,
        ],
```

```
            200
        );

    }
    public static function responseWeb($sts, $redir_url = '')
    {
        $status       = $sts;
        $redirect_url = $redir_url;
        //$payment_link = $pay_link;
        return view(
            'payment.status',
            compact(
                'status',
                'redirect_url'
            )
        );

    }
}
```

AuthorizeAccessController

This controller will be modified to offer service to the first three controller classes you
created earlier, so it will not be tied to a route either. This class will specifically be used
to determine if a user is authorized to access a resource. To edit this controller, open the
AuthorizeAccessController.php file and add the code in bold shown in Listing 6-23.

Listing 6-23. Modifying the AuthorizeAccessController.php File

```
<?php

//app/Http/Controllers/Custom/AuthorizeAccessController.php

namespace App\Http\Controllers\Custom;

use App\Models\Transaction;


class AuthorizeAccessController
{
```

```php
    //
    public static function checkAccessRightToTransaction(
        $user_id,
        $txn_ref) {

        if (Transaction::where('user_id', $user_id)->where('transaction_
        ref', $txn_ref)->Exists()) {
            //
            return true;
        }
        return false;

    }
}
```

Using Token Ability Middleware

In Chapter 5 (see the "Implementing the DashboardPagesController Controller Class" section), you learned how to generate two tokens, each with different abilities—secret and public. Using this technique, you can determine whether the token used by a user trying to access a route (endpoint) in the API is authorized to do so. Generally, a secret key can be used to access any route in the API, while a public key can only access some, less risky routes (e.g., read-only routes). As a result of this, secret keys must be kept secret and should be used only from the backend (the server side). Public keys, on the other hand, can be used from the frontend and the backend. This section explains how to define the appropriate middleware aliases in your application's bootstrap/app.php file so that you can use the abilities you attached to the token to authorize or deny access to a given route in the API. Open the file and update it, as shown in Listing 6-23a.

Listing 6-23a. Updating the bootstrap/app.php File

```php
<?php
//bootstrap/app.php

use Illuminate\Foundation\Application;
use Illuminate\Foundation\Configuration\Exceptions;
use Illuminate\Foundation\Configuration\Middleware;
```

271

```
use Laravel\Sanctum\Http\Middleware\CheckAbilities;
use Laravel\Sanctum\Http\Middleware\CheckForAnyAbility;

return Application::configure(basePath: dirname(__DIR__))
->withRouting(
 web: __DIR__.'/../routes/web.php',
 api: __DIR__.'/../routes/api.php',
 commands: __DIR__.'/../routes/console.php',
 health: '/up',
 )
->withMiddleware(function (Middleware $middleware) {

 $middleware->alias([
 'abilities' => CheckAbilities::class,
 'ability' => CheckForAnyAbility::class,
 ]);

})
->withExceptions(function (Exceptions $exceptions) {
//
})->create();
```

With these changes implemented, you can now use the token ability in the API routes.

Implementing Your Routes

Next, you learn how to define the routes that'll allow clients to access your controllers in order to use the API. In all, there are seven routes, as listed in Listing 6-24.

Listing 6-24. Seven Routes

```
1.POST payment/initiate       : It initializes payment
2.POST payment/charge         : for completing payment
3.GET transaction/{{id}}      : Retrieves a transaction
4.GET transactions            : Retrieves transactions
5.GET transaction/verify/{{id}}: Verifies payment
6.GET wallet/balance          : Retrieves wallet balance
7.POST wallet/withdraw        : Withdraws fund to bank account
```

Next, you need to add these routes to your route list. Open the routes/api.php file and update it to look like Listing 6-25.

Listing 6-25. Updating the routes/api.php File

```php
<?php

//routes/api.php

use App\Http\Controllers\Api\V1\PaymentController;
use App\Http\Controllers\Api\V1\TransactionController;
use App\Http\Controllers\Api\V1\WalletController;
use Illuminate\Support\Facades\Route;

Route::group(['prefix' => 'v1'], function () {

    // Routes that only require authentication
    Route::group(['middleware' => 'auth:sanctum'], function () {

        Route::get('/transaction/{id}', [TransactionController::class,
        'getTransaction'])->name('transaction.get');
        Route::get('/transactions', [TransactionController::class,
        'getTransactions'])->name('transactions.get');
        Route::get('/wallet/balance', [WalletController::class,
        'getWalletBalance'])->name('wallet.get');

        // Routes that also require the 'secret' ability
        Route::middleware('abilities:secret')->group(function () {
            Route::get('/transaction/verify/{id}',
            [TransactionController::class, 'verifyTransaction'])-
            >name('transaction.verify');
            Route::post('/payment/initiate', [TransactionController::class,
            'initTransaction'])->name('payment.init');
            Route::post('/wallet/withdraw', [WalletController::class,
            'withdrawFund'])->name('wallet.withdraw');
        });

    });
```

```
// Public route
Route::post('/payment/charge', [PaymentController::class,
'processPayment'])->name('payment.charge');
});
```

Notice that the seven routes have been placed into a group with a prefix of v1. This means that you must prefix the URI of your route with api/v1. For example, take the first route in the group, /transaction/{id}. To be able to visit this route, you must write its URI as api/v1/transaction/{id}. Otherwise, Laravel will think you are pointing to a different route. Instead of writing the URL as http://localhost/transaction/34245, you need to write it as http://localhost/api/v1/transaction/34245.

Note the following also:

1. The POST /api/v1/payment/ route does not require authentication; the route can be accessed without using a token.

2. The three routes—GET /api/v1/transaction/{id}, GET /api/v1/transactions, and GET /api/v1/wallet/balance—can be accessed by any key (secret or public).

3. The remaining three routes—GET /api/v1/transaction/verify/{id}, POST /api/v1/payment/initiate, and POST/api/v1/wallet/withdraw—can only be accessed using secret keys. This higher security is due to the sensitive nature of these three routes.

API Documentation Viewing and Basic Functional Testing with Scramble

To do basic testing on the API using Scramble, you first need to open the generated documentation. To open the documentation, visit http://localhost/docs/api (generally, base_url/docs/api) from your browser.

Note   To access the generated documentation, especially the first time, you may need to connect to the Internet.

If everything goes well, you should see a page similar to the one in Figure 6-7.

Note   As a first test, go through the documentation generated for the API endpoints and be sure they convey what you intended. Links to the endpoints are located on the left side of the documentation under the endpoint label, see Figure 6-7. Click each group to reveal the contained endpoints and click each endpoint to access its documentation. If you make any changes to the annotations, comments, or attributes in any of the documented methods, simply reloading the documentation will regenerate it and reflect the changes.

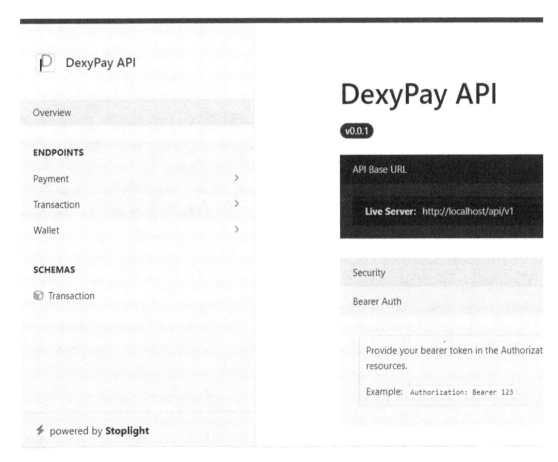

Figure 6-7. *The home page of the generated API documentation*

Note   If you haven't done so yet, you should log in to the API user dashboard and generate your public and secret keys. Have them handy, as you'll need them in the following tests.

Next, you see how to do a basic functional test with Scramble. You'll test the Initialize Payment endpoint as an example. To access this endpoint on the documentation page, locate the left sidebar and click Transaction under the Endpoints label. Then click the Initializes Payment endpoint; see Figure 6-8. Clicking the Initializes Payment endpoint link will open the Initialize Payment documentation page, as shown in Figure 6-9.

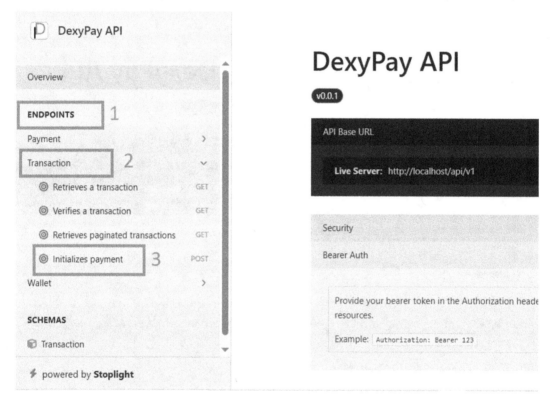

Figure 6-8. *Accessing the generated documentation for the InitPayment endpoint*

Initializes payment

Figure 6-9. *The InitPayment documentation page*

On the opened Initialize Payment page shown in Figure 6-9, enter your secret key. Update the request body with the appropriate values for the transaction to be initiated, then click the Send API Request button to submit the request and test the endpoint. After some seconds, there should be a response. It will either indicate a successful test or a failed one. If the call to the endpoint was successful, the response should show something like Figure 6-10. Note that some values in the response will differ, depending on the values you sent through the request body. You may have to scroll down to the bottom of the documentation page to see the returned response.

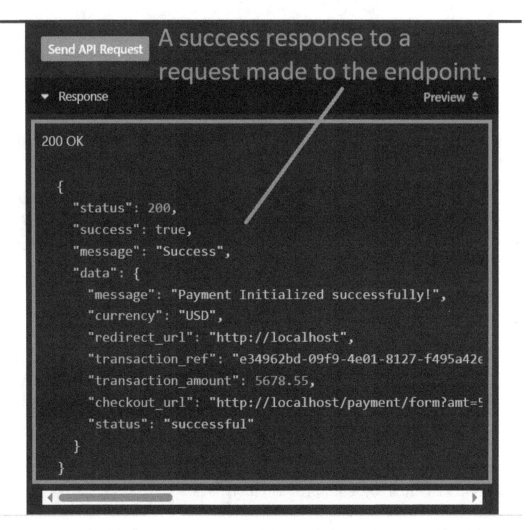

Figure 6-10. *A success response*

If, on the other hand, the request to the endpoint results in an error, you may see a response like the one in Figure 6-11. (The message that's returned depends on what caused the error.)

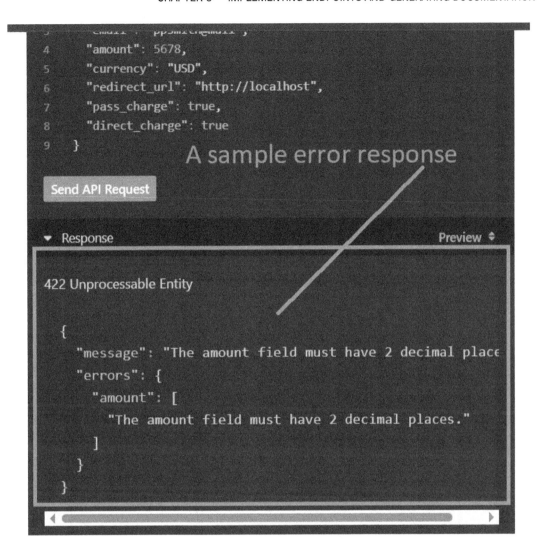

Figure 6-11. A sample error response

You can follow the same steps to test the other endpoints in your API.

Now that you know how to run a quick basic functional test of your API endpoints, you can take this a step further by trying automated functional testing of your API using EchoAPI.

Committing Your Changes

Commit your changes in this chapter to Git by running the command in Listing 6-25.

Listing 6-25. Comitting Your Changes to Git

```
git add . && git commit -m "Chapter 6"
```

Conclusion

This chapter showed you how to start building your payment processor API. You implemented the API models and the migrations, controllers, and routes. You also took a look at Scramble, which helps you generate documentation, and you ran through some basic API testing.

## CHAPTER 7

Automated Functional Testing with EchoAPI

In the last chapter, you learned how to develop the core of the API and use Scramble for API documentation generation and basic testing. In this chapter, you look at another tool, called *EchoAPI*. You'll learn how to use it to run API automated functional testing.

Testing with EchoAPI

To test the API in the last chapter, you had to manually enter request body parameters and carry out the test from one endpoint to another. This means that to test your API, say ten times in a row, you would need to manually enter all the values for the request body and click the Send API Request button for each of the endpoints in turn. Then you would have to repeat the whole process ten times. This will result in at the least 70 manual operations (seven endpoints x ten cycles of API testing).

With EchoAPI, you can set your test up so that the values needed for each endpoint's request body are automatically generated and sent with each request, without having to manually add them. In addition, you only need to specify the number of times to repeat the testing of the endpoints (the entire API endpoints); EchoAPI will do it for you automatically. You can also carry out *Assertions* operations on your API end points to see if the values received are as expected.

EchoAPI initially requires additional time in order to set up the testing specs; however, once it's set up, it makes the testing experience much less stressful, more flexible, and more powerful.

© Adegoke Akintoye 2025
A. Akintoye, *API Development with Laravel*, https://doi.org/10.1007/979-8-8688-1576-8_7

Basic EchoAPI Concepts

Before you get started testing with EchoAPI, it's important to understand a few basic concepts related to this tool.

Environment Management and Environment Variables

At any given point, your app or API lifecycle will pass through two or more of the following stages or environments—the development, staging, and production environments . Each of these environments will have a copy of your app. Let's explore these further:

1. **Development environment**: This environment contains a copy of your app on a local or isolated server. This is usually where your app development starts. This is where features are built and bugs are fixed. It uses mock or test data for testing the app as you're building it.

2. **Staging environment**: Once you verify that your app can be used by real users in a real-world environment, you can make a copy of it to another server, called a *staging server*. It's like a "dress rehearsal" environment configured to mirror the production environment as closely as possible—same software versions, nearly identical datasets—and it's used for final QA (Quality Assurance) and performance testing. The copy of your app in this environment is tested further to ascertain its suitability for real-world usage before being deployed.

3. **Production environment**: Once you're certain of the quality of the app in the staging environment, you can make a copy to another server, called the *production server*. This is the live system serving real users and real data. Changes here directly impact end users, so stability, security, and monitoring are paramount. However, this will still be tested in its own way.

The copy of your API in each of these stages still requires testing and it'll have different parameters and settings unique to each stage—like the URL, for example. EchoAPI allow you to create what it refers to as an *environment* that represents the copy of the API you are testing. You can give the environment a name that reflects the stage of the copy of the API you are testing—for example, development, staging, or production. Each environment can contain the data unique to it, referred to as the *environment variables.* The advantage of this is that your API can be tested for different stages by just switching to the corresponding environment in the EchoAPI user interface.

You can create an environment and the environment variables from the EchoAPI dashboard.

To use an environment variable in your code and even via the dashboard, you can wrap the name of the environment variable within two sets of curly brackets like this: {{Environment_var_name}}.

You can also get and set the value of an environment variable from within your post-request and pre-request scripts (more on these later). You do this by using the methods shown in Listing 7-1.

Listing 7-1. Methods for Setting and Retreiving Environment Variables

```
//Get a single environment variable
pm.environment.get(variableName);

//Set a single environment variable
pm.environment.set(variableName, variableValue);

//Replace the included dynamic variables in the string with their actual
values, such as {{variable_name}}
pm.environment.replaceIn(variableName);

//Set a single environment variable
pm.environment.set(variableName, variableValue);
```

Cookie Management

EchoAPI's cookie manager automatically stores all cookies returned by the server during any request and attaches them to subsequent requests to the same domain, handling session-based APIs seamlessly. You can also view, edit, or clear cookies via the debugging interface by clicking the cookie icon next to the Environment drop-down menu.

Global Parameters

Your API will often require the same request values for things like headers, query parameters, body parameters, authentication settings, cookies, pre-request and post-response scripts, and so on, for two or more endpoints. Defining them once reduces repetitive work and ensures consistency. You can manage these global parameters from the EchoAPI dashboard.

Global Variables

When you have values that are the same across two or more environments, you can save them as global variables. Global variables are accessible to all environments. Using global variables enhances reusability and maintainability. You can manage your global variables from the EchoAPI dashboard.

To use a global variable in your code and even via the dashboard, you can wrap the name of the global variable within two sets of curly brackets like this: {{global_var_name}}.

You can also get and set the value of a global variable from within your post-request and pre-request scripts (more on these later) using the methods shown in Listing 7-2.

Listing 7-2. Methods for Setting and Retreiving Global Variables

```
//Get a single global variable
pm.globals.get(variableName);

//Set a single global variable.
pm.globals.set(variableName, variableValue);

//Replace the included dynamic variables in the string with their actual
values, such as {{variable_name}}
pm.globals.replaceIn(variableName);

//Check if a certain global variable exists.
pm.globals.has(variableName);
```

Dynamic Values

EchoAPI's dynamic value feature lets you generate realistic, variable test data without writing any code. By using dynamic values, you can generate random values for emails, phone numbers, names, addresses, dates, and so on. Once specified, these values will be automatically injected into the specified request by EchoAPI before sending it.

Pre-request Script

This is a, usually tiny, JavaScript code snippet you write and place in the Pre-request tab of either an endpoint or as a global parameter. (You see how to do this later.) EchoAPI makes writing these code snippets even easier by providing you with code fragments you can use in writing your code. Before EchoAPI sends your HTTP request, it executes the script. The script can, for example, set or update variables, add or change headers, or tweak the request body in one way or another. With all your script's changes applied, the API call is sent to the server. An example script is shown in Listing 7-3.

Listing 7-3. Example Pre-request Script

```
//Sets global variable GlobalAge to a random age between 0 and 100
pm.globals.set("GlobalAge",getRandomAge());

// returns a random age between 0 and 100
function getRandomAge() {
  return Math.floor(Math.random()*101);
}
```

Post-request Script

This is a JavaScript code snippet that you write and place in the Post-request tab of either an endpoint or as a global parameter. As soon as the server response is received, EchoAPI will run your post-response script. In your script, you can parse the response, make checks (assertions), save values into variables for later, log info for debugging, and so on. An example script is shown in Listing 7-4.

Listing 7-4. Example Post-request Script

```
//Logs the responseText to the console
console.log(response.raw.responseText);
```

The request Object

The request object holds information about the request being made to an endpoint. The object can be accessed from within your pre-request scripts. Listing 7-5 shows the kind of information accessible from this object.

Listing 7-5. Example request Object

```
{
    "id": "3a6a9839f8f007",
    "name": "InitPayment",
    "headers": {
        "accept-encoding": "gzip, deflate, br",
        "user-agent": "EchoapiRuntime/1.1.0",
        "connection": "keep-alive",
        "accept": "application/json"
    },
    "method": "POST",
    "url": "http://localhost/api/v1/payment/initiate",
    "data": {
        "email": "{{$email}}",
        "amount": "{{amount}}",
        "currency": "USD",
        "redirect_url": "http://localhost",
        "pass_charge": "1",
        "direct_charge": "0"
    },
    "request_headers": {
        "accept-encoding": "gzip, deflate, br",
        "user-agent": "EchoapiRuntime/1.1.0",
        "connection": "keep-alive",
        "accept": "application/json"
    },
    "request_bodys": {
        "email": "{{$email}}",
        "amount": "{{amount}}",
        "currency": "USD",
```

```
        "redirect_url": "http://localhost",
        "pass_charge": "1",
        "direct_charge": "0"
    },
    "request_querys": {},
    "request_variables": {},
    "mode": "form-data",
    "uri": {
        "protocol": "http",
        "path": ["api", "v1", "payment", "initiate"],
        "host": ["localhost"],
        "query": [],
        "variable": []
    }
}
```

Listing 7-6 shows how to access some properties of the request object.

Listing 7-6. Accessing Properties of the request Object

```
//returns the request method
request.method;
//returns the user agent
request.headers.user-agent;
//returns the endpoint's URL
request.url;
```

The response Object

The response object contains information about the response visiting an endpoint. The object can be accessed from within your post-request scripts. Listing 7-7 shows the kind of information accessible from this object.

Listing 7-7. Example response Object

```
{
    "headers": {
        "date": "Tue, 22 Apr 2025 13:53:10 GMT",
        "server": "Apache",
```

```
    "vary": "Authorization,Accept-Encoding,User-Agent",
    "x-powered-by": "PHP/8.3.0",
    "cache-control": "no-cache, private",
    "access-control-allow-origin": "*",
    "content-encoding": "gzip",
    "keep-alive": "timeout=5, max=100",
    "connection": "Keep-Alive",
    "transfer-encoding": "chunked",
    "content-type": "application/json"
},
"cookies": {},
"raw": {
    "responseText": "{\"status\":200,\"success\":true,\"message\":
    \"Success\",\"data\":{\"message\":\"Payment Initialized succes
    sfully!\",\"currency\":\"USD\",\"redirect_url\":\"http:\\/\\/
    localhost\",\"transaction_ref\":\"bea88bcc-c33e-48ff-8492-8
    6029a77b71a\",\"transaction_amount\":\"9618.31\",\"checkout_
    url\":\"http:\\/\\/localhost\\/payment\\/form?amt=9618.31&expire
    s=1745366000&tx_ref=bea88bcc-c33e-48ff-8492-86029a77b71a&signature=
    2c39c126c44cf4219af39f1d60f4e951c36951e6d8feb89f267e7b5411bc0f75\
    ",\"status\":\"successful\"}}",
    "json": {
        "status": 200,
        "success": true,
        "message": "Success",
        "data": {
            "message": "Payment Initialized successfully!",
            "currency": "USD",
            "redirect_url": "http://localhost",
            "transaction_ref": "bea88bcc-c33e-48ff-8492-86029a77b71a",
            "transaction_amount": "9618.31",
            "checkout_url": "http://localhost/payment/form?amt=9618.31
            &expires=1745366000&tx_ref=bea88bcc-c33e-48ff-8492-86029a
            77b71a&signature=2c39c126c44cf4219af39f1d60f4e951c36951e6
            d8feb89f267e7b5411bc0f75",
```

```
            "status": "successful"
        }
    },
    "status": 200,
    "responseTime": 11808
},
"json": {
    "status": 200,
    "success": true,
    "message": "Success",
    "data": {
        "message": "Payment Initialized successfully!",
        "currency": "USD",
        "redirect_url": "http://localhost",
        "transaction_ref": "bea88bcc-c33e-48ff-8492-86029a77b71a",
        "transaction_amount": "9618.31",
        "checkout_url": "http://localhost/payment/form?amt=9618.31&expi
        res=1745366000&tx_ref=bea88bcc-c33e-48ff-8492-86029a77b71a&sign
        ature=2c39c126c44cf4219af39f1d60f4e951c36951e6d8feb89f267e7b54
        11bc0f75",
        "status": "successful"
    }
}
}
```

Listings 7-8 and 7-9 show how to extract information contained in the object.

Listing 7-8. Extracting Information Contained in the `response` Object

```
//Returns response status code
response.raw.status;
```

```
//Returns response time (milliseconds)
response.raw.responseTime;
```

Listing 7-9. Extracting Information Contained in the response Object

```
//Returns response type (json, etc.)
response.raw.type;
```

```
//Returns response text
response.raw.responseText
```

Assertions

An assertion checks that an API response meets a specific expectation—such as "status code is 200," "Content-Type is application/json," or "the JSON field userId equals 42." Assertions turn raw responses into pass/fail results, so you can get specific answers about what really matters.

You can write your assertions in a JavaScript script and EchoAPI will run them. Listing 7-10 shows an example of such a script with comments explaining how it works.

Listing 7-10. Example Assertion Scripts

```
//1.  Test to check if the response status code is 200 (OK)
pm.test("Status code is 200", () => {
  // Asserts that the response has a status code of 200
  pm.response.to.have.status(200);
});
```

```
//2. Test to verify that the response is in JSON format
pm.test("Response is JSON", () => {
  // Asserts that the response's Content-Type is application/json
  pm.response.to.be.json;
});
```

```
//3. Test to ensure that the response body contains a userId field that is
a number
pm.test("User ID exists", () => {
  // Parses the response body as JSON and assigns it to the variable 'data'
  const data = pm.response.json();
  // Asserts that the 'userId' field in the parsed JSON is of type 'number'
  pm.expect(data.userId).to.be.a("number");
});
```

One good thing about writing your assertion script is that EchoAPI has assertion code fragments that you can put together to create a full script.

Automated Functional Testing with EchoAPI

It's time to implement an automated functional testing flow for your API.

Prerequisites for Setting Up the Test

Here are some prerequisites for setting up this test:

1. Thos API is about helping merchants receive payment online, and to test it, you'll need secret keys to gain access to the API like a merchants have. Therefore, you'll need to create some accounts and copy the secret keys of these accounts to test the API. Visit the dashboard created earlier and submit emails (dummy emails will do) in order to log in and copy the secret keys. In demonstrating this test, four secret keys are used. Copy the keys into a text file (.txt) in the format shown here and save it as test_secret_keys.txt:

    secret_key1,secret_key2,secret_key3,secret_key4

    I'm assuming you have created four merchant accounts and copied their secret keys. You can create and add as many secret keys as you want. Just make sure they are separated by commas. However, do not put a comma at the end of the last secret key.

2. Download the OpenAPI specification file from the API documentation page generated by Scramble. Click the Export drop-down menu on the top-right side of the page; see Figure 7-1. Then choose the Original option. Wait a couple of minutes for the file to finish downloading.

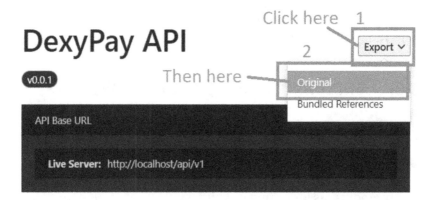

Figure 7-1. *Downloading the OpenAPI specification for the API*

- Create a folder inside your Laravel installation folder and give the folder a name, say openapi_specs. Copy the downloaded file into this folder. Assuming the name of the downloaded file is document.json, it should be located in the Laravel file structure shown in Figure 7-2.

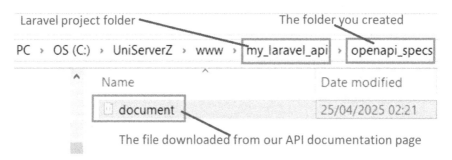

Figure 7-2. *The downloaded OpenAPI specs*

- Install the Openapi-to-Postman library to convert the OpenAPI specs to the corresponding Postman collection. To install the library, run the command in Listing 7-11a.

Tip   Keep your Internet on while running this command.

Listing 7-11a. Installing the Openapi-to-Postman Library

```
composer require adexyme/openapi-to-postman
```

3. Convert the OpenAPI specifications contained in the downloaded
file to a Postman collection that you can easily export into
EchoAPI. Run the command in Listing 7-11b at the command-line
terminal interface from within your Laravel project folder.

Listing 7-11b. Converting the OpenAPI specs to a Postman Collection

```
php artisan postman:generate openapi_specs/document.json openapi_
specs/my_api_collection.json --folder="Process Payment API V1"
```

This command takes three parameters:

a. `openapi_specs/document.json`: The path where the file
containing the OpenAPI specs is located.

b. `openapi_specs/my_api_collection.json`: The path to the
generated Postman collection file. To locate this file inside
your Laravel installation folder, check inside `storage/app/
private`. This means that from within your Laravel installation
folder, the path to this file is `storage/app/private/openapi_
specs/my_api_collection.json`.

c. `--folder="Process Payment API V1"`: Although this
parameter is technically optional, you should use it, as it'll
make your job easier later. Whatever string you pass to the
folder parameter, in this case `Process Payment API V1`, will
be used to create a folder that'll contain all your endpoints
when you eventually export your Postman collection into
EchoAPI.

4. Next, you need to transfer the data about each endpoint
from the Scramble API documentation to EchoAPI to create
a corresponding endpoint. To do this, import the Postman
collection that you generated earlier into EchoAPI. From within
EchoAPI in VS Code, on the top-left side of the page, click the
HTTP1/2 Request drop-down menu. Then choose the Import
Data option; see Figure 7-3.

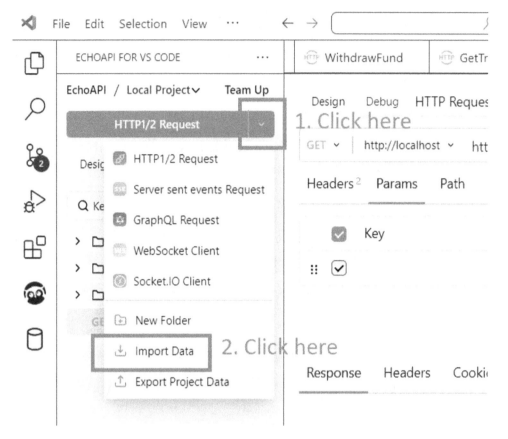

Figure 7-3. *Accessing the Import Data menu in EchoAPi inside VS Code in order to import the generated Postman collection*

Choosing the Import Data option will open the Import Data page shown in Figure 7-4.

Select the Postman option as shown in Figure 7-4, then click the box labeled Upload File. Clicking the Upload File box will open a file chooser. Navigate to the location of the Postman collection file generated earlier (`storage/app/private/openapi_specs/my_api_collection.json`) and select the file.

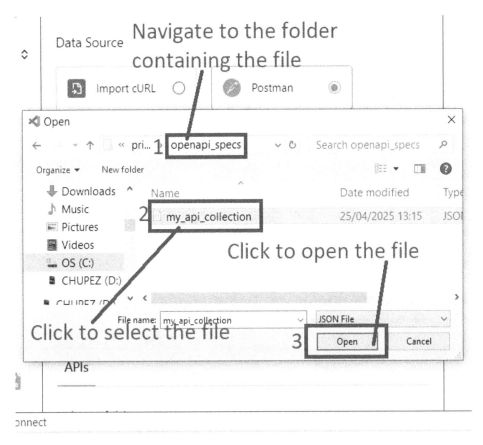

Figure 7-4. *Select the Postman option and navigate to the folder containing the Postman collection; then click the Open button to import it into EchoAPI from within VS Code*

Once you choose the right file, click the Import Now button; see Figure 7-5.

Figure 7-5. *Click the Import Now button to import the selected file*

Clicking the Import Now button will import the file contents. After a while, you should see all the endpoints from your API documentation appear on the left pane of EchoAPI, as shown in Figure 7-6.

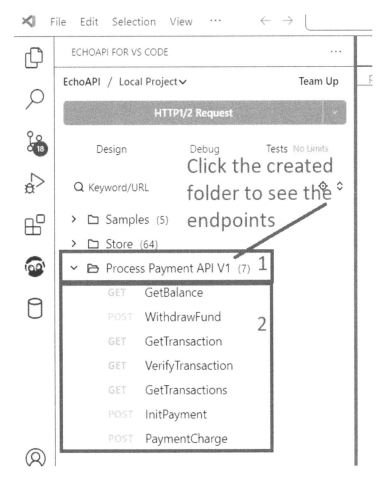

Figure 7-6. *The imported endpoints*

High-Level View of the Test Flow

It'll be helpful to have a high-level view of how this test will work. The following steps will occur during each test cycle:

1. EchoAPI will randomly retrieve a secret key from the list of secret keys you provided to it and store it as an environment variable linked to all the endpoints to be used for the test. A random amount is generated and stored as an environment variable as well; this is the amount to be paid to the merchant whose secret key is being used for this cycle of test.

2. Next, EchoAPI tests the GetBalance endpoint by calling it. If the test is successful, the response will contain the merchant's wallet balance. This balance is then added to the amount to be paid the merchant and saved in an environment variable as the expected balance of the merchant at the end of this test cycle.

3. Next, EchoAPI tests the InitPayment endpoint by calling it with the required body parameters, generated randomly using EchoAPI's dynamic values (except for the amount, which is retrieved from the environment variable you created earlier). A successful response from this endpoint should include the amount to be paid (which must equal the amount you randomly generated earlier) and a transaction reference code, which should be saved in an environment variable for use by other endpoints later in this test cycle.

4. Next to be tested is the PaymentCharge endpoint. The body parameters required for making payment are passed to the endpoint, including the details of the card to be used for payment—like the card holder's name, card number, card secret, and so on—all generated randomly using the dynamic variable feature of EchoAPI. Other body parameters, like transaction references and the amount to pay, are taken from environment variables set earlier in the test cycle. A successful response should include the amount paid, the fee charged for processing the payment, and the transaction reference, which should tally with the transaction reference obtained from initializing the payment. The amount returned should also equal the one randomly generated at the beginning of the test cycle. You should then subtract the fee from the expected balance stored in the environment variable earlier.

5. Next, EchoAPI will test the VerifyTransaction endpoint. To test this route, you only need to pass a transaction's reference to verify the payment transaction. Since you are verifying the payment transaction made in the last test, you simply retrieve the transaction reference saved in an environment variable

earlier and pass it to the route. A successful response should contain the transaction amount, reference, currency, and status. The transaction amount and reference should match the values contained in the corresponding environment variables set earlier.

6. The `WithdrawFund` endpoint will be tested next. To test it, you generate a random amount to be withdrawn from the merchant's balance. If the random amount suggested is greater than the merchant's expected balance, the program will set the amount to withdraw to 0.00. This amount will be sent to the endpoint for withdrawal from the merchant's account. A successful response should include the amount withdrawn and the merchant's balance. The amount withdrawn should equal the random amount sent for withdrawal to the endpoint. The balance should equal the expected balance stored in the environment variable.

7. The next two tests involve the `GetTransaction` and the `GetTransactions` endpoints. The `GetTransaction` endpoint does the same thing as the `VerifyTransaction` endpoint and their test is thus similar. The `GetTransactions` endpoint, on the other hand, returns the transactions of the current merchant in batches of 10. Each set of transactions is returned as an array. So you want to check that you are receiving an array at least if the test is successful.

8. Lastly, the `GetBalance` endpoint is tested again to retrieve the balance at the end of the test cycle in order to confirm that it's equal to the expected value stored in the environment variable.

You can repeat this test cycle as much as you want, by simply telling EchoAPI how many times to repeat it. It will carry out all the instructions without any further input needed.

Rearranging the Endpoints

You need to rearrange the imported endpoints so that they align with the test flow outlined in the preceding section. To do that, you simply click and drag each endpoint up or down so it's placed in its correct position. They should be arranged as shown in Figure 7-7.

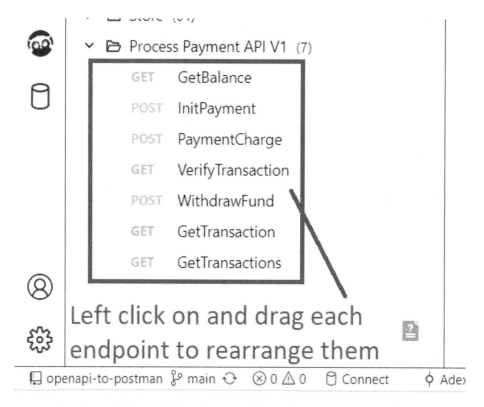

Figure 7-7. *You can click and drag to rearrange the endpoints*

Duplicating the GetBalance Endpoint

In the test flow overview, you might have noticed that the GetBalance endpoint was called (tested) twice, once at the beginning and once at the end of the flow. This allows you to compare the final balance to the initial balance after taking into consideration the amount paid and the amount withdrawn during a test cycle. You therefore need to duplicate the GetBalance endpoint so you have one at the beginning and another at the end of the test flow. To do this, right-click the GetBalance endpoint and choose the Duplicate option; see Figure 7-8. This action will duplicate the endpoint, as shown in Figure 7-9.

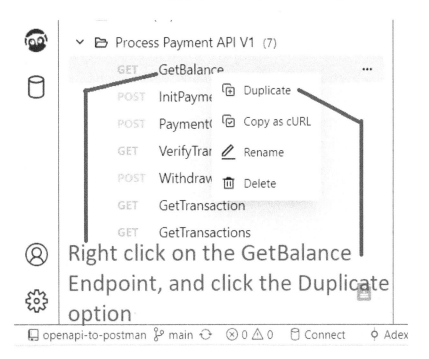

Figure 7-8. *Duplicating an endpoint*

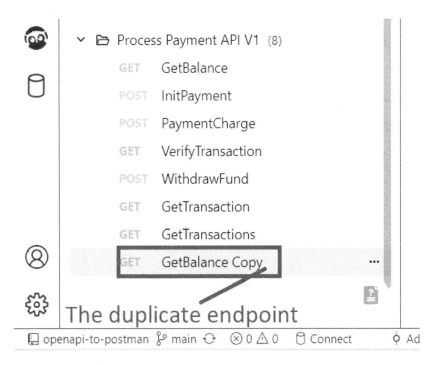

Figure 7-9. *A duplicated endpoint*

Notice in Figure 7-9 that the duplicated endpoint is also automatically placed at the end of the endpoints list, which is what you want.

Creating the Global Variable

You need to store the secret keys (saved as comma separated values, CSV) you retrieved from the dashboard earlier in a global variable. See Figure 7-10.

Figure 7-10. *The secret keys saved in a text file as comma separated values (csv)*

To navigate to the Global Variable page in EchoAPI, click the ellipses (three dots) at the top-left. See Figure 7-11. Choose the Environment option.

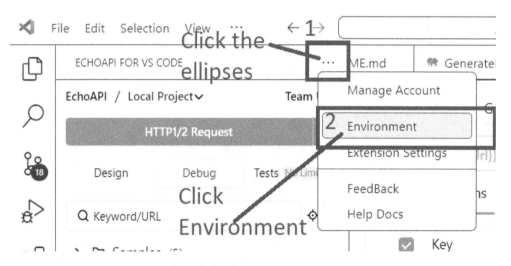

Figure 7-11. *Navigating to the Global Variable page*

On the opened page, click Global Variables. See Figure 7-12.

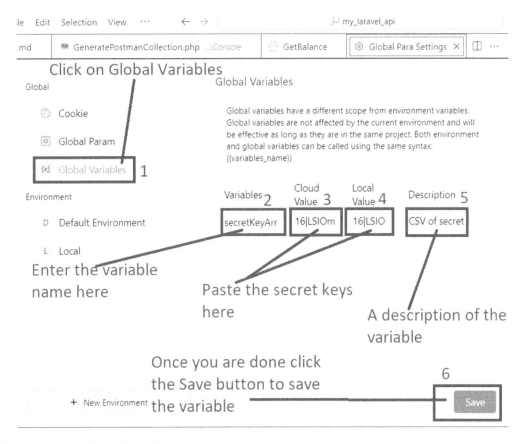

Figure 7-12. *The Global Variable page*

In the opened page in Figure 7-12, enter a name for the global variable; copy and paste the comma separated secret key into the Cloud Value and Local Value text boxes. You can also give a description of the global variable in the Description text box. Finally, click the Save button to save the global variable. This last step ensures that you don't the changes you've made.

Creating the Environment and Environment Variables

In this section, you learn how to create an environment as well as the environment variables needed for this test. Still on the Global Variable page from the last section, click the + New Environment button at the bottom of the page. See Figure 7-13.

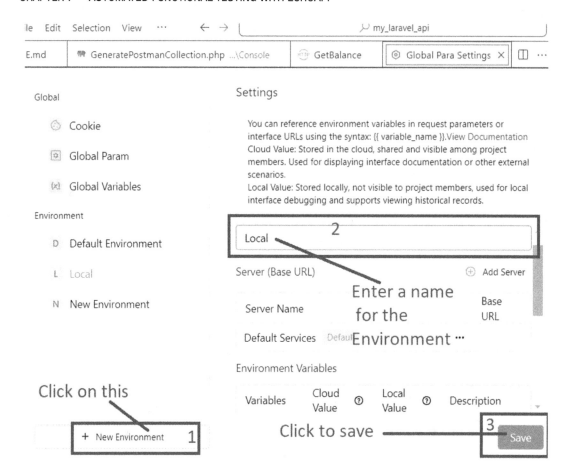

Figure 7-13. *Global Variable page*

Table 7-1 provides details about the environment variables you will create for this test.

Table 7-1. *Environment Variables To Be Created for This Test*

SN.	Variable	Cloud Value	Local Value	Description
1	amount	0.00	0.00	Amount to pay
2	txnid	-	-	Transaction reference ID
3	token	-	-	Currently elected secret key
4	expectedBalance	0.00	0.00	Initial balance plus amount to be paid
5	amount2Withdraw	0.00	0.00	Amount to withdraw from the current merchant balance
6	payment_fee	0.00	0.00	Payment processing fee; deductible from amount paid to the merchant
7	baseUrl	http:// localhost	http:// localhost	The base URL for all endpoints

In EchoAPI, scroll down the Environment page to show the Environment Variable section, where you can create the needed environment variables using the values in Table 7-1. Don't forget to click the Save button in order to save your edits.

Once you create them, the environment variables should appear as shown in Figure 7-14.

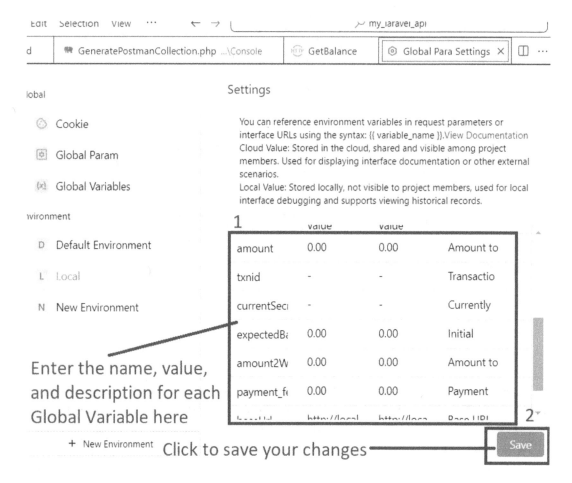

Figure 7-14. *The environment variables*

Adding Global Parameters

With a global parameter, you can set a single value for a given parameter globally. This means that EchoAPI will automatically apply this value to every endpoint that uses this parameter when sending requests to the endpoint. The value given to a global parameter can be a fixed value or a value obtained from a global or environment variable.

There is a JavaScript script used by more than one of the endpoints in their pre-request and post-response scripts. You can set this script up as a global parameter so that you don't to have to add it individually to all the endpoints that need it.

The script is shown in Listing 7-12.

Listing 7-12. JavaScript Script

```
function getARandomValueFromCSV(randValCSVKey) {
  //Get a global variable, & convert the csv stored in it to
  //an array of the csv values
  let retArr = pm.globals.get(randValCSVKey).split(',');

  //get a random number between zero and the length of the
  // array retArr
  let i = Math.floor(Math.random() * retArr.length);

  //use the random number i to retrieve a random value from
  //retArr
  return retArr[i];

}

function getRandomDecimal(min=10, max=10000) {
  // 1. Generate base random [0, 1)
  const base = Math.random();

  // 2. Scale to [min, max)
  const scaled = base * (max - min) + min;

  // 3. Round to 2 decimal places and convert back to Number
  return scaled.toFixed(2);
}
```

The script contains two functions. The first of these functions, getARandomValueFromCSV(), retrieves a random value from any global variable containing comma separated variables (CSVs). Specifically, you'll use it to retrieve random secret keys from the secretKeyArr global variable. The second function, getRandomDecimal(), returns a random number to two decimal places, and it serves as the amount to pay.

To add this script, ensure that you are on the Global Param page, then click the Pre-request script tab. Then click the + Add Task button and then select the Processing Script option. See Figure 7-15.

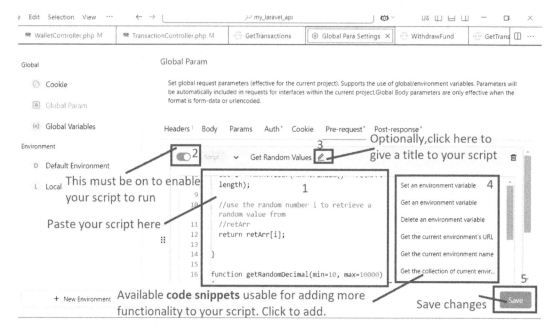

Figure 7-15. *Global Param page*

Clicking the Processing Script option will open a text box into which to paste your script; see Figure 7-16. Don't forget to save your changes.

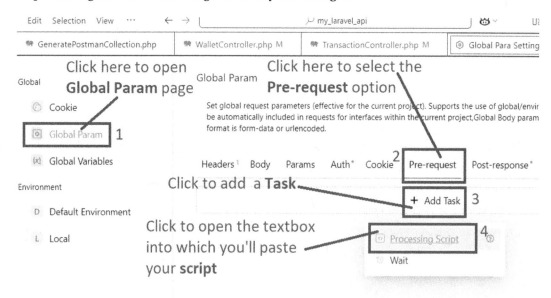

Figure 7-16. *Adding a pre-request script*

The endpoints will now automatically have access to this script, since you saved it as a global parameter (pre-request) script.

Next, you need to add the same script as a global parameter (post-response) script, so that it can be made available to the endpoints' post-response scripts as well. To do this, first click the Post-response tab, then follow the same steps you took for the global pre-request script. See Figure 7-17.

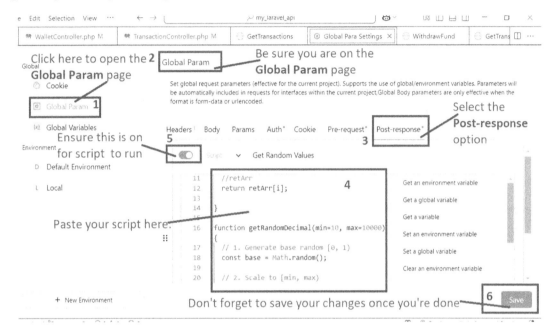

Figure 7-17. *Adding a post-response script*

Adding Dynamic Values

In EchoAPI, dynamic values—random values—can be generated for request parameters whose values need to change from one request to another (i.e., from one test to the next). If you need to test an endpoint requiring parameters like email, full name, phone number, credit card detail, and so on, you can use EchoAPI dynamic value feature to automatically generate random values for this parameters for each test. Dynamic values can be obtained via environment variables and global variables, including EchoAPI's built-in global variables.

To instruct EchoAPI to generate a dynamic value for say, a body parameter needing a random email value for each test, select the endpoint whose parameter you want to make dynamic and select the Body option. Then enter two opening curly brackets into the Value text box of the parameter to display the available environment variables and global variables. Search for and select the dynamic variable for email. Figure 7-18 shows how we set the email field of the InitPayment endpoint body parameter to be generated dynamically.

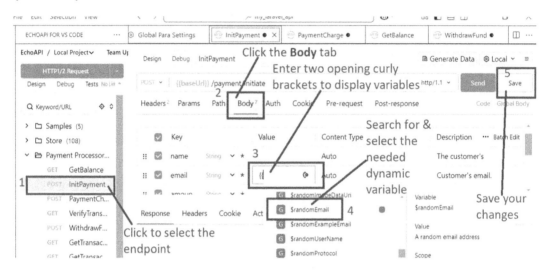

Figure 7-18. *Specifying request data to be automatically generated using environment or global variables for an endpoint during testing*

Although implementing dynamic variables using environment or global variables, as you did here, is easier, the Faker library that comes with EchoAPI offers more flexibility.

This section explains how to add a dynamic value using the Faker library. As an example, you'll add a credit card number to the card_num field of the PaymentCharge endpoint's body parameter.

Click the PaymentCharge endpoint to select it; then click the Body tab. Locate the card_num field and click its Value text box to reveal a tiny icon to the right. Click the tiny icon to display three options; Figure 7-19.

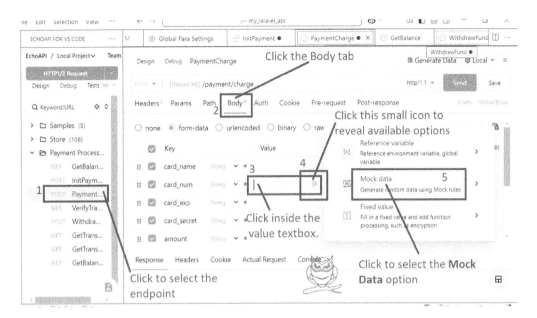

Figure 7-19. *Specifying request data to be automatically generated using the Faker library for an endpoint during testing*

Then select the Mock Data option to display another interface for choosing the appropriate Faker data. See Figure 7-20.

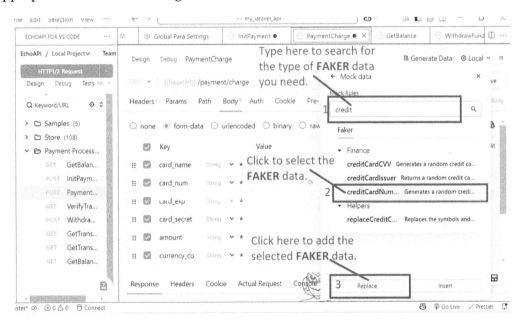

Figure 7-20. *Specifying request data to be automatically generated using the Faker library for an endpoint during testing*

Try searching for the type of Faker data you need, using the search box. Then scroll through the search results and click to select the appropriate one. Then click the Replace button to add the selected Faker data type to the endpoint's body parameter's field. See Figure 7-20.

Figure 7-21 shows the selected Faker data assigned to the card_num field. Now, anytime a request is sent to this endpoint, a random credit card number will be generated and sent with the request.

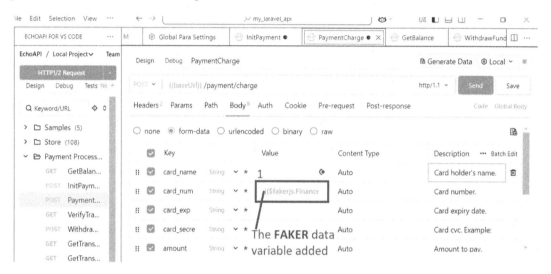

Figure 7-21. *Dynamic data added using the Faker library*

Table 7-2. *Endpoints with the Dynamic Data They Require*

SN	Endpoint	Field	Dynamic Data Type	Dynamic Data Value
1	PaymentCharge	card_name	Global variable	{{$randomFullName}}
2	PaymentCharge	card_num	Faker data	{{$fakerjs.Finance. creditCardNumber}}
3	PaymentCharge	card_exp	Fixed value	09/45
4	PaymentCharge	card_secret	Faker data	{{$fakerjs.Finance. creditCardCVV}}

(continued)

Table 7-2. (*continued*)

SN	Endpoint	Field	Dynamic Data Type	Dynamic Data Value
5	PaymentCharge	payment_method	Fixed value	card
6	PaymentCharge	amount	Environment variable	{{amount}}
7	PaymentCharge	currency_code	Fixed value	USD
8	PaymentCharge	transaction_ref	Environment variable	{{txnid}}
9	PaymentCharge	direct_charge	Fixed value	1
10	InitPayment	name	Global variable	{{$randomFullName}}
11	InitPayment	amount	Environment Variable	{{amount}}
12	InitPayment	email	Global variable	{{$randomEmail}}
13	InitPayment	currency	Fixed value	USD
14	InitPayment	redirect_url	Fixed value	http://localhost
15	InitPayment	pass_charge	Fixed value	1
16	InitPayment	direct_charge	Fixed value	1
17	WithdrawFund	amount	Environment variable	{{amount2Withdraw}}

Table 7-2 contains endpoints with the dynamic data that they require. Use the information in the table with the aid of the previous two examples to add this dynamic data to the endpoints. When you're done, the dynamic data should be as shown in Figures 7-22, 7-23, and 7-24.

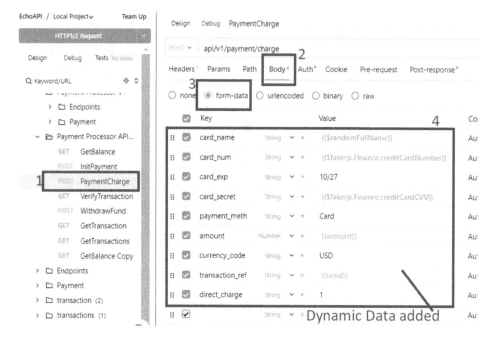

Figure 7-22. *Dynamic data for the PaymentCharge endpoint*

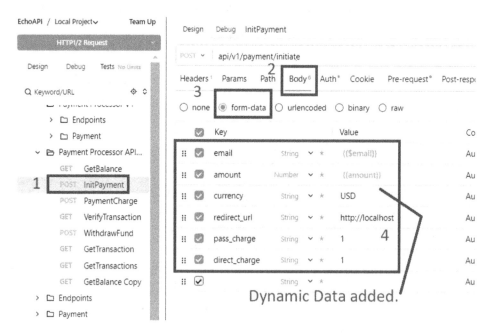

Figure 7-23. *Dynamic data for the InitPayment endpoint*

Figure 7-24. *Dynamic data for the WithdawFund endpoint*

Integrating the Pre-request and Post-response Scripts

Lastly, before you run your test, you need to implement the pre-request and post-response scripts needed by the individual endpoints.

Tables 7-3 and 7-4 contain endpoints with their pre-request and post-response scripts, respectively. Use the information to integrate each endpoint's scripts appropriately.

Table 7-3. *Endpoints with their Pre-Request Scripts*

SN	Endpoint	Pre-Request Script	Explanation

1	GetBalance	`let randSecKey = getARandomValueFromCSV("secretK`
		`eyArr");`
		
		`pm.environment.set("token", randSecKey);`	

2	WithdrawFund	`let amt2Withdraw = getRandomDecimal();`
		
		`pm.environment.set("amount2Withdraw", amt2Withdraw);`
		
		`//get the expected balance`
		`expBal = pm.environment.get('expectedBalance');`
		
		`console.log('amt2Withdraw: '+amt2Withdraw);`
		
		`console.log('expBal: '+expBal);`
		
		`if(parseFloat(expBal) > parseFloat(amt2Withdraw)){`
		
		`pm.environment.set("amount2Withdraw", amt2Withdraw);`
		`}else{`
		
		`pm.environment.set("amount2Withdraw", '0.00');`
		`}`	

Table 7-4. *Endpoints with Their Post-Response Scripts*

SN	Endpoint	Post-Response Script	Explanation

1	GetBalance	```let randAmt = getRandomDecimal();```
		```pm.environment.set("amount", randAmt);```
		
		```let iniBal = response.json.data.wallet_```
		```balance;```
		```let expBal = (parseFloat(randAmt) +```
		```parseFloat(iniBal)).toFixed(2);```
		
		```console.log('randAmt: ' + randAmt);```
		```console.log('iniBal: ' + iniBal);```
		```console.log('expBal: ' + expBal);```
		
		```//Set the expected balance```
		```pm.environment.set('expectedBalance',```
		```expBal);```
		
		```pm.test("Status code is 200", () => {```
		
		```pm.expect(pm.response.code).to.eql(200);```
		```});```	

(continued)

Table 7-4. (*continued*)

SN	Endpoint	Post-Response Script	Explanation

2	InitPayment	```let txnref = response.json.data.transaction_ref;```
		```console.log('txnref: ' + txnref);```
		
		```pm.environment.set("txnid", txnref);```
		```pm.test("Status code is 200", () => {```
		```pm.expect(pm.response.code).to.eql(200);```
		```});```
		```pm.test("Response property amount matches global variable amount", function () {```
		
		```pm.expect(pm.response.json().data.transaction_amount).to.eql(pm.environment.get("amount"));```
		```});```
		```console.log('response: ' + JSON.stringify(response));```
		```//console.log('response.raw.responseText: '+response.raw.responseText)```	

(*continued*)

Table 7-4. (*continued*)

SN	Endpoint	Post-Response Script	Explanation
3	PaymentCharge	```let retFee = response.json.data.fee;
console.log(retFee);
if(retFee){
let expectBal = pm.environment.
get('expectedBalance');
expectBal = (parseFloat(expectBal) -
parseFloat(retFee)).toFixed(2);

pm.environment.set('expectedBalance',
expectBal);

pm.environment.set('payment_fee', retFee);
}

pm.test("Status code is 200", () => {

pm.expect(pm.response.code).to.eql(200);
});

pm.test("Response property amount matches
global variable amount", function () {

pm.expect(pm.response.json().data.amount).
to.eql(pm.environment.get("amount"));
});

pm.test("Sum of response properties
amount_less_fee plus fee matches global
variable amount", function () {

pm.expect((parseFloat(pm.response.json().
data.amount_less_fee) + parseFloat(pm.
response.json().data.fee)).toFixed(2)).
to.eql(pm.environment.get("amount"));
});``` | |

(*continued*)

Table 7-4. (*continued*)

SN	Endpoint	Post-Response Script	Explanation
		`pm.test("Response property transaction_ref matches global variable txnid", function () {`	
		`pm.expect(pm.response.json().data.transaction_ref).to.eql(pm.environment.get("txnid"));` `});`	
4	VerifyTransaction	`pm.test("Status code is 200", () => {`	
		`pm.expect(pm.response.code).to.eql(200);` `});`	
		`pm.test("Response property transaction_amount matches global variable amount", function () {`	
		`pm.expect(pm.response.json().data.transaction_amount).to.eql(pm.environment.get("amount"));` `});` `pm.test("Response property transaction_ref matches global variable txnid", function () {`	
		`pm.expect(pm.response.json().data.transaction_ref).to.eql(pm.environment.get("txnid"));` `});`	

(*continued*)

Table 7-4. (*continued*)

SN	Endpoint	Post-Response Script	Explanation

5	WithdrawFund	```let amtWithdrawn = response.json.data.amount_withdrawn;```
		 ```console.log(amtWithdrawn);```
		 ```if(amtWithdrawn){```
		 ```let expectBal = pm.environment.get('expectedBalance');```
		 ```expectBal = (parseFloat(expectBal) - parseFloat(amtWithdrawn)).toFixed(2);```
		
		 ```pm.environment.set('expectedBalance', expectBal);```
		
		 ```}```
		
		 ```pm.test("Status code is 200", () => {```
		
		 ```pm.expect(pm.response.code).to.eql(200);```
		 ```});```
		
		 ```let retBal = (pm.response.json().data.balance).toFixed(2);```
		
		 ```console.log('retBal: '+retBal)```
		
		 ```pm.test("Response property balance matches global variable expectedBalance", function () {```
		
		 ```pm.expect(retBal).to.eql(pm.environment.get("expectedBalance"));```
		 ```});```	

(*continued*)

Table 7-4. (*continued*)

SN	Endpoint	Post-Response Script	Explanation

6	GetTransaction	`pm.test("Status code is 200", () => {`
		
		`pm.expect(pm.response.code).to.eql(200);`
		`});`
		`pm.test("Response property transaction_ref matches global variable txnid", function () {`
		
		`pm.expect(pm.response.json().data.transaction_ref).to.eql(pm.environment.get("txnid"));`
		`});`	

7	GetTransactions	`pm.test("Status code is 200", () => {`
		
		`pm.expect(pm.response.code).to.eql(200);`
		`});`
		`pm.test("json.data is an array", () => {`
		`pm.expect(pm.response.json().data).to.be.an("array");`
		`}`
		`);`	

8	GetBalance Copy	`pm.test("Status code is 200", () => {`
		
		`pm.expect(pm.response.code).to.eql(200);`
		`});`
		
		`pm.test("Response property wallet_balance matches environment variable expectedBalance", function () {`
		
		`pm.expect(pm.response.json().data.wallet_balance).to.eql(pm.environment.get("expectedBalance"));`
		`});`	

This section explains how to add pre-request and post-response scripts to an endpoint using the GetBalance endpoint as an example. In EchoAPI, start by clicking the GetBalance endpoint; then click the Pre-request tab. Click + Add Task to reveal two options. Select the Processing Script option to open the text box where you'll paste the script. Paste the script into the text box and don't forget to click the Save button once you are done. See Figures 7-25 and 7-26.

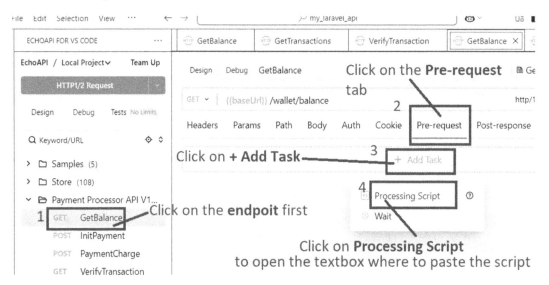

Figure 7-25. *Adding a pre-request script to the GetBalance endpoint*

Figure 7-26. *Adding a pre-request script to the GetBalance endpoint*

Next, you learn how to add a post-response script to an endpoint using the GetBalance endpoint as an example. Again, start by clicking the GetBalance endpoint. Then click the Post-response tab. Click + Add Task to reveal four options. Choose the Processing Script option to open the text box where you'll paste the script. Paste the script into the text box; don't forget to click the Save button once you are done. See Figures 7-27 and 7-28.

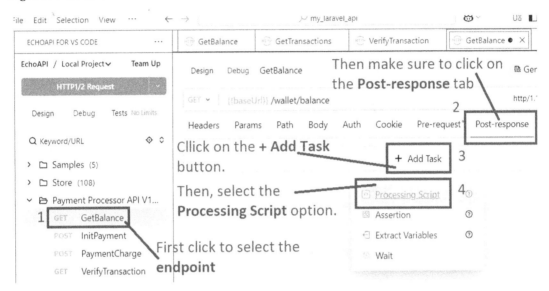

Figure 7-27. *Adding a post-response script to the GetBalance endpoint*

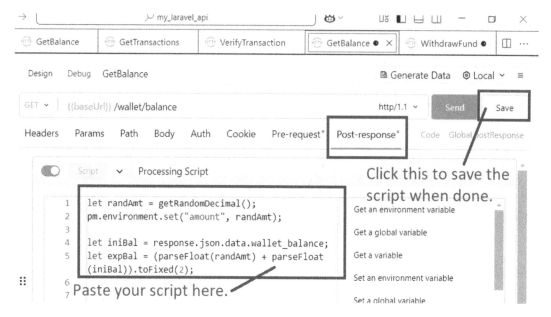

Figure 7-28. *Adding a post-response script to the GetBalance endpoint*

Using the information provided in Tables 7-3 and 7-4, add the pre-request and post-response scripts to the remaining endpoints.

Running the Automated Test

To run your test, right-click the project folder, as shown in Figure 7-29, and click the Run All option from the list of options displayed. This will open the test page, as shown in Figure 7-29.

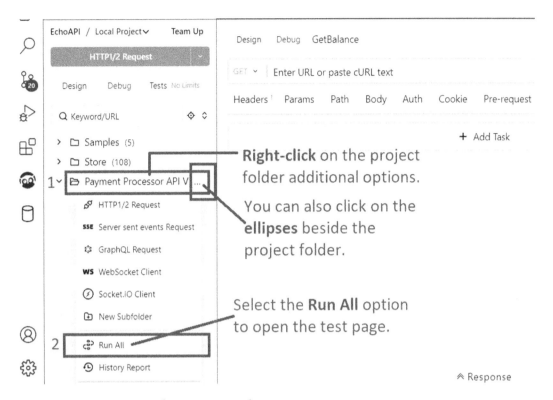

Figure 7-29. *Opening the automated test page*

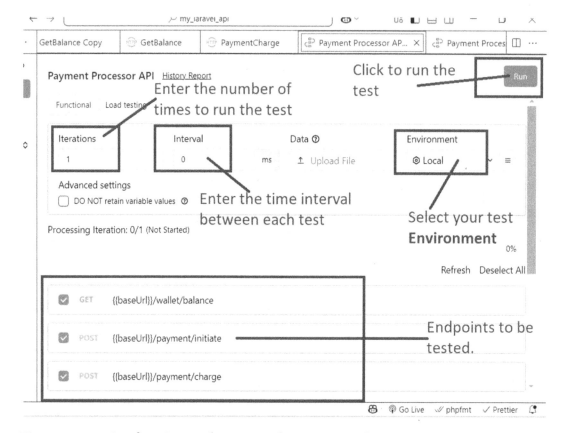

Figure 7-30. *Configuring and running the automated test*

Clicking the Run button will start the test. The number of times the test will run is determined by the iteration counts entered before running the test; see Figure 7-30. Figure 7-31 shows a summary report of a test that's been run.

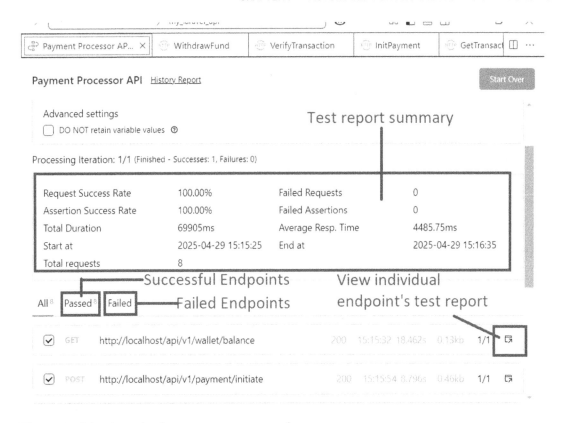

Figure 7-31. *A typical summary report of a test*

Handling Failed Tests

Here's what you can do when a test fails:

1. **Failed assertion**: Check your script to see whether the assumption behind your assertions is valid. Check the actual response obtained from the endpoint to see if it is as expected. You may need to rewrite your assertion or adjust your API code to send an appropriate response.

2. **Failed request**: Try to test the failed endpoint using Scramble. If the test passes in Scramble, then ensure that your secret key (token) is correct and enabled; see Figure 7-32. If the test fails in Scramble, you may want to check your API code and your secret key.

Figure 7-32. *Locating and confirming the correctness of your secret key*

Committing Your Changes

Commit your changes in this chapter to Git by running the command in Listing 7-13.

Listing 7-13. Command to Commit Changes to Git

```
git add . && git commit -m "Chapter 7"
```

Conclusion

In this chapter, you looked at EchoAPI. You learned how to use it to run API automated functional testing.

## CHAPTER 8

Implementing Webhook and Asynchronous Notifications

In the last chapter, you learned how to run automated feature testing on your API using EchoAPI. This chapter explores how to implement webhooks, which enable you to send email using queued jobs.

Implementing Webhooks

Webhooks are powerful mechanisms for enabling real-time communication between applications. They allow systems to send HTTP POST requests to specific URLs whenever an event occurs. In the context of the Payment Processor API, you can send a webhook notification to the URL supplied by the API users to notify them about payments into their account. This URL is supplied by the API user and it usually points to a script on their server. That script includes code for handling the webhook and for updating their records regarding payments received. In this chapter, you learn how to implement a webhook notification system for your API, so that your API users can be notified via webhooks any time a payment is made into their account.

As mentioned, the user must supply the URL where their webhook notification will be sent; users must also submit a *secret*, which is essentially a string. It can be a phrase, a collection of random words, a collection of alphanumeric characters, and so on. The

329

© Adegoke Akintoye 2025
A. Akintoye, *API Development with Laravel*, https://doi.org/10.1007/979-8-8688-1576-8_8

secret is supposed to be known only by the user and the API, enabling the user to verify that the received webhook notification is from the API. The user can submit both via the API dashboard. Both the URL and secret are stored in the user table in the database.

Note   The source code for this book is available on GitHub via the book's product page, located at `https://github.com/Apress/API-Development-with-Laravel`.

Creating a Job to Send Webhook Notifications

You'll start by creating a Laravel job. Inside the job, you'll indicate the information to be sent via the webhook notification using the given secret and then send the notification to the submitted URL. Let's start by creating a job. To generate the job, run the command in Listing 8-1 from within your Laravel project folder in the command-line terminal.

Listing 8-1. Command to Create the Job

```
php artisan make:job SendWebhookNotification
```

Then update the app/Jobs/SendWebhookNotification.php file, as shown in Listing 8-2.

Listing 8-2. Updating the app/Jobs/SendWebhookNotification.php File

```php
<?php
//app/Jobs/SendWebhookNotification.php

namespace App\Jobs;

use Illuminate\Bus\Queueable;
use Illuminate\Contracts\Queue\ShouldQueue;
use Illuminate\Foundation\Bus\Dispatchable;
use Illuminate\Queue\InteractsWithQueue;
use Illuminate\Queue\SerializesModels;
use Illuminate\Support\Facades\Http;
use Illuminate\Support\Facades\Log;
```

```php
class SendWebhookNotification implements ShouldQueue
{
    use Dispatchable, InteractsWithQueue, Queueable, SerializesModels;

    protected string $signature;

    /**
     * Create a new job instance.
     *
     * @param string $webhookUrl
     * @param string $subscriberSecret
     * @param array  $payload
     */
    public function __construct(
        protected string $webhookUrl,
        protected string $subscriberSecret,
        protected array $payload
    ) {
        $this->signature = $this->generateSignature(json_encode($this->
        payload), $this->subscriberSecret);
    }

    /**
     * Execute the job.
     *
     * @return void
     */
    public function handle()
    {
        try {
            $response = Http::withHeaders([
                'X-Signature'  => $this->signature,
                'Content-Type' => 'application/json',
            ])->post($this->webhookUrl, $this->payload);
            // Throws an exception for client or server error responses
            $response->throw();
```

```php
            Log::info('Webhook sent successfully', ['url' => $this-
            >webhookUrl]);

        } catch (\Exception $e) {
            Log::error('Failed to send webhook', [
                'url'   => $this->webhookUrl,
                'error' => $e->getMessage(),
            ]);
            // Optionally, implement retry logic or mark the subscriber
                for review
        }
    }

    /**
     * Generate an HMAC signature for the payload using the user-
       provided secret.
     *
     * @param string $payload
     * @param string $secret
     * @return string
     */
    protected function generateSignature(string $payload, string
    $secret): string
    {
        return hash_hmac('sha256', $payload, $secret);
    }

    public function failed(\Throwable $e)
    {
        \Log::error('Job failed: ' . $e->getMessage(), ['trace' => $e->
        getTraceAsString()]);
    }
}
```

Dispatching the Webhook Notification When a Payment Is Successful

You will dispatch the webhook notification and send email messages whenever a successful payment event occurs. This means that you need to modify the sendWebhookNotification() method of the PaymentController controller to send a webhook notification whenever such an event occurs.

Update the sendWebhookNotification() method in the app/Http/Controllers/v1/PaymentController.php file, as shown in Listing 8-3a (the changes are shown in bold).

Listing 8-3a. Updating the sendWebhookNotification() Method in the app/Http/Controllers/v1/PaymentController.php File

//app/Http/Controllers/v1/PaymentController.php

```
private function sendWebhookNotification($user){

    // Dispatch a job for the user's webhook URL using their secret
    SendWebhookNotification::dispatch(
        $user->webhook_url,
        $user->webhook_secret,
        $this->successData($txn)
    );

}
```

Now, when you call the sendWebhookNotification() method, the webhook notification should be queued and eventually sent.

Sending Emails Asynchronously

Now you will update the sendMail() method in the app/Http/Controllers/v1/PaymentController.php file, as shown in Listing 8-3b (changes are shown in bold). These changes allow the emails being sent to be added to the queue and sent in the background.

Listing 8-3b. Updating the sendMail() Method in the app/Http/Controllers/
v1/PaymentController.php File

//app/Http/Controllers/v1/PaymentController.php

```php
private function sendMail($txnn){

 $subject = 'Payment Receipt Notification';

 $mailData = [
 'mailView' => 'emails.success-customer',
 'subject'  => $subject,
           'amount'   => $txnn->amount,
           'refid'    => $txnn->transaction_ref,
           'email'    => $txnn->email,

        ];

        Mail::to($txnn->email)->queue(new \App\Mail\
        PaymentMail($mailData));

        $mailData['subject'] = 'Payment Notification';

        $mailData['mailView'] = 'emails.success-merchant';

        $mailData['email']    = $txnn->user->email;

        Mail::to($txnn->user->email)->queue(new \App\Mail\
        PaymentMail($mailData));

    }
```

Lastly, in this section, you'll update the requestLink() method in the app/Http/
Controllers/Auth/AuthController.php file, as shown in Listing 8-3c (changes are
shown in bold). This simply changes Mail::to($user->email)->send(new \App\
Mail\MagicLinkMail($link)) to Mail::to($user->email)->queue(new \App\Mail\
MagicLinkMail($link)). This change also allows the emails being sent to be added to
the queue and sent in the background.

Listing 8-3c. Updating the requestLink() Method in the app/Http/
Controllers/Auth/AuthController.php File

//app/Http/Controllers/Auth/AuthController.php

```php
    public function requestLink(Request $request)
    {
        $request->validate([
            'email' => 'required|email',
        ]);

        // Find or create user
        $user = User::firstOrCreate(['email' => $request->email]);

        // Generate a magic link token
        $token    = Str::random(64);
        $expiresAt = Carbon::now()->addMinutes(15); // Link valid for
        15 minutes

        // Store token in database
        MagicLink::create([
            'user_id'    => $user->id,
            'token'      => $token,
            'expires_at' => $expiresAt,
        ]);

        // Generate login link
        $link = URL::temporarySignedRoute(
            'auth.login',
            $expiresAt,
            ['token' => $token]
        );

        // Send email
        Mail::to($user->email)->queue(new \App\Mail\MagicLinkMail($link));
        //
        $masked_email = substr_replace($user->email, '****', 0, 3);
        //return response()->json(['message' => 'A login link has been sent
        to your email.']);
```

```
    return redirect()->route('sent_email_notifier', ['email' =>
    $masked_email]);
}
```

Setting Up the Queue Database

Each webhook notification and email you'll send (dispatch) is configured and stored as a Laravel job, with *Queue Worker* taking each job and executing it. Laravel Queue Worker has different types of drivers that it can use to connect with the jobs to be executed. This book uses the *database driver*. The jobs will be stored (queued) in a database table. To tell Laravel that you are using the database driver, you need to update your Laravel project's .env file. Open the .env file and ensure that the QUEUE_CONNECTION option is set to database, as shown in Listing 8-4.

Listing 8-4. Ensure that QUEUE_CONNECTION Is Set to database

```
QUEUE_CONNECTION=database
```

Next, you need to set up the necessary database tables—if they have not already been created by Laravel—to store your jobs. To do that, run the Artisan command shown in Listing 8-5.

Listing 8-5. Artisan Commands to Set Up the Database Tables

```
php artisan queue:table
php artisan queue:failed-table
php artisan migrate
```

These commands will generate and run migrations that create a jobs table (and a failed_jobs table if you want to log failed jobs). You should see the jobs and failed_jobs tables in your database after migration.

Configuring and Running the Queue Worker

You can run the Queue Worker from a terminal so that it can take the webhook notifications and sent email jobs and execute them for you, one after the other. To set the Queue Worker up, run the command shown in Listing 8-6.

Listing 8-6. Command to Run Queue Worker

```
php artisan queue:work --tries=3 --timeout=90 --sleep=3
```

This command starts a worker that will continuously look for new jobs in the jobs table. The --tries=3 option means that Laravel will try a failing job up to three times before marking it as failed. The --timeout=90 setting ensures that any job that runs longer than 90 seconds is killed (to avoid hanging). Adjust the specs as needed. If you're testing just one job and want it to exit after that, use --once instead of a continuous worker.

Testing the Webhook and Email

To determine if your webhook notifications and emails are being sent, keep the command-line interface used for the command in Listing 8-6 open. Then run a test on the API that results in a successful payment. If the webhook notification is being sent, the command-line interface you opened earlier should indicate that. Figure 8-1 shows what the command-line interface should look like.

```
Adegoke Akintoye@LAPTOP-FDSFCFRB MINGW64 /c/UniServerZ/www/my_laravel_api (maste
r)
$ php artisan queue:work --tries=3 --sleep=3

   INFO  Processing jobs from the [default] queue.

  2025-05-02 15:22:35 App\Jobs\SendWebhookNotification ............... RUNNING
  2025-05-02 15:23:06 App\Jobs\SendWebhookNotification .............. 30s DONE
  2025-05-02 15:23:06 App\Mail\PaymentMail ........................... RUNNING
  2025-05-02 15:24:12 App\Mail\PaymentMail ....................... 1m 5s DONE
  2025-05-02 15:24:12 App\Mail\PaymentMail ........................... RUNNING
  2025-05-02 15:24:13 App\Mail\PaymentMail ..................... 580.31ms DONE
```

Figure 8-1. *A list of queued jobs being processed*

In Figure 8-1, note that successful jobs are marked as DONE and failed jobs are marked as FAILED.

What To Do When a Job Fails

Here are the steps you should take when a job fails:

1. Assuming you are using EchoAPI for your API test, check the endpoints being tested. If any of the endpoints failed, check the response for clues as to what might be causing the error. See Figure 8-2,

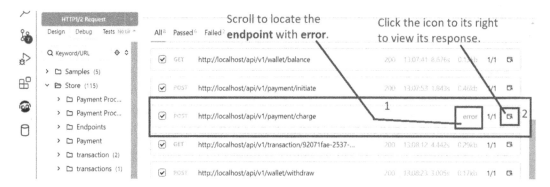

Figure 8-2. *Accessing the error message attached to a failed endpoints in EchoAPI*

Clicking the icon labeled 2 in Figure 8-2 will open a page containing details about the error; see Figure 8-3.

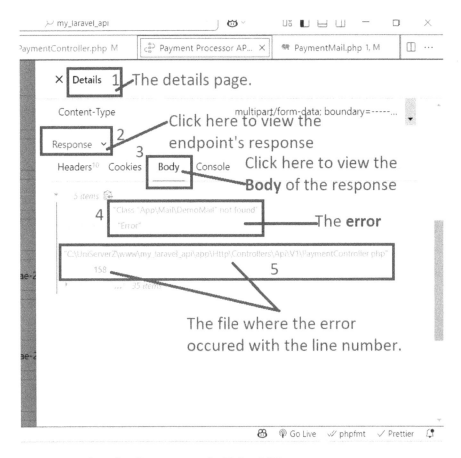

Figure 8-3. *Accessing the Error page in EchoAPI*

2. There may be times when your jobs fail, but none of your
    endpoints tests fail. In that case, open the Uniform Server
    Controller and launch the phpMyAdmin web interface. See
    Figure 8-4.

Figure 8-4. *Accessing the phpMyAdmin interface*

Clicking the phpMyAdmin button shown in Figure 8-4 will open phpMyAdmin in your web browser; see Figure 8-5.

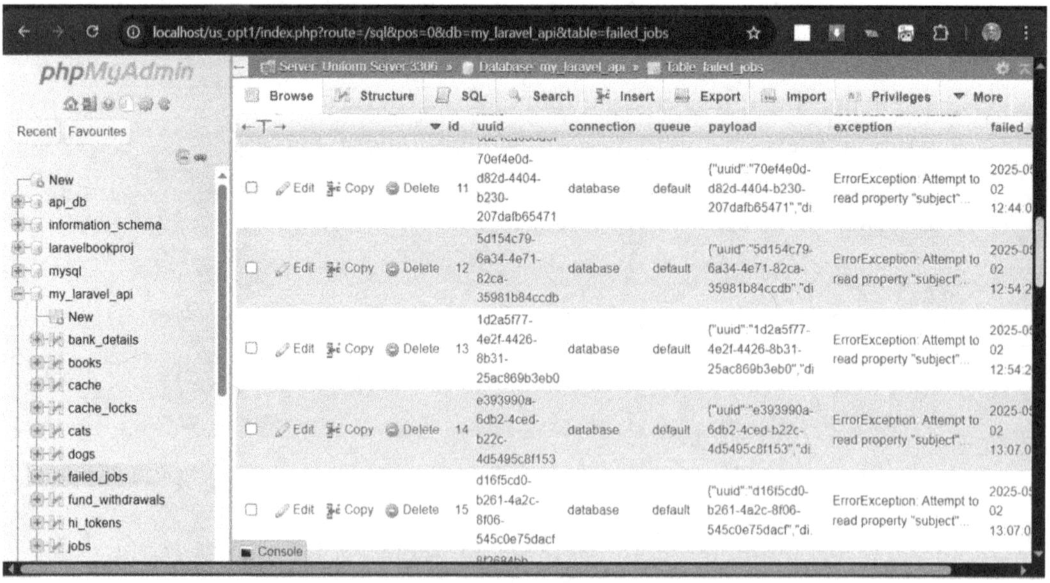

Figure 8-5. *The* failed_jobs *table in the phpMyAdmin interface*

On the opened page, click your application database name and then the failed_jobs table. See Figure 8-6.

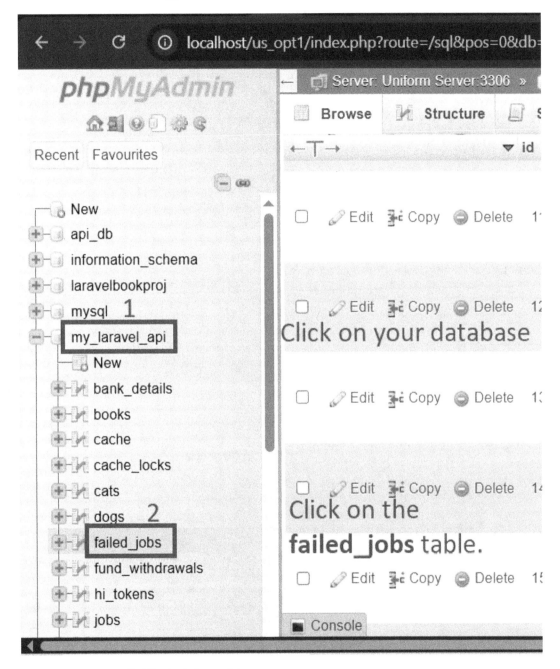

Figure 8-6. The failed_jobs table

Clicking the failed_jobs table will load records of failed jobs. Scroll down to the latest record and find the Exception column to view the cause of the job's failure. See Figure 8-7. You can copy and paste the description into Notepad to read it fully. It will likely point you to the cause of the error.

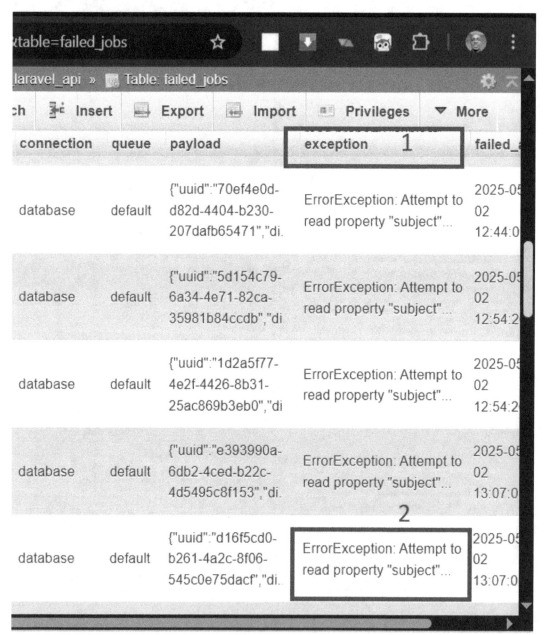

Figure 8-7. *Accessing the cause of a failed job*

3. If the error keeps occurring, even when you're sure you've fixed it, it may be due to the cache. Try the following steps:

    a. Close the command-line terminal from which you invoked the Queue Worker earlier; see Figure 8-1.

    b. Run the Artisan command shown in Listing 8-7.

Listing 8-7. Artisan Command

```
php artisan optimize:clear
```

    c. Then restart the Queue Worker by running the command shown in Listing 8-8.

Listing 8-8. Restarting the Queue Worker

```
php artisan queue:work --tries=3 --timeout=90 --sleep=3
```

    d. Now you can restart your test. If you have corrected the error, you shouldn't receive the previous error again, unless it occurs in more than one location in your code.

    e. Good luck.

Committing Your Changes

Commit your changes in this chapter to Git by running the command in Listing 8-9.

Listing 8-9. Command to Commit Changes to Git

```
git add . && git commit -m "Chapter 8"
```

Conclusion

In this chapter, you learned how to implement webhooks and send emails using queued jobs so that your API's performance is not degraded.

CHAPTER 9

Deploying and Scaling Your API Using CapRover

This chapter looks at how to deploy the API so that it can be accessible to and used by your customers (users) to receive payment. This chapter also discusses how to scale your API to meet increasing usage as your customer base increases.

There are many ways that your API can be deployed and many of them are as proprietary products or dependent services. I try as much as possible to follow paths that do not tie you to a proprietary product or service, unless the knowledge gained can still be generally applicable. I try as much as possible to use open-source tools.

Getting a Virtual Private Server

A *virtual private server* (VPS) is a virtualized server environment provided by hosting companies that gives you dedicated resources—such as CPU, RAM, and storage—within a larger physical server. It uses a hypervisor to split one physical machine into multiple isolated "mini-servers," each with its own operating system and administrative access. This setup offers better performance and security than shared hosting, but at a lower cost and complexity than renting an entire dedicated server.

You can buy a VPS from myriads of web hosting companies online. The following list is a sample, as there are far more web hosting companies than these. The cost of a VPS typically starts from around $3/month.

1. `contabo.com`

2. `webdock.io`

3. `time4vps.com`

© Adegoke Akintoye 2025
A. Akintoye, *API Development with Laravel*, https://doi.org/10.1007/979-8-8688-1576-8_9

4. go54.com

5. interserver.net

6. scalarhosting.com

7. domainking.ng

8. namecheap.com

9. ssdnodes.com

To continue, visit the web hosting company of your choice, sign up, and buy a VPS or get one for trial if available. The selected VPS should meet the following conditions:

1. 2GB of RAM (minimum)

2. 10GB of storage space (minimum)

3. A clean Ubuntu OS (i.e., without any preinstalled control panel, web server, database server, etc.)

For SSH access to your VPS, a username and password will either be created for you and sent to you via email, or you'll be required to create one yourself. In either case, keep the username and password handy, as you'll need them to access your server. In addition, at least one IP (Internet Protocol) address will be assigned to your VPS. Each Internet-connected device is normally assigned an IP address, which identifies it and facilitates effective inter-device communication online. There are major types of IP addresses—IPv4 (e.g., 128.168.90.87) and IPv6 (e.g., 2001:0db8:0000:0000:0000:0000:0000:0001). You'll most certainly be assigned an IPv4, and likely an IPv6 in addition. You'll need your server's IP address later, so keep it handy too.

Domain Name Registration

Next, you need to register a *domain name*. To register one, you can do a search for domain name registration via Google to locate an organization to register with. Most web hosting companies also sell domain names. The company you bought your VPS from may likely handle domain name registrations too, so you might be able to buy a domain name from them. Here is a short list of some web hosting companies that also handle domain name registrations:

1. namecheap.com

2. lcn.com

3. domainking.ng

4. go54.com

5. domains.cloudflare.com

6. freehostia.com

Most web hosting sites provide a search bar so that you can search for domain names; see Figure 9-1. If your desired domain name is not available, choose from the suggested options or try another domain name to see if it's available there.

Figure 9-1. *Searching for a domain name to buy*

To buy any of the available domains, simply add them to the cart and checkout to make payment. If you are not already logged in to the site, you'll be required to sign up before making payment. After you successfully purchase the domain, a confirmation email will be sent to you. You'll need your login details later to access the site in order to use or renew the domain name.

DNS Records

This section explains how to create DNS (Domain Name System) records. These records help you link the IP (Internet Protocol) address of the computer (server) that hosts your application to your domain name. The domain name is converted to the IP address of your server (assuming you've set your DNS records), allowing your application to be reached.

DNS records are typically managed through your domain name registrar (the company/site you bought your domain name from). To create or edit a DNS record, you typically log in to your domain registrar's site and locate the DNS record page in order to create a new record or edit an existing one. You'll see an example of how to do this later.

Creating an A Record for Your Primary Domain Name

The domain name you registered earlier will serve as your primary domain name. As you'll see later, you can derive other domain names from a primary domain name; these derived domain names are referred to as *subdomain* names.

To set an *A* record for the primary domain name, visit the domain name registrar page where you can add or edit DNS records, as shown Figure 9-2.

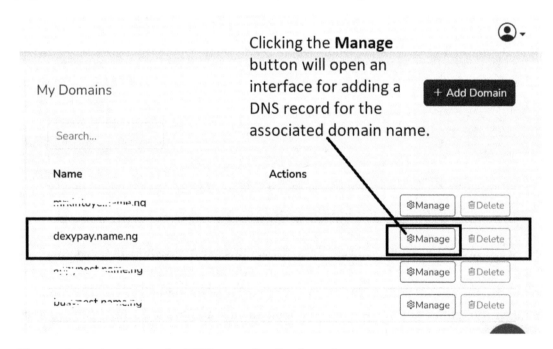

Figure 9-2. *Accessing the DNS records of a domain name*

In this example (your own case might be slightly different), after logging in to the domain registrar's site and locating the page listing the domains with the registrar, you click the Manage button attached to the domain name. This action will take you to another page, where you can add the record. On the opened page, shown in Figure 9-3, you click the +Add Record button to display the form for entering the record. On this form, choose A under Type, enter the @ symbol into the Name text box, then enter your VPS server's IPv4 address into the IPv4 text box. Finally, click the Add button to add the record. The record should now appear under the list of records, as shown in Figure 9-4.

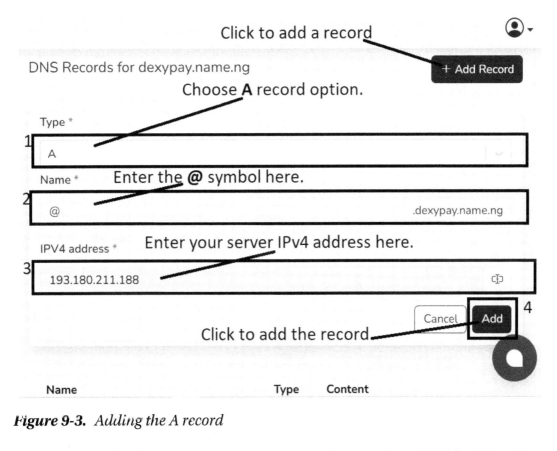

Figure 9-3. *Adding the A record*

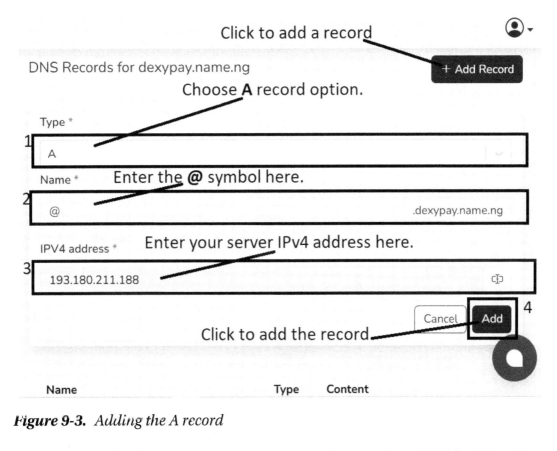

Name	Type	Content
@	A	193.180.212.211

Figure 9-4. *The added A record*

Creating an A Record for Your Subdomain Name

You need a domain name for the control panel you'll use to deploy the application later in this chapter. For this, you need to create a wildcard subdomain name based on the primary domain name. To create a wildcard subdomain, I simply prefixed the primary domain name with *.dp2., resulting in *.dp2.dexypay.name.ng. You are free to replace dp2 with whatever alphanumeric string you want in order to create your own wildcard subdomain name. Of course, don't forget to also replace the dexypay.name.ng part with your own primary domain name.

Next, you'll create an A record for the wildcard subdomain name. On your domain registrar's site, locate the page for adding DNS records (see the preceding section). Figure 9-5 shows how to add an A record to your wildcard domain name. Select A under Type, enter *.dp2 into the Name text-box, and then enter your VPS server's IPv4 address into the IPv4 text-box. Finally, click the Add button to add the record. The record should now appear under the list of records, as shown in Figure 9-6.

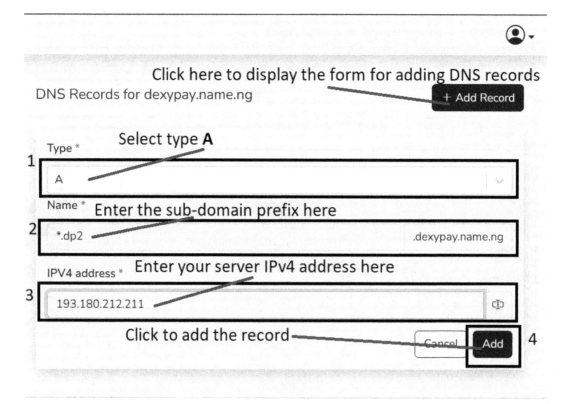

Figure 9-5. *Setting the A record of the subdomain name*

| *.dp2.dexypay.name.ng. | A | 193.180.212.211 |

Figure 9-6. The added A record

Deploying Your App

To deploy your app, you'll be using an open-source tool called **CapRover**. With this tool, you can easily deploy and scale your app. However, you first need to install Docker in order to install and use CapRover. The installations that follow assume that you have installed a clean Ubuntu 24.04 OS on your VPS. Figure 9-7 shows the CapRover home page.

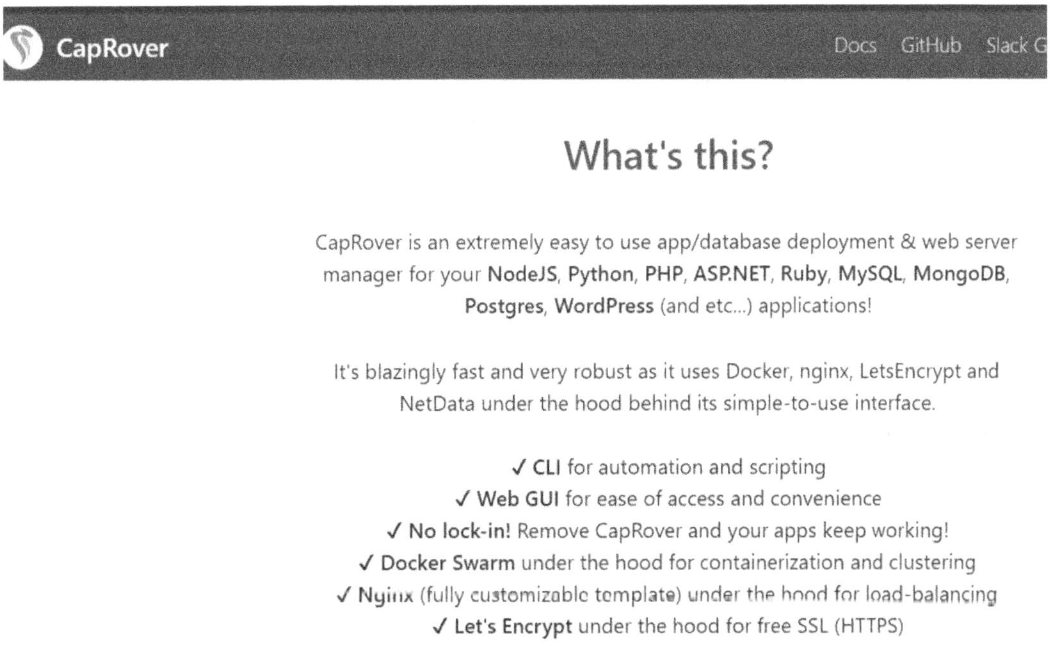

What's this?

CapRover is an extremely easy to use app/database deployment & web server manager for your **NodeJS, Python, PHP, ASP.NET, Ruby, MySQL, MongoDB, Postgres, WordPress** (and etc...) applications!

It's blazingly fast and very robust as it uses Docker, nginx, LetsEncrypt and NetData under the hood behind its simple-to-use interface.

✓ **CLI** for automation and scripting
✓ **Web GUI** for ease of access and convenience
✓ **No lock-in!** Remove CapRover and your apps keep working!
✓ **Docker Swarm** under the hood for containerization and clustering
✓ **Nginx** (fully customizable template) under the hood for load-balancing
✓ **Let's Encrypt** under the hood for free SSL (HTTPS)

Figure 9-7. The CapRover home page

Docker Installation

While connected to the Internet, open your command-line terminal and run the command shown in Listing 9-1. Replace username with VPS SSH username, and vps-IP-address with the IP address of your VPS. Then press the Enter key.

Tip   Keep your Internet on while running the following commands.

Listing 9-1. Connecting to your VPS

```
ssh usernname@vps-IP-address
```

You'll be prompted to enter your password. Enter the password for your VPS SSH and press the Enter key to continue.

Once connection has been established with your VPS, enter the command in Listing 9-2 and press the Enter key. You may be prompted for your SSH user password. Enter the password and press the Enter key again.

Listing 9-2. Gaining sudo access

```
sudo su
```

Next, to install Docker, copy and paste the command in Listing 9-3 into the command-line terminal and press the Enter key.

Listing 9-3. Installing Docker

```
sudo bash <<'EOF'
apt-get remove -y docker docker-engine docker.io containerd runc
apt-get update -y
apt-get install -y ca-certificates curl gnupg lsb-release
curl -fsSL https://download.docker.com/linux/ubuntu/gpg \
  | gpg --dearmor -o /usr/share/keyrings/docker-archive-keyring.gpg
echo "deb [arch=$(dpkg --print-architecture) signed-by=/usr/share/keyrings/
docker-archive-keyring.gpg] \
  https://download.docker.com/linux/ubuntu $(lsb_release -cs) stable" \
  | tee /etc/apt/sources.list.d/docker.list > /dev/null
```

```
apt-get update -y
apt-get install -y docker-ce docker-ce-cli containerd.io docker-buildx-
plugin docker-compose-plugin
systemctl enable docker.service
systemctl start docker.service
usermod -aG docker $USER
newgrp docker
docker version
EOF
```

If the Docker installation is successful, the version of Docker that's been installed will be displayed.

Installing CapRover

To install CapRover, copy and paste the command in Listing 9-4 into the command-line terminal you opened earlier and press the Enter key to run it.

Tip   Keep your Internet on while running this command.

Listing 9-4. Installing CapRover

```
docker run -p 80:80 -p 443:443 -p 3000:3000 -e ACCEPTED_TERMS=true -v /var/
run/docker.sock:/var/run/docker.sock -v /captain:/captain caprover/caprover
```

Upon successful execution of the command in Listing 9-4, CapRover should be installed. To verify that the CapRover installation was successful, you can visit http://[IP_OF_YOUR_VPS]:3000 in your browser and log in to CapRover using the default password, captain42.

Installing Node

If it's not already installed on your local machine, you'll need to install Node. To verify if you have Node, open a command-line terminal on your local machine and run the command in Listing 9-5.

Listing 9-5. Verifying Node Installation

```
node -v
```

If Node is installed, the version should be displayed. If Node is not installed, visit `https://nodejs.org` to download and install it. It's available for most operating systems.

Setting Up CapRover on Your Local Computer

As mentioned in the preceding section, you need Node in order to install CapRover on your computer. To install CapRover locally, run the command in Listing 9-6 from the command-line.

Tip   Keep your Internet on while running the following commands.

Listing 9-6. Installing CapRover Locally

```
npm install -g caprover
```

Afterward, run the command in Listing 9-7 to link your local CapRover installation to your remote server (VPS).

Listing 9-7. Linking Your Local CapRover Installation to Your Remote Server

```
caprover serversetup
```

When you run the command in Listing 9-7, you'll be prompted to answer some questions; see Figure 9-8:

1. Have you already started CapRover container on your server?: Enter Y and press the Enter key to continue.

2. IP address of your server: Enter your VPS IP address and press the Enter key to continue.

3. CapRover server root domain: Enter the wildcard subdomain, excluding the preceding * and . symbols (i.e., `dp.dexypay.name.ng`) and press the Enter key to continue..

4. New CapRover password (minimum eight characters): Enter a new password and press the Enter key to continue.

5. Enter new CapRover password again: Enter the new password again and press the Enter key to continue.

6. Valid email address to get certificate and enable HTTPS: Enter a valid and functional email address and press the Enter key to continue.

7. CapRover machine name, with whom the credentials are stored locally: Enter a name or just accept the default and press the Enter key to continue.

```
Adegoke Akintoye@LAPTOP-FDSFCFRB MINGW64 /c/UniServerZ/www/my_laravel_api (master)
$ caprover serversetup

Setup CapRover machine on your server...

? have you already started CapRover container on your server? Yes
? IP address of your server: 193.180.211.188
? CapRover server root domain: dp2.dexypay.name.ng
? new CapRover password (min 8 characters): [hidden]
? enter new CapRover password again: [hidden]
? "valid" email address to get certificate and enable HTTPS: adexyme@gmail.com
? CapRover machine name, with whom the login credentials are stored locally: DexyPay

CapRover server setup completed: it is available as DexyPay at https://captain.dp2.dexypay.name.ng
```

Figure 9-8. *Setting up CapRover*

Creating Applications on CapRover

CapRover uses Docker-based containers to host your applications. You can thus break the application into subunits, with each unit being hosted on its own assigned container. All these containers will communicate and work together.

In this example, you'll break down the app into the following units, so that each unit can be hosted in its own container:

1. **Web server/PHP**: Here, you'll use Apache web server and PHP8.3. These will be packaged together as a standalone app in a container. The Laravel-based code will be hosted here. This subunit (app) will be non-persistent, as you are not storing data on the web server but rather on the database. After you create this app, you'll upload the API code here.

2. **MariaDB database**: This is where you'll store the API-generated data, and as such it'll be persistent. Unlike Apache and PHP, MariaDB is available as a One-Click app. One-Click apps are CapRover-curated apps and can be easily installed by simply filling in a form and clicking to submit it.

3. **PhpMyAdmin**: You'll also install this as a container for administering the database. It's non-persistent and available as a One-Click app.

4. **Mail server**: This allows you to manage and send email from within the application. It's also persistent.

5. **File manager**: This allows you to view, edit, and upload files. It's a non-persistent app.

To create these apps, visit the CapRover installation on your VPS from the web browser at `https://captain.dp2.dexypay.name.ng` (this URL may be different for you, depending on the subdomain name you used during CapRover installation). Visiting the URL should load a login page similar to Figure 9-9.

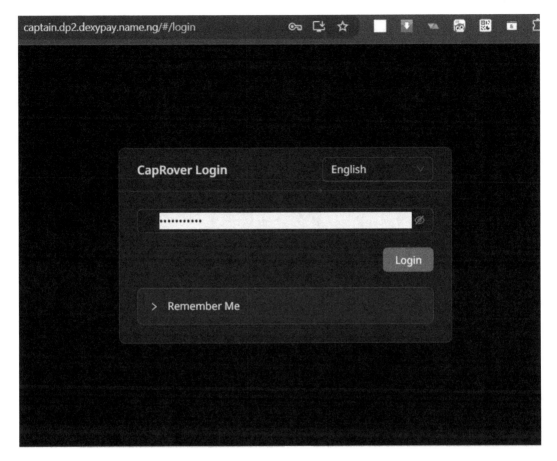

Figure 9-9. *The CapRover login page*

Enter your CapRover password and click the Login button to log in to the CapRover control panel. Upon successful login, you'll be taken to a page similar to Figure 9-10.

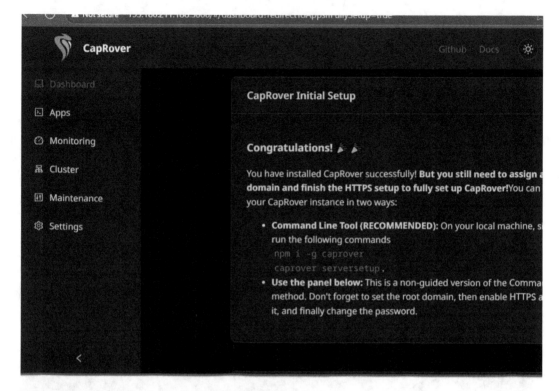

Figure 9-10. *The CapRover Welcome page after logging in*

Creating the MariaDB Database App

Click the Apps and Create A New App buttons, as shown in Figure 9-11, to open the Create A New App page. On the Create A New App page, click the One-Click Apps/ Databases button to open the One Click App page, as shown Figure 9-12.

Figure 9-11. *Creating an app in CapRover*

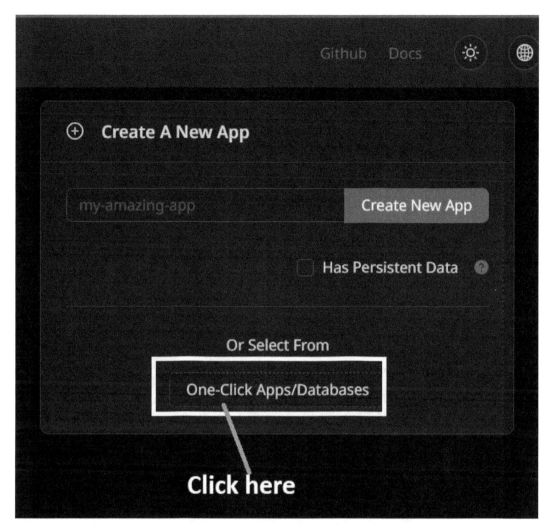

Figure 9-12. *Accessing CapRover's One-Click Apps/Databases button*

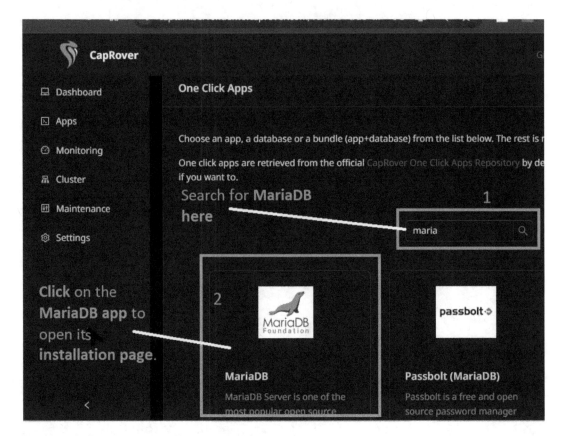

Figure 9-13. *Seaching for the MariaDB database*

Search for MariaDB and click it to open its installation page, as shown in Figure 9-13. On the installation page, enter a name for the app. Scroll down and enter a password, then click the Deploy button to install the database. See Figure 9-14.

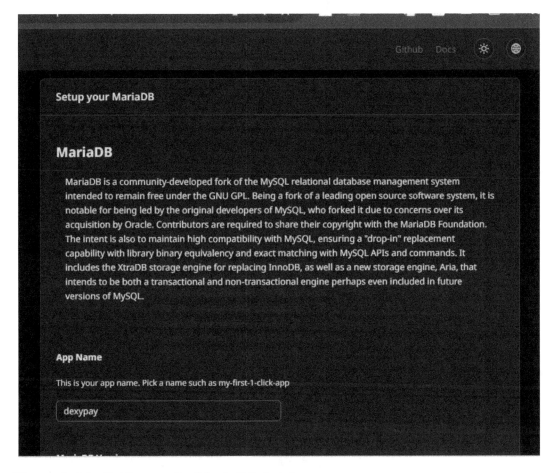

Figure 9-14. *Setting up the MariaDB database*

Creating the PhpMyAdmin App

Next, you install PhpMyAdmin to administer your MariaDB database. To install it, click the Apps and Create A New App buttons; this opens the Create A New App page. On the Create A New App page, click the One-Click Apps/Databases button to open the One Click App page (refer back to Figures 9-11 and 9-12 if needed).

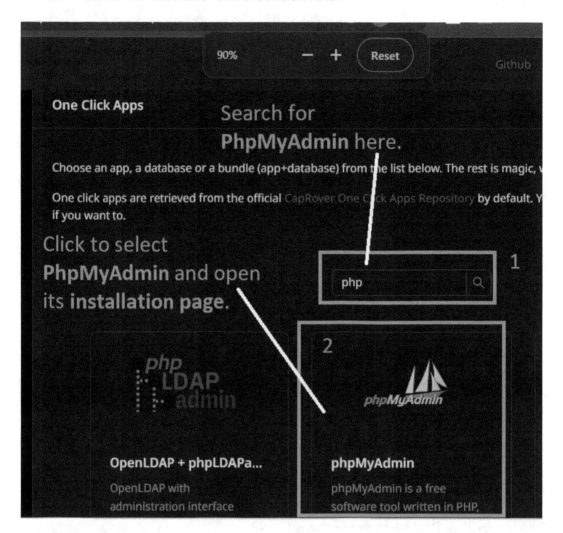

Figure 9-15. *Seaching for the phpMyAdmin app*

Search for and click PhpMyAdmin to open its installation page, as shown in
Figure 9-15. On the installation page, enter a name for the app. Scroll down and click the
Deploy button to install the database. See Figure 9-16.

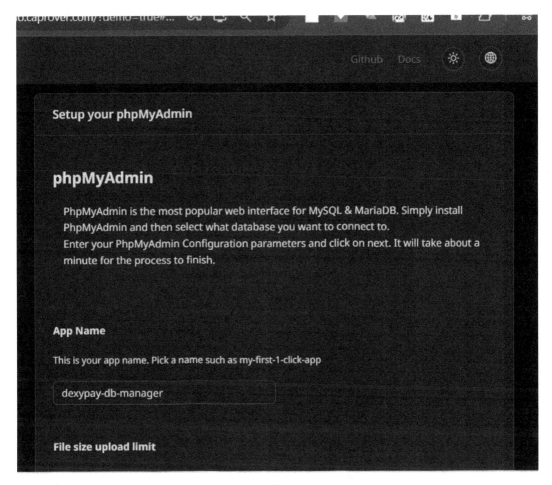

Figure 9-16. Setting up phpMyAdmin

Creating the Mail Server App

Now you'll install the iRedMail server, which is used to administer the MariaDB database. To install it, click the Apps and Create A New App buttons; this opens the Create A New App page. On the Create A New App page, click the One-Click Apps/ Databases button to open the One Click App page (refer back to Figures 9-11 and 9-12 if needed).

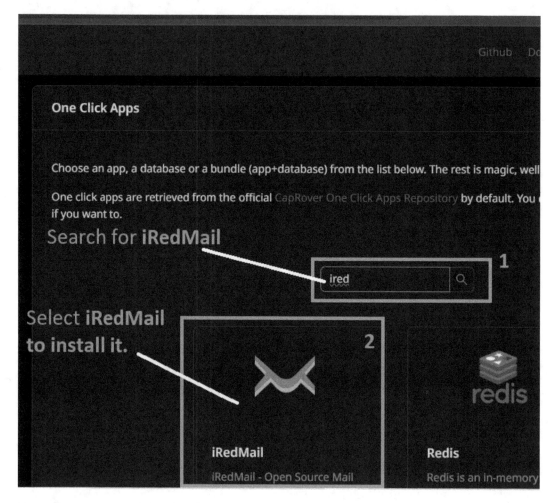

Figure 9-17. *Searching for the iRedMail app*

Search for and click iRedMail to open its installation page, as shown in Figure 9-17. On the installation page, enter `mail` as the name of the app. Scroll down and enter the admin's password and click the Deploy button to install the app. See Figure 9-18.

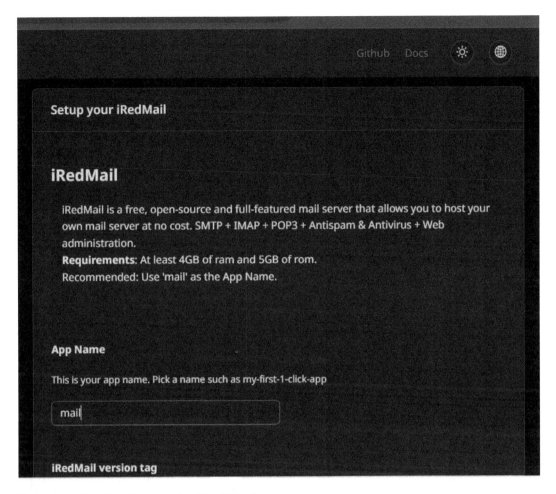

Figure 9-18. *Setting up the iRedMail app*

Creating the File Manager App

Lastly, you'll install filebrowser, a web-based interface for managing your files. To install it, click the Apps and Create A New App buttons; this opens the Create A New App page. On the Create A New App page, click the One-Click Apps/Databases button to open the One Click App page (refer back to Figures 9-11 and 9-12 if needed).

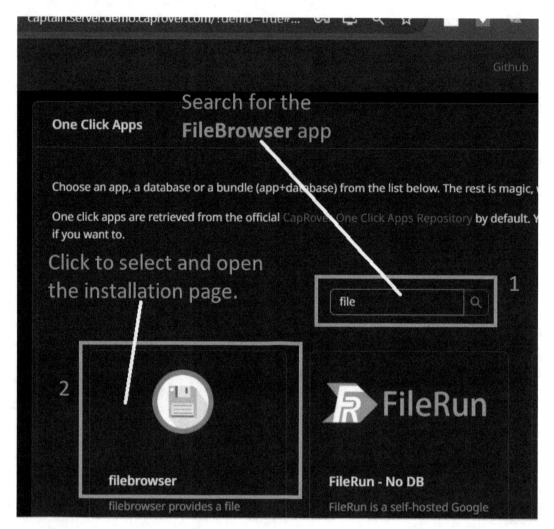

Figure 9-19. *Searching for filebrowser*

Search for and click filebrowser to open its installation page, as shown in Figure 9-19. On the installation page, enter a name for the app. Scroll down and click the Deploy button to install the app. See Figure 9-20.

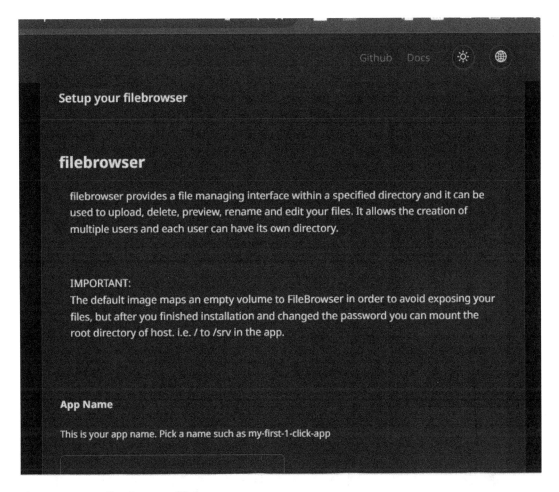

Figure 9-20. Setting up filebrowser

Creating the Apache Web Server/PHP8.3 App

Click the Apps and Create A New App buttons to open the Create A New App page; see Figure 9-21.

Figure 9-21. Creating the Apache Web Server/PHP8.3 App

On the Create A New App page (see Figure 9-22), enter a name for the app and ensure that the Has Persistent Data option is not ticked. Then click the Create New App button to create the app.

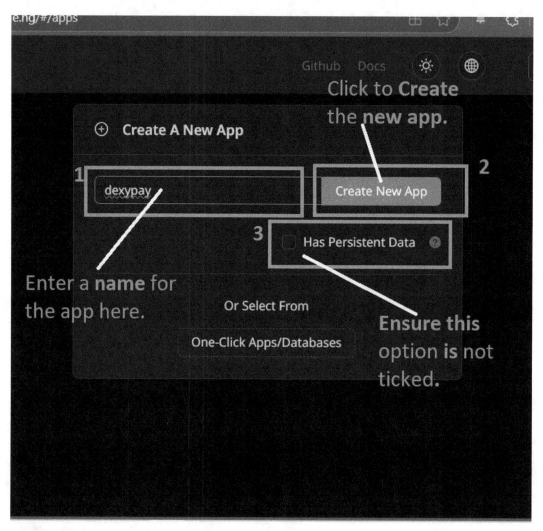

Figure 9-22. Enter the app's details and click the Create New App button

Installing Apache and PHP8.3 and Uploading Your Laravel Code

Next, you'll complete this installation by installing the Apache web server and PHP8.3, and deploying the Laravel code into this app (container).

To install the Apache web server and PHP8.3, and to upload your Laravel code, CapRover requires that you put a `captain-definition` file inside the root folder of the Laravel application. In addition, you'll be adding two files inside the root folder—a Dockerfile and a `.dockerignore` file. The Dockerfile will be referenced from within the `captain-definition` file. Here's what these two files do:

1. `captain-definition`: A *captain definition file* (usually named `captain-definition`, with no extension) is the primary way you tell CapRover how to build and deploy your application. It lives at the root of your project and uses simple JSON code. Listing 9-8 shows the `captain-definition` file you'll use to install the Apache server and PHP8.3, and deploy the application to the VPS.

Listing 9-8. The `captain-definition` File

```
{
  "schemaVersion": 2,
  "dockerfilePath": "./Dockerfile"
}
```

This points to a Dockerfile in the root directory of your application.

2. **Dockerfile**: A Dockerfile is simply a text file that contains a set of step-by-step instructions for building a Docker image. Think of it as a recipe or blueprint that tells Docker the following:

    a. Which base image to start from. This gives you a preconfigured OS (and sometimes a runtime) to build upon.

    b. Which commands to run inside the image. Like installing system packages (`RUN apt-get install ...`), enabling services, or compiling code.

    c. How to add your application code. Using `COPY` or `ADD` to bringing files from your local machine into the image.

d. Which directory to work in. For example, WORKDIR /app tells Docker, "from now on, run all commands in /app".

e. Any environment variables or configuration settings. For example:

ENV NODE_ENV=production or ENV APACHE_DOCUMENT_ROOT=/var/www/html/public

f. What command to launch by default. For example:

With CMD ["php", "artisan", "serve"] or ENTRYPOINT ["npm", "start"], you tell Docker what to execute when you run a container from this image.

Listing 9-9 contains the contents of the Dockerfile file you'll use to install the Apache server and PHP8.3, and to deploy the application to the VPS.

Listing 9-9. Docker File to Install the Apache Server and Deploy the Application to the VPS

```
FROM php:8.3-apache

# Install dependencies
RUN apt-get update && \
    apt-get install -y \
    libzip-dev \
    zip

# Enable mod_rewrite
RUN a2enmod rewrite

# Install PHP extensions
RUN docker-php-ext-install pdo_mysql zip

ENV APACHE_DOCUMENT_ROOT=/var/www/html/public
RUN sed -ri -e 's!/var/www/html!${APACHE_DOCUMENT_ROOT}!g' /etc/apache2/sites-available/*.conf
RUN sed -ri -e 's!/var/www/!${APACHE_DOCUMENT_ROOT}!g' /etc/apache2/apache2.conf /etc/apache2/conf-available/*.conf
```

```
# Copy the application code
COPY . /var/www/html

# Set the working directory
WORKDIR /var/www/html

# Install composer
RUN curl -sS https://getcomposer.org/installer | php -- --install-dir=/usr/
local/bin --filename=composer

# Install project dependencies
RUN composer install

# Set permissions
RUN chown -R www-data:www-data /var/www/html/storage /var/www/html/
bootstrap/cache
```

    g. Installs a Linux environment with PHP8.3 and Apache preinstalled
       and configured:

```
FROM php:8.2-apache
```

    h. Installs system dependencies:

```
RUN apt-get update && \
    apt-get install -y \
    libzip-dev \
    zip
```

    i. Turns on Apache's mod_rewrite module, which lets you rewrite
      URLs (Laravel needs this for "pretty" URLs):

```
RUN a2enmod rewrite
```

    j. Installs PHP extensions:

```
RUN docker-php-ext-install pdo_mysql zip
```

    k. Changes Apache's document root:

```
ENV APACHE_DOCUMENT_ROOT=/var/www/html/public
RUN sed -ri -e 's!/var/www/html!${APACHE_DOCUMENT_
ROOT}!g' /etc/apache2/sites-available/*.conf
```

```
RUN sed -ri -e 's!/var/www/!${APACHE_DOCUMENT_
ROOT}!g' /etc/apache2/apache2.conf /etc/apache2/conf-
available/*.conf
```

l. Copies your application code into the web server folder:

```
COPY . /var/www/html
```

m. Sets the working directory:

```
WORKDIR /var/www/html
```

Any subsequent commands (like RUN, CMD, or relative COPY)
will default to /var/www/html.

n. Installs Composer (PHP's package manager):

```
RUN curl -sS https://getcomposer.org/installer \

| php -- --install-dir=/usr/local/bin
--filename=composer
```

o. Installs your PHP dependencies:

```
RUN composer install
```
Reads your composer.json and composer.lock, then
downloads and installs all the libraries (e.g., Laravel
framework and packages) into vendor/.

Note   By default, this runs in the WORKDIR you set, so it installs in /var/
www/html.

---

p. Adjusts file permissions:

```
RUN chown -R www-data:www-data /var/www/html/storage
/var/www/html/bootstrap/cache
```
chown -R www-data:www-data ... changes the owner (and
group) of those directories to www-data (Apache's user). Why?
Because Laravel needs write access to storage/ (for logs,
cache, file uploads) and bootstrap/cache/. This ensures that
Apache can read/write there.

3. .dockerignore: A .dockerignore file is a simple text file, placed in the root of your project (next to your Dockerfile), that tells Docker which files and directories to exclude when it sends your "build context" to the Docker daemon. Think of it like a .gitignore for Docker builds. It helps exclude unnecessary files or files that contain secret information.

Listing 9-10 shows the contents of the .dockerignore file you'll use in this example.

Listing 9-10. The .dockerignore File

```
node_modules
vendor
.env
```

With these three files added to the root of your Laravel project, your project folder structure should look like Figure 9-23.

s PC › OS (C:) › UniServerZ › www › my_laravel_api

Name	Date modified	Type	Size
.git	20/05/2025 09:13	File folder	
.scribe	24/04/2025 14:55	File folder	
app	24/04/2025 18:49	File folder	
bootstrap	13/12/2024 14:57	File folder	
config	13/05/2025 15:14	File folder	
database	10/01/2025 17:47	File folder	
public	30/04/2025 23:26	File folder	
resources	13/12/2024 14:57	File folder	
routes	05/03/2025 07:02	File folder	
storage	04/04/2025 11:11	File folder	
tests	13/12/2024 14:57	File folder	
vendor	20/05/2025 09:12	File folder	
.dockerignore	20/05/2025 00:37	DOCKERIGNO...	1 KB
.editorconfig	13/12/2024 14:57	Editor Config ...	1 KB
.env	13/05/2025 15:21	ENV File	2 KB
.env.example	13/12/2024 14:57	EXAMPLE File	2 KB
.gitattributes	13/12/2024 14:57	Text Document	1 KB
.gitignore	13/05/2025 08:14	Text Document	1 KB
.phpunit.result.cache	17/03/2025 13:02	CACHE File	1 KB
artisan	13/12/2024 14:57	File	1 KB
captain-definition	20/05/2025 06:46	File	1 KB
composer	20/05/2025 09:12	JSON File	3 KB
composer.lock	20/05/2025 09:12	LOCK File	338 KB
Dockerfile	20/05/2025 08:17	File	1 KB
my_laravel_api	11/04/2025 09:19	CODE-WORKS...	1 KB
openAPI	27/04/2025 14:50	JSON File	35 KB

Figure 9-23. *The project folder structure*

To deploy the application to your remote VPS while also installing the Apache web server and PHP8.3, you'll need to run the command in Listing 9-11 from within the root folder of the application.

Note   CapRover requires that your application be a Git repository. That means only the changes you've committed will be uploaded. Even the changes made to your `captain-definition`, Dockerfile, and `.dockerignore` files must be committed for them to take effect while deploying your app. Therefore, if you haven't done so already, run the following commands from the root folder of your application: 1. `git init` 2. `git add .` 3. `git commit -m "a comment to accompany your commit"`.

Listing 9-11. Deploying the Application

```
caprover deploy
```

When you run the command in Listing 9-11, you'll be prompted to answer some questions in order for CapRover to deploy your app; see Figure 9-24:

1. Select the CapRover machine name you want to deploy to: You'll be presented with one or more remote server(s), depending on the number of remote server(s) you installed CapRover on. Use the Up and Down arrow keys to select the name of the remote server you want to deploy to and press the Enter key to continue.

2. Select the app name you want to deploy to: You'll be presented with a list of available app(s) from CapRover machine (server) you selected in the last question. Select the app you want to deploy to and press the Enter key to continue.

3. Git branch name to be deployed: Here, you provide the name of your Git repository branch you want to deploy to. Press the Enter key to continue. For example, you might have branches you've named production, staging, and development that you want to push to similarly named remote machines (servers).

4. Note that any uncommitted and gitignored files will not be pushed to server! Are you sure you want to deploy?: If so, type Yes and press the Enter key.

    CapRover will start to install the specified software and upload your Laravel app; see Figure 9-24.

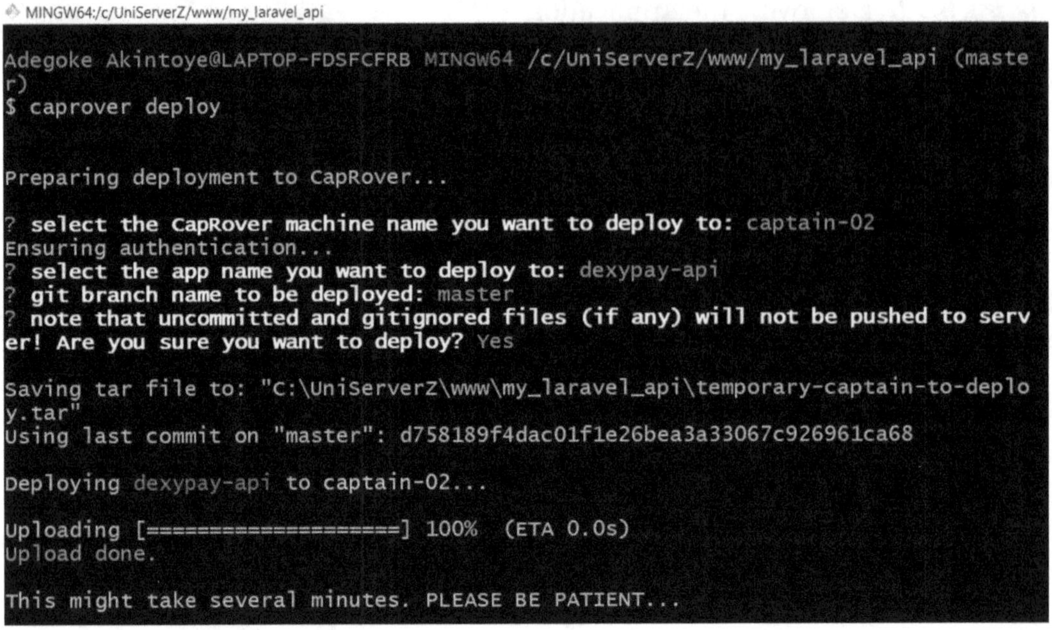

MINGW64:/c/UniServerZ/www/my_laravel_api

```
Adegoke Akintoye@LAPTOP-FDSFCFRB MINGW64 /c/UniServerZ/www/my_laravel_api (maste
r)
$ caprover deploy


Preparing deployment to CapRover...

? select the CapRover machine name you want to deploy to: captain-02
Ensuring authentication...
? select the app name you want to deploy to: dexypay-api
? git branch name to be deployed: master
? note that uncommitted and gitignored files (if any) will not be pushed to serv
er! Are you sure you want to deploy? Yes

Saving tar file to: "C:\UniServerZ\www\my_laravel_api\temporary-captain-to-deplo
y.tar"
Using last commit on "master": d758189f4dac01f1e26bea3a33067c926961ca68

Deploying dexypay-api to captain-02...

Uploading [====================] 100%  (ETA 0.0s)
Upload done.

This might take several minutes. PLEASE BE PATIENT...
```

Figure 9-24. *Deploying the Laravel app*

Upon successful completion of the deployment operation, you'll be notified; see Figure 9-25. If the deployment fails, you'll be given a clue as to the cause of the failure.

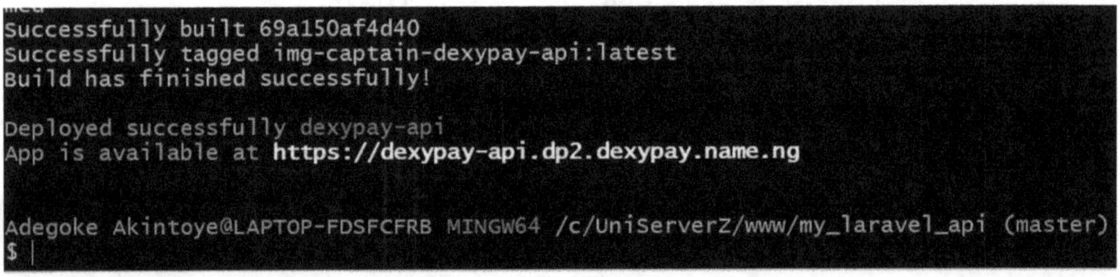

```
Successfully built 69a150af4d40
Successfully tagged img-captain-dexypay-api:latest
Build has finished successfully!

Deployed successfully dexypay-api
App is available at https://dexypay-api.dp2.dexypay.name.ng

Adegoke Akintoye@LAPTOP-FDSFCFRB MINGW64 /c/UniServerZ/www/my_laravel_api (master)
$ |
```

Figure 9-25. *The app was successfully deployed*

Pointing Your Primary Domain Name to the App

In Figure 9-25, notice that the URL generated by CapRover for your app is a subdomain (https://dexypay-api.dp2.dexypay.name.ng) based on your primary domain name. To link your primary domain—in this case dexypay.name.ng—open the CapRover Control Panel and choose Apps ➤ dexypay (dexypay is the name you gave the app you created earlier) to open the app's HTTP Settings page; see Figure 9-26.

376

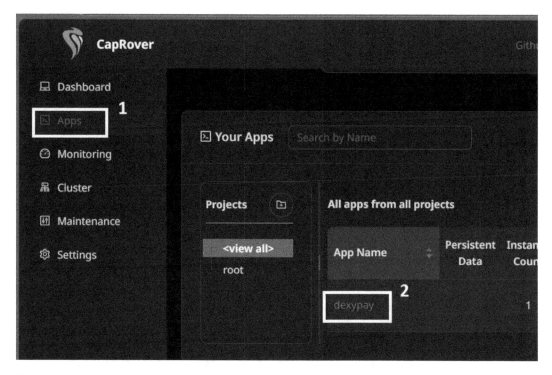

Figure 9-26. *Accessing your app on CapRover*

On the page shown in Figure 9-27, enter the domain name to be linked and click the Connect New Domain button to link the domain name to the app. You should also add the variant of the primary domain name prefixed with `www.`, such as `www.dexypay. name.ng`.

Figure 9-27. *Linking the primary domain to the app*

Once the domain names has been added, click the Enable HTTPS button for each domain name to force `https`. Then click the Save & Restart button; see Figure 9-28.

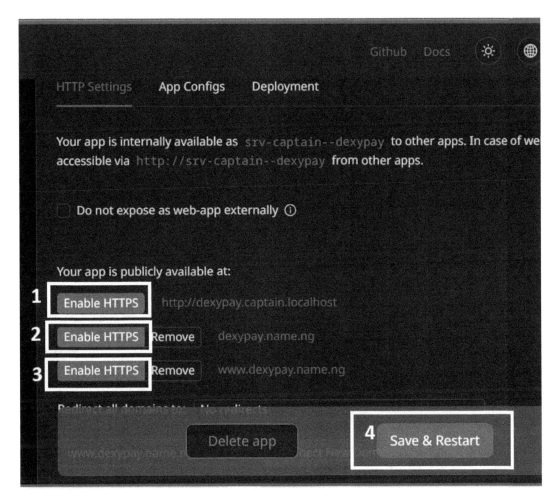

Figure 9-28. *A list of URLs linked to your app*

Setting Your App's Environment Variables

To add your Laravel app's environment values, choose App Configs and then click
the Bulk Edit button; see Figure 9-29. Copy the contents of your app's .env file and
paste them into the Environment Variables text box. Edit them as appropriate for the
environment you are deploying to—staging, production, and so on. Click the Save &
Restart button to have your changes take effect.

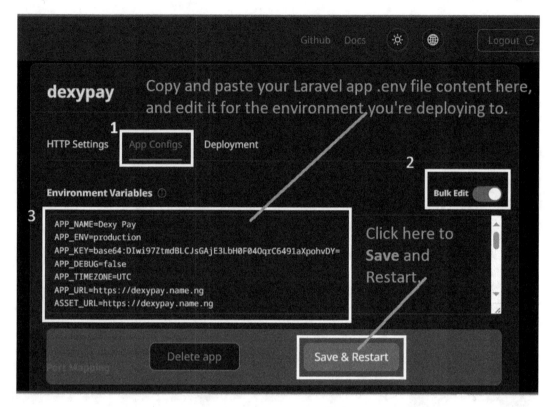

Figure 9-29. *Adding your app's environment variable via CapRover's dashboard*

The ASSET_URL Environment Variable

It is important to set this environment variable too, so that your assets (CSS, JS, and image files) can be properly loaded. Just set this variable to your base_url using https. See Figure 9-29 and Listing 9-12. Replace https://dexypay.name.ng with your own primary domain name.

Listing 9-12. Setting the ASSET_URL Environment Variable

```
ASSET_URL=https://dexypay.name.ng
```

Running a Migration for Your First Deployment

Since this is the first deployment of your app from your development server to your remote VPS server (production or staging), it is safe to carry out database migration. To migrate your database from the development environment to the current environment, you need to run the appropriate Artisan command from within your app's container. To open the app's (container) command-line, connect via SSH to your VPS and run the command shown in Listing 9-13.

Listing 9-13. Open the App's (Container) Command-Line

```
docker exec -it dexypay bash
```

To carry out the migration, run the command in Listing 9-14.

Listing 9-14. Running the Migration

```
php artisan migrate
```

You'll be greeted with a warning, asking you if you want to proceed with the migration process. See Figure 9-30.

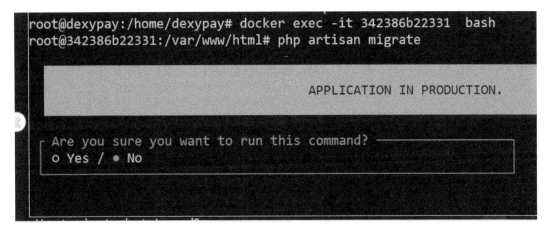

Figure 9-30. *Running the database migration*

Choose Yes and then press the Enter key to continue with the migration.

Launching Your AP

To launch your app, visit any of its URLs, in this case, `https://dexypay.name.ng`, `https://www.dexypay.name.ng`, and so on. Visiting any of these URLs, should open your app's welcome page, as shown in Figure 9-31.

Figure 9-31. *The app dashboard's welcome page*

Scaling Your App

This section explains how to scale your application to handle increase demand as your userbase increases. There are basically two ways to scale your application—vertically or horizontally.

Vertical Scaling

This involves adding more resources (CPU, RAM) to a single server. It's simple but limited by hardware. To implement this, you simply upgrade your server to one with more resources. This usually requires you to pay more. This can be useful for scaling apps that have persistent data and cannot be easily scaled using CapRover (such as a database app).

Horizontal Scaling

Horizontal scaling involves adding more machines or instances to your system to handle increased load. Instead of upgrading a single server (which is vertical scaling), you add more servers and distribute the work among them. To implement this, you add more instances (containers/servers) behind a *load balancer*. This approach offers better redundancy and unlimited growth potential. CapRover makes doing this very easy.

You can also scale horizontally by deploying multiple instances of your app on multiple servers or on the same server.

Horizontal Scaling via Multiple App Instances

The easiest way to implement horizontal scaling using CapRover is to deploy multiple instances of the app on the same server. For example, for the RESTful API application, you can add multiple instances of the container hosting the Apache web server, PHP8.3, and the Laravel code. To do this, from within your VPS CapRover Control Panel, first choose Apps ➤ dexypay (dexypay is the name you gave the app/container when you created it). This will open the app's HTTP Settings page, as shown in Figure 9-32. Next, click the App Configs button. Scroll down the App Configs page to locate the Instance Count text box, shown in Figure 9-33. Increase the Instance Count value from 1 to 2 or more, depending on the resources (RAM, CPU) available on your VPS.

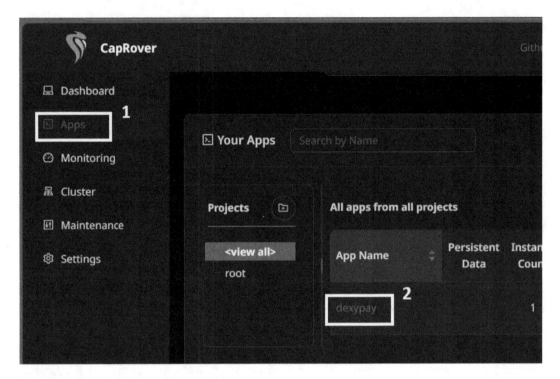

Figure 9-32. *Accessing the app on CapRover*

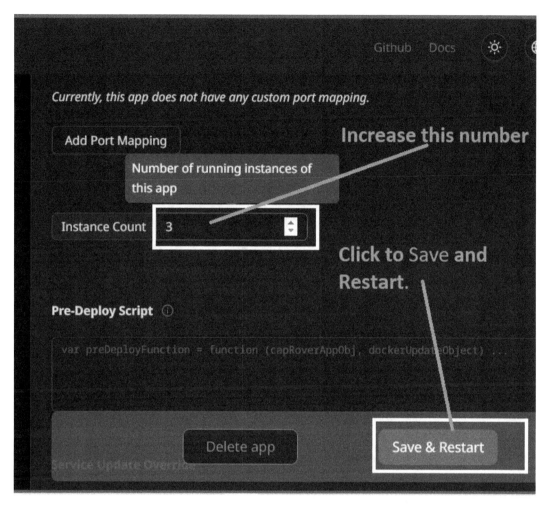

Figure 9-33. *Increasing the number of running instances of the app*

That is it. From now on, CapRover will share requests to your app among these instances, ensuring that they handle the requests in parallel. If any of these instances should go down, CapRover will automatically create another one, ensuring that you have the same number of instances working at any given time.

Horizontal Scaling via Multiple Server Connection

Horizontal scaling using multiple servers is a bit more complex. To implement it, from within your current VPS CapRover Control Panel, choose Cluster and then click the Add Self-Hosted Registry and Enable Self-Hosted Registry buttons. See Figure 9-34.

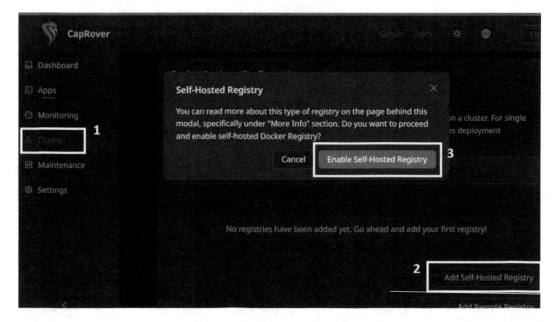

Figure 9-34. *Enabling a self-hosted registry*

Provision a new VPS (using the same OS as the previous VPS—Ubuntu 24.04) with Docker installed. Ensure that the new node can be SSH'ed into by the main server. On your primary CapRover server, copy the root user's SSH public key to the new node's / root/.ssh/authorized_keys path. This allows the CapRover UI (on the leader) to SSH into it. Then, in the CapRover dashboard, click Cluster. In the Nodes section, enter the following:

- **CapRover IP (remote)**: The public IP of your main server

- **New node IP**: The IP of this new server

- **SSH key**: The private key of the main server's root user (usually /root/.ssh/id_rsa)

- **Node type:** Choose worker (or manager if you want this node to also be a Swarm manager)

Finally, click Join Cluster. CapRover will SSH into the new node and run the docker swarm join command.

Behind the scenes, CapRover will use Docker Swarm commands to join the cluster. After this, you have one Swarm leader (the original manager) and one worker. CapRover will automatically distribute new app instances across both nodes. For example, if you scale an app to six instances, CapRover "will spin up instances on the other server... and automatically load balance the requests."

Conclusion

This chapter explained how to deploy your API so that it can be accessible to and used by your customers (users) to receive payment. It also explained how to scale the API to meet increasing usage as your customer base increases.

Index

© Adegoke Akintoye 2025
A. Akintoye, *API Development with Laravel*, https://doi.org/10.1007/979-8-8688-1576-8

GPSR Compliance
The European Union's (EU) General Product Safety Regulation (GPSR) is a set
of rules that requires consumer products to be safe and our obligations to
ensure this.

If you have any concerns about our products, you can contact us on

ProductSafety@springernature.com

In case Publisher is established outside the EU, the EU authorized
representative is:

Springer Nature Customer Service Center GmbH
Europaplatz 3
69115 Heidelberg, Germany